WOMEN WHO LAUNCH

Also by Marlene Wagman-Geller

Still I Rise: The Persistence of Phenomenal Women

Behind Every Great Man: The Forgotten Women Behind the World's Famous and Infamous

And the Rest is History: The Famous (and Infamous) First Meetings of the World's Most Passionate Couples

Eureka! The Surprising Stories Behind the Ideas That Shaped the World

Once Again to Zelda: The Stories Behind Literature's Most Intriguing Dedications

WOMEN WHO LAUNCH

Women Who Shattered Glass Ceilings

Marlene Wagman-Geller

Published by Mango Publishing Group, a division of Mango Media Inc.

Cover, Layout & Design: Morgane Leoni

For permission requests, please contact the publisher at:
Mango Publishing Group
2850 Douglas Road, 3rd Floor
Coral Gables, FL 33134 U.S.A.
info@mango.bz

For special orders, quantity sales, course adoptions and corporate sales, please email the publisher at sales@mango.bz. For trade and wholesale sales, please contact Ingram Publisher Services at customer.service@ingramcontent.com or +1.800.509.4887.

Women Who Launch: Women Who Shattered Glass Ceilings

Library of Congress Cataloging
ISBN: (p) 978-1-63353-695-1, (e) 978-1-63353-696-8
Library of Congress Control Number: 2017962523
BISAC - SOC028000 SOCIAL SCIENCE / Women's Studies
    - BUS046000 BUSINESS & ECONOMICS / Motivational

Printed in the United States of America

To the memory of my mother Gilda Wagman.
With love for my daughter Jordanna Shyloh Geller.

"Somewhere over the rainbow
Skies are blue
And the dreams that you dare to dream
Really do come true."

—Judy Garland as Dorothy (1939)

CONTENTS

PROLOGUE

Ladies Who Lunched

If a sociologist held a mirror to the 1950s, it would have reflected a flat line in the march to level the gender playing field. The term "ladies who lunched" described the era's wealthy wives—Mrs. So-and-Sos who used both their husbands' given and surnames—handmaidens to the mundane. Their outlet was to frequent the best restaurants to see and to be seen. These establishments served small portions for high prices; skimpy servings were no problem, though, as the weight-conscious females did very little eating. The sauce for their meals was gossip.

The ladies who "lunched" in Manhattan were an especially well-heeled subset of the breed. The Colony in New York was the first restaurant in the 1930s to import Dom Pérignon, and the only one where the ladies could check their Yorkies and pugs along with their minks and chinchillas. A Van Cleef & Arpels was an adjacent concession. One of the members of this elite group, the Duchess of Windsor, was sadly serious when she famously—and fatuously—delivered her maxim, "A woman can't be too rich or too thin." She also made the lesser-known but equally expected pronouncement, "All my friends know I'd rather shop than eat." Yes, these well-heeled matrons seemed so glamorous in their dresses with the nipped-in waists and their elegant black pumps. The crack in the pretty picture was that the '50s was the era of the captive wife. Fanny Brice in *Funny Girl* sang a tongue-in-cheek reference to the arid desert of matrimony: "I'm Sadie, Sadie, married lady,/Still in bed at noon,/Racking my brain deciding/Between orange juice and prune . . ."

In sharp juxtaposition, there were intrepid women who launched rather than lunched—instead of waiting for a glass slipper, they shattered glass ceilings. One of these, Josephine Esther Mentzer, began life in an apartment over her Hungarian father's hardware store in Queens. Armed with her uncle's cold creams and her own innate chutzpah, she reinvented herself into the cosmetics queen Estée Lauder. Among her roster of friends and clients were Princesses Grace and Diana, First Lady Nancy Reagan, and the Duchess of Windsor. When she passed the torch to her sons—the Kennedys of the beauty world—she left them a legacy of billions. Her son Ronald Lauder's $135 million purchase of Klimt's world-famous painting *Woman in Gold*, a luxurious fin de siècle icon from her father's native Hungary, would have met with her smile of approval. Similarly, Estée would have nodded her head—always perfectly coiffed—at her daughter-in-law Evelyn's pink ribbon campaign, which became the ubiquitous symbol of the battle against breast cancer.

The founding of museums usually connotes male prerogative: the Guggenheim, after Solomon R.; the Smithsonian, after James Smithson; the Tate, after Sir Henry. Women's lot was to have their likenesses hang on their walls, encased in gilded, often evocative poses. What added estrogen to this mix was waxworker wunderkind Marie Grosholz—the architect of Madame Tussauds, a hall of wonders that has remained for two centuries and is one of London's crown jewels.

When one thinks of the newspapers of yesteryear, the image that comes to mind is men with ink-stained fingers bending over their printing presses. And the media tycoons behind the scenes cast the giant shadows of Joseph Pulitzer and William Randolph Hearst. In the contemporary era, the formerly testosterone-fueled media has been impacted by Greek-born Arianna Huffington. On a shoestring budget, she launched the eponymous *Huffington Post*, which was subsequently sold to AOL for $315 million. As a well-connected wielder of political clout—she has the world leaders on her smartphone's speed dial—if angered, she can huff and puff. . . .

The nemesis of women scaling to new heights can be attributed to the Lex Luthor of female empowerment: gender stereotyping. For our mothers, sexism was explicit. Their stories would make any Title IX compliance officer of today perform a full-body heave. My father told me that it was OK for girls not to do well in math, and that the only respectable profession was to be a housewife. However, he did make the concession that if I had to work, I could become a teacher—which I did. When my mother stated she wanted a job, her remark was met with hostility; he said that when a wife worked, it denigrated her husband's ability as a provider. It would never have occurred to him to shop, cook, or change a diaper. In his defense, my old-country father was in good stead with the societal mores of the time. Letters for my mother were addressed to "Mrs. Harry Wagman." It was a milieu where credit cards were only issued in a husband's name, a female physician was so rare that she would inevitably be referred to as "the woman doctor," and juries excluded the possessors of estrogen.

A conundrum faced by women is if they stay boxed in by the dictates of the paradigm—passive, sweet, agreeable—they may not be viewed as mover-and-shaker material. But if they try to break free from this mold—decisive, aggressive, and assertive—are often perceived as bossy. During the 2016 election, men held up iron my shirt signs, showing that sexism still has not been put to rest. To combat this mindset, Sheryl Sandberg, with her Lean In Foundation, has done her utmost to help combat collective chauvinism.

William Wordsworth, in his poem "My Heart Leaps Up," wrote, "The Child is father of the Man"—our youth is a preface to the future. Deeply ingrained bias can be traced to the paradigm that boys are brought up believing they need to get jobs and make money; their fire engines and toy cars put them in the driver's seat. Girls are raised to marry good providers, their dolls and dollhouses conditioning them for their roles as mothers. It is time for the blending of the blue and the pink. Until the traditional mindset is altered, men will continue to hunt trophy wives and women will continue in their perspective that husbands are ATM dispensers.

Many felt that the righteous postscript to this long and winding road of sexism would be a woman in the White House. Amidst many of her supporters' tears—long felt a woman's prerogative—in her concession speech Mrs. Clinton stated, "I know that we still have not shattered that highest and hardest glass ceiling, but someday someone will." Let's cling to that note of optimism. After all, we have the staunchest of shoulders upon which to stand. And when all people are created and treated with equality we, in Wordsworth's vein, can live his words, "My heart leaps up when I behold/A rainbow in the sky. . . ."

Here's to the ladies—the kick-ass heroines—who launched careers and businesses exhibiting the words and belief of Rosie the Riveter: "We can do it!"

CHAPTER # 1

Seen the Glory (1861)

 Songs have oftentimes encapsulated the spirit of protest and become synonymous with a movement. In 1772, former slave trader turned abolitionist John Newton penned "Amazing Grace," an ode against slavery. In 1969, during his "bed-in," John Lennon composed "Give Peace a Chance" against the Vietnam War. In 1972, Helen Reddy, the voice from Down Under, became the roar of Women's Liberation. Another paean was born during a clash between the Blue and the Gray.

Nineteenth-century women—like children—were expected to be seen and not heard, unless the latter was in praise of their husbands. Julia Ward was born in 1819 into early New York power and privilege; her silver spoon came from her father Samuel, one of the country's first bankers. Julia and her five siblings lived in a succession of opulent Manhattan mansions on Bond Street; what transformed these into prisons were her religious father's restrictions on his daughters. Julia's burning aspiration was to be a great literary light and to "write the novel or the play of the age." Another outlet was singing, in which she excelled, and which led to her nickname, "The Diva." That moniker could also have come from her constant thirst for attention. This petite, Titian-haired beauty enjoyed rides around the city in her lemon-yellow carriage, dreaming of a prince to come to her rescue.

During an 1841 visit to Boston, Julia was smitten by Samuel Gridley Howe, a man eighteen years her senior. He was a celebrity in literary and philanthropic circles, and he had spent years in Greece in support of that country's struggle for independence from the Ottoman Empire. He returned home with Lord Byron's helmet as a relic of the poet, a feat that fired Julia's romantic imagination. For his service, the King of Greece bestowed on him the title of Chevalier of the Order of St. Savior—which gave rise to his nickname, Chev. As a Harvard-educated doctor, he obtained a position as the head of the new Perkins School for the Blind, an institution he made famous through his accomplishments with a deaf and blind student, Laura Bridgman.

Samuel was also interested in the twenty-two-year-old Julia—she and her sisters were known as the Three Graces of Bond Street. He wrote his friend Henry Wadsworth Longfellow about how his lady was "gushing over with tenderness & love." He felt he had found in her a helpmeet—a woman who would be happy as the wife of a busy man, not to mention the mother of many hoped-for children. When Samuel asked for her hand, Julia declared, "The Chevalier's way will be a very charming way, and is, henceforth, to be mine." Because of Ward's immense wealth from her father's will, her brother Sam and uncle John required Samuel to sign an "antenuptial agreement," wherein the bride's inheritance would remain under the control of her male relatives. This legality was included because they viewed Chev as a "confounded bit of Boston granite." Longfellow likewise harbored reservations about his friend's fiancée, saying that she was "a damsel of force and beauty . . . carrying almost too many guns for any man who does not want to be firing salutes all the time." Julia, in an uncharacteristic move for the era, retained her maiden name, and became Julia Ward Howe.

15

The couple moved in rarified circles alongside the Lowells, the Cabots, Louisa May Alcott (who could not abide Julia), Horace Mann, the Brownings, and Henry James. Ward Howe met Charles Dickens on his trip to America, and decades later had Oscar Wilde as a houseguest. Although the dashing doctor and the beautiful poetess presented a pretty picture of marital bliss, cracks soon appeared in the union of

Chev and the Diva. Julia craved autonomy, while Samuel assumed her father's role as domestic dictator. A red alert sounded when Samuel told his young wife he wanted her kept in a chrysalis, declaring that if she ever emerged and grew wings, "I shall unmercifully cut them off, to keep you prisoner in my arms." Julia wrote her sisters, "The Dr. calls me child." Another problem might have been that Samuel was hiding in a Victorian closet, secretly in love with Charles Sumner, the best man at his wedding. Two hours after he returned from his honeymoon, Howe wrote Charles, "Julia often says Sumner ought to have been a woman & you to have married her." Tensions were exacerbated on their sixteenth-month wedding anniversary to Europe. Samuel was "London's lion" because of his halcyon Grecian past, burnished by his Perkins School accomplishment. Literary lights such as Thomas Carlyle invited the Howes to lunch, where Samuel served as the sun around which the host and guests orbited. The Diva was not impressed; she was not content to bask in spousal glory.

Despite the doctor's questionable sexual orientation and Julia's growing disdain, she became pregnant soon after tying the knot. Samuel wrote of the news to Charles, "Only a year ago, Julia was a New York belle. Now she is a wife who lives only for her husband & a mother who would melt her very beauty, were it needed, to give a drop of nourishment to her child." That is not how Mrs. Ward Howe saw it. She wrote her sister Louisa, "In giving life to others, do we lose our own vitality, and sink into dimness, nothingness, and living death?" What wore at the fabric of her soul was the worry that she did not care for her sons and daughters to the acceptable degree. "I am alas one of those exceptional women who do not love their children," she wrote, and then crossed out "do not love" with the words "cannot relate to."

16

Another source of resentment was Samuel did not permit Julia the comfort of ether during her six deliveries. His rationale: women needed discipline. He stated, "The pains of childbirth are meant by a beneficent creator to be the means of leading them back to lives of temperance, exercise, and reason." In 1847, Howe confided to her sister that her life had become unspeakable and unbearable: "You cannot know the history, the inner history of the last four years." Secretly, she began writing a novel, *The Hermaphrodite*. She never sought publication, knowing full well that her husband, as well as antebellum America, would not approve. However, in 1854 she anonymously published a volume of poetry, *Passion-Flowers*, without her husband's consent. In thinly veiled prose, it revealed marital misery. Nathaniel Hawthorne declared that Julia "ought to have been soundly whipt for publishing them." Samuel raged that the poems "border on the erotic," and the couple engaged in a period of estrangement. Finally, Samuel demanded that his wife resume sexual relations, or he would initiate divorce. Faced with the prospect of losing her children, Julia acquiesced. She confessed, "I made the greatest sacrifice I can ever be called upon to make."

In 1861 the couple was in Washington, where Julia met the President and observed "the sad expression of Mr. Lincoln's deep blue eyes." It was four months since the Union defeat at the First Battle of Bull Run, and from her room at the Willard Hotel, she spied an advertisement for a business that embalmed and forwarded the bodies of the dead. That evening, the words to a song drifted into her mind. Fearful she would forget the lines by the morning, she wrote down the verse that compared the sacrifices of the Northern soldiers to the crucifixion of Christ: "As He died to make men holy, let us die to make men free."

Samuel, no doubt, rolled his eyes at his wife's latest literary endeavor—*The Battle Hymn of the Republic*—which she sent to the editor of the *Atlantic Monthly*, receiving a remuneration of five dollars for its publication in February 1862. The ethereal poem became one of the world's most beloved hymns and showered upon her the recognition she had always sought.

Sadly, this success did not heal the fabric of their marriage. Julia commented, "I have been married twenty-two years today, and in the course of this time I have never known my husband to approve of any act of mine which I myself valued . . . everything has been contemptible or contraband in his eyes." But he had not succeeded in silencing her spirit. In 1876, the day after her husband's funeral, Julia wrote, "Began my new life today." She had been married for thirty-three years and would live another thirty-four, during which she struggled alongside Lucy Stone and Susan B. Anthony for women's rights.

Howe's hymn was destined to become an intrinsic fabric of the world's tapestry. In 1939, at his wife's suggestion, Steinbeck used one of its lines for the title *The Grapes of Wrath*. In 1965, it was the opening hymn at the funeral of Winston Churchill, and Martin Luther King, Jr.'s last public address, delivered the night before his assassination, ended with the line, "Mine eyes have seen the glory of the coming of the Lord." In 1968, as the twenty-one-car funeral bearing the body of Robert F. Kennedy crept through Baltimore, thousands of people lining the tracks sang the century-old lyrics, "Glory, glory hallelujah . . ." Its haunting memory was also heard at the Washington National Cathedral after the terrorist attacks of 2001. Less reverently, in 2016 George W. Bush swayed to its accompaniment at the memorial for five slain Dallas police officers.

A week before Julia's passing in 1910 at age ninety, Smith College conferred upon her an honorary degree, with a chorus of two thousand white-clad girls singing her hymn at the ceremony. Although she had engaged in a three-decade-long civil war with her husband, she was vindicated through literary immortality; despite everything, her eyes had "seen the glory."

CHAPTER # 2

Success Was Sure to Go (1863)

 Hamlet railed, "Frailty, thy name is woman!" and in this vein, female Victorians struggled against the slings and arrows of misogyny: they could not vote, serve on jury duty, or attend university. Their corseted bodies mirrored the shackles society placed on their minds. Despite these restrictions, one lady launched not just one, but two beloved pieces of Americana. Although her contributions differed in nature, they shared the commonality of involving animals—one a lamb, the other a turkey.

This mother of invention, Sarah Josepha, was born in 1788 on a farm in Newport, New Hampshire, to Revolutionary War hero Captain John Gordon and Martha Buell. Contrary to the mores of her era, her parents believed in education for girls, and her elder brother Horatio, a graduate of Dartmouth, served as her tutor. At age eighteen, she took on the nontraditional role of a teacher at a private school, and in her spare time, she penned poetry. Sarah married lawyer and Freemason David Hale in 1813; when she was pregnant with their fifth child, her husband died from pneumonia. The widow, as Queen Victoria did after the passing of Albert, never wore any color but black.

As his will left her only slightly wealthier than Old Mother Hubbard, Sarah turned to writing and, with the support of David's Masonic lodge, published a collection of poems followed by an 1827 novel, *Northwood; or, Life North and South*. This book made her the country's first female author, as well as the first to write about the evils of slavery. Its premise was that slaves should be relocated to Liberia rather than toil as American beasts of burden.

The novel attracted the attention of the Reverend John Blake, who made Hale the country's first female editor when he hired her for his Boston publication, *The Lady's Magazine*; after this became *Godey's Lady's Book*—the *Good Housekeeping* of its day—she settled in Philadelphia. The periodical, renowned as much for its dress patterns as for its uplifting articles, was referred to as the Victorian Bible of the Parlor. Hale became the last word on fashion and manners in one hundred and fifty thousand homes, and she remained at its helm until age ninety, a year before her death. Sarah wielded her pen not only to tell women what to wear, but also to shape public sentiment. Its 1830 edition included Sarah's poem, "Mary's Lamb," which would later become the beloved nursery rhyme, "Mary Had a Little Lamb." Legend has it that the poem was inspired by Mary Elizabeth Sawyer, whose pet lamb followed her to school—a prank suggested by her brother. Devoutly religious, Hale intended it as a religious allegory for children: Mary as the mother of God, the lamb as Jesus, "with a fleece as white as snow" that symbolized the purity of Christianity. In 1877, Thomas Edison invented the phonograph, and the world's first recording was the scientist reciting "Mary Had a Little Lamb."

Sarah was the Martha Stewart of the pre-Civil War era, filling her hugely popular magazine with advice on how to build a dream cottage, cook a seven-course dinner, and decorate the perfect spring hat. Under her leadership, *Godey's Lady's Book* popularized white wedding dresses and Christmas trees, trends often credited to Queen Victoria. She also published the works of well-known authors such as Harriet Beecher Stowe, Nathaniel Hawthorne, Washington Irving, Henry Wadsworth Longfellow, and Ralph Waldo Emerson. In 2012, an anonymous bidder purchased a letter from Edgar Allan Poe to Ms. Hale for $164,000; in it, the mystery writer declined to write an article for her magazine because, after a recent bout of illness, he was too caught up in other literary obligations.

Sarah was a cheerleader of many causes, and women's education was a priority for her. She deplored the widespread illiteracy among her sex, and in her role as editor she was instrumental in supporting Matthew Vassar's successful venture to found his eponymous women's college. Sarah also helped solicit the thirty thousand dollars (equivalent to eight hundred thousand dollars today) needed for the completion of the Bunker Hill Monument in Boston, and she also worked to obtain property ownership rights for wives. Despite her strides toward the goal of female emancipation, she still subscribed to the cult of "true womanhood" which entailed that the highest calling for her sex was to maintain a Christian nursery, one ruled by the Lamb.

Hale already had a formidable roll call of accomplishments, but her greatest one was yet to come. After Christmas, the busiest travel day of the year is Thanksgiving. The good china makes an appearance, and it is acceptable to watch football all day and to eat oneself into a turkey coma—the reason many don the unofficial festive garb of pants with elastic waists. The turkey consolidated its position of honor at the center of the table thanks to the late nineteenth-century marketing efforts of the poultry industry. Had it not been for this campaign, a different animal would be receiving the President's annual Thanksgiving pardon. Most assume we have the Pilgrims to thank for the turkey, but like for most things, there is a backstory. More than those who alighted from the Mayflower, it was Sarah Josepha Hale who gave America Thanksgiving. Until she came along, the only national holiday was Independence Day, which exclusively featured men parading down the street, creating large explosions and consuming massive quantities of liquor. Women were relegated to the role of spectator, waving handkerchiefs or serving as décor on the occasional float. In *Northwood*, Hale included an entire chapter about a traditional New England Thanksgiving celebration, and as the north/south conflict deepened, she became ever more committed to this holiday's cause. She believed that regional observances should be national, and as such would help bind the fractured country. In an 1859 editorial, she wrote, "Everything that contributes to bind us in one vast empire together, to quicken the sympathy that makes us feel from the icy north to the sunny south that we are one family, each a member of a great and free nation, not merely the unit of a remote locality, is worthy of being cherished."

Although Thanksgiving had been observed since 1621 when William Bradford, the governor of Plymouth Plantation, called for a day of prayer and thanksgiving, it had evolved as a haphazard tradition. Thanksgiving occurred on different days in various states—mostly in autumn—while some parts of the country ignored it in the spirit that it violated the separation of church and state. These ad hoc celebrations were primarily invoked in response to specific events. They were religious in nature, intended to ask God's help in coping with hardships, or to offer a day of prayer for times of prosperity. In 1863, Lincoln designated four Thanksgiving days, including one to celebrate Gettysburg and Vicksburg, while Jefferson Davis proclaimed Thanksgivings after each of the two Confederate victories at Manassas.

In vain, Sarah had petitioned Presidents Fillmore, Pierce, and Buchanan to set aside a uniform day, but for thirty-six years her pleas fell on deaf ears. She hit pay dirt when her letter reached Abraham Lincoln. She wrote, "Sir, permit me as editress of 'Lady's Book,' to request a few minutes of your precious time, while laying before you a subject of deep interest to myself and—as I trust—even to the President of the Republic of some importance. This subject is to have the day of our annual Thanksgiving made a national and fixed union festival." She added that the latter should occur on the last Thursday of November, because that was when George Washington had declared the first observance in 1789.

On October 3, 1863, five days after receiving Sarah's letter, President Lincoln declared, "I do therefore invite my fellow citizens in every part of the United States, and also those who are at sea and those who are sojourning in foreign lands, to set apart and observe the last Thursday of November next, as a day of Thanksgiving and Praise to our beneficent Father who dwelleth in the Heavens." In that fall, Lincoln had precious little of which to be thankful. The Union victory at Gettysburg the previous July had come with a terrible price—a combined fifty-one thousand estimated casualties and nearly eight thousand dead. Enraged by the draft laws, rioters in Northern cities such as New York went on bloody rampages. Moreover, the President and his wife Mary were in mourning for the loss of their eleven-year-old son Willie, who had died the year before. Lincoln's fervent hope was that a standardized celebration would help unite a divided United States.

Sarah Josepha Hale remains an unsung heroine. However, there is a memorial to her in Newport that showcases her role as America's first female novelist and editor, foundational fundraiser for Vassar College, the composer of "Mary Had a Little Lamb," and the mother who birthed a national holiday. It features a bronze bust of the Victorian woman—arms in shackles to highlight her anti-slavery views—that sits atop a black pillar, representative of her long widowhood. Her name also lives on in her hometown, where an annual award is presented to distinguished writers. Its first recipient was Robert Frost; John F. Kennedy reluctantly turned down the honor because of a prior—and fateful—commitment in Dallas.

Looking back at the accomplishments of an indefatigable woman, everywhere that Sarah went—like Mary's lamb—success was sure to go.

CHAPTER # 3

Five Stone Lions (1883)

 If the amber-hued liquid inside a classic bottle could speak, it would tell the tale of the convergence of an American sex symbol, a German officer, and a French legend. The black lettering on the bottle contains an eponymous name and a lucky number, and a story as extraordinary as the woman who willed it into existence.

For Coco Chanel, the Duchess of Windsor's declaration that "You can never be too rich or too thin" was holy writ. The icon who became synonymous with haute couture started life in poverty. Gabrielle Bonheur Chanel, the second daughter of an unmarried couple, hailed from the small town of Saumur, France. Her father, Henri-Albert, was an itinerant peddler, and her mother, Jeanne DeVolle, worked in the poorhouse where Gabrielle was born. When Gabrielle was twelve, her mother passed away and Albert (as he was known), now left with five offspring, took to travelling permanently. Gabrielle found herself in an orphanage where joyless nuns taught her to sew.

When Gabrielle made her escape, she found work as a cabaret singer, where her trademark song, a favorite of the soldiers, was "Qui qu'a vu Coco." She shed her name Gabrielle (as she had been christened, after the nun who had delivered her) and became Coco, from the lyric and because it was the shortened version of "cocotte," French for "kept woman." Escape beckoned with the patronage of Étienne Balsan, a textile heir who set her up in a shop on 31 rue Cambon to pursue her "little hat hobby." She lived in his grand manor, and he introduced his friends to her chapeaus (the antithesis of the flower-themed ones then in vogue), and they became wildly popular. During this period Coco met a friend of Balsan, Arthur Capel, nicknamed "Boy," an English polo-playing businessman who became the love of her life.

Coco became a fashion force to be reckoned with because of a black dress she designed from an old jersey in order to stay warm on a chilly day; previously the material had been used solely for men's underwear. In addition to warmth, it allowed liberty of movement, something that garters and the tight-fitting whalebone corsets of the day did not. The demand for the LBD (little black dress) was overwhelming; she explained her clothing philosophy thusly: "Luxury must be comfortable; otherwise it is not luxury." She had taken a color associated with mourning and transformed it into the height of fashion for evening wear. Her philosophy was that women should dress for other women—and undress for men. She also, through a mishap, introduced the flapper-styled bob when, preparing for the opera, her gas heater blew up and singed her long, lustrous locks. She cut off a foot of her damaged tresses and the style inspired the *garçon* boyish style that became *de rigueur* for flappers.

Boy married an aristocratic English beauty; however, the C's in Coco Chanel never stood for "conventional," and she continued the affair. In 1919, en route to their rendezvous, he died in a car accident on the Côte d'Azur. Chanel stated that 1919 was "The year I woke up famous and the year I lost everything."

After Boy there were other lovers, such as Hugh "Bendor" Grosvenor, 2nd Duke of Westminster—the richest man in Europe. Through him, Coco established connections with heavyweights such as David Lloyd George, Charlie Chaplin, and Winston Churchill. She refused her lover's marriage proposal with the pronouncement, "There have been several Duchesses of Westminster—but there is only one Chanel."

Chanel became the first female to head a fashion house, maintained a suite at the Ritz, vacationed on the Riviera (which she popularized as a holiday destination), befriended Pablo Picasso, and had an affair with composer Igor Stravinsky. Her shop, with its logo of mirror-image C's, became a mecca for those who desired to sheathe themselves in the ultimate status label. As the Queen of the opulent castle on 31 rue Cambon, Mademoiselle (as her staff of three hundred called her) became the mother of reinvention—a French equivalent of Gatsby. She reminisced how her doting dad had used "coco" as a term of endearment, altered the date of her birth to make herself ten years younger, and changed the locale of her birth. Through steely determination, she trod the road from courtesan to doyenne of high society, from seamstress to celebrated couturier. Yet her crowning achievement was her empire's greatest jewel: the eponym that made her name iconic.

The amber-hued perfume had its genesis in the collaboration of Chanel and Ernest Beaux—former perfumer to the Tsar of Russia— whom she had met through her lover, the recently deposed Grand Duke Dmitri Romanov. The perfume bottle's design remains a masterful example of classic elegance; its iconic glass cap was inspired by an antique mirror in her Ritz home, and its label (the first to feature a designer's name) still bears an understated "No. 5", a number with superstitious significance for Chanel. A fortune-teller had told her that five was her lucky number, and Coco released her famous perfume on May 5, 1921. When a young woman inquired where one should use perfume, Chanel replied, "Wherever one expects to be kissed." In a similarly sensual vein, when a reporter asked Marilyn Monroe what she wore to bed, the sex symbol responded, "Three drops of Chanel No. 5." This comment began the tradition of the perfume's association with the world's most desired women. In the 1970s, Catherine Deneuve purred, "You don't have to ask for it. He knows what you want: Chanel." Coco herself was enamored of her eponymous scent: her assistants sprayed it in her spiral staircase whenever she made her entrance, so she could waltz in through a haze of her signature scent. Chanel No. 5 made its entrance into pop art history when Andy Warhol produced the image of its iconic bottle dozens of times on canvas. Coco's couture also made it into American history: Jacqueline Kennedy was wearing a pink Chanel suit at her husband's assassination. When Lady Bird Johnson asked the new widow why she kept the blood-spattered garment on for her husband's impromptu inauguration aboard Air Force One, Mrs. Kennedy replied, "Let them see what they have done."

World War II was the event where Coco's talisman "5" deserted her. The war years proved to be the time when the creator of the world's best-selling fragrance came away smelling not so sweet. During the Occupation of Paris, she embarked on an affair with Nazi officer Baron Hans Günther von Dinklage that carried the fringe benefit of allowing her to remain in her suite at the Ritz. The once homeless orphan was willing to become the "cocotte" once more. She served as a willing agent for the German high command, partly driven by anti-Semitism. In return she was granted favors that included the release of her nephew from a German prisoner-of-war camp. Moreover, under the laws of Vichy France, she sought to dispossess the Jewish Pierre Wertheimer of his 90-percent ownership stake in Les Parfums Chanel. However, before Pierre fled to New York City, he transferred his shares to the Christian industrialist Felix Amiot. After the war, Wertheimer bought back the company and his two grandsons' fortunes are currently valued at $19.2 billion.

Nevertheless, the degree of her involvement with the enemy is shrouded in the gray arena of conjecture. Her defenders argue that her transgression was solely on a horizontal level, driven by love rather than avarice. Her detractors view her as a master manipulator, flawed, hard, and pitiless, like the nuns who had raised her. She had become rich by catering to the rich, and at age fifty her fortune was worth the equivalent of almost one billion in today's dollars. Her success stemmed from her Golden Rule of never following anyone else's rules. Coco was always able to land on her feet—or someone else's—and move on to the next man, the next collection, or the next patron.

After the war, female collaborators had their heads shaved and were paraded through the streets; through Churchill's intervention, she was spared the indignity. However, she could not elude the court of public opinion that condemned her for sleeping with the enemy, and Chanel retreated to her Elba—a self-imposed exile in Switzerland.

After eight years, she returned to her suite at the Ritz, the place where she had conducted affairs with the most celebrated men of the twentieth century; however, in the end, she was alone. Coco's greatness, putting aside her legacy, lay in how she proved that she did not define herself by the many men who had desired and deserted her. Chanel's personal tragedy was that her life never delivered the unalloyed sweetness of her iconic scent.

The grand doyenne of fashion passed away at age eighty-seven, hard at work up to the end—designing, controlling, and dictating, inspiring equal parts admiration and fear in Madame's employees. Her last words were to her maid Celine: "You see, this is how you die." On her casket lay a spray of white flowers in the shape of a tailor's shears. The attendees at her funeral were clad in Chanel; interment was at the Cimètiere du Boise-de-Vaux in Lausanne. Her headstone bears the name Gabrielle Chanel—inscribed under five bas-relief stone lions, a nod to her astrological sign and her immortal scent.

CHAPTER # 4

You Can't Beat (1903)

 From time immemorial, relationships have often been expressed through gifts. Some, like Eve's apple and the Trojan Horse, proved unkind to those who received them, while other gifts have been odes to romance. Few women have received as wondrous a present as Cosima Wagner did when Richard composed the *Siegfried Idyll* for her birthday. Tsar Alexander's Fabergé egg gained him mileage with his young bride, as did Burton's sixty-eight-carat diamond for his ladylove. Resplendent as the symphony, the egg, and the ring may be, nothing could rival a son's tribute to his mother.

In 1865, Frenchman Frédéric Auguste Bartholdi conceived a giant statue to send across the sea to commemorate the centennial of America's freedom from monarchy. The robed figure represented the Roman goddess Libertas, and the seven spikes of her crown symbolized the seven continents and the seven seas. Her rib cage was an engineering marvel of Gustave Eiffel, while her face was a portrait of Charlotte Bartholdi, the sculptor's mother. He baptized his lady "Liberty Enlightening the World."

The game plan was for France to absorb the cost of the statue's creation and the United States to pay for its pedestal; however, many Americans were not convinced they needed a gigantic, European statue. Joseph Pulitzer, a Hungarian Jewish immigrant, disgusted by this parsimony, spearheaded a fundraiser through his newspaper, the *New York World*. This campaign included an auction to bid for the works of eminent writers; Mark Twain and Walt Whitman sent in their work as an inscription for its pedestal.

One of the authors who picked up her pen to give words to the Lady was Emma Lazarus. She was the fourth of seven children, six of them girls, born in 1849 into a secular Jewish family who had lived in America since before the Revolution. Her great-great-uncle had welcomed George Washington to Newport, Rhode Island. They enjoyed annual visits to Saratoga and other fashionable resorts for "the upper ten thousand" of the richest families in New York. Her father, Moses, who had made his fortune in sugar, was proud of his daughter's literary skills, and, when she was seventeen, paid for the publication of her poems. The book was more than two hundred pages long and was dedicated "To My Father"; Moses and Emma were thrilled when, a year later, a commercial press issued a second edition. The publication attracted the notice of literary celebrities such as Ralph Waldo Emerson, then sixty-five, whom Emma met through the Transcendentalist Samuel Gray Ward. A line from one of his letters to the eighteen-year-old poetess indicates he would have been pleased to serve as her Abelard: "I would like to be appointed your professor." Her indifference may have stemmed from their age difference—or something else. In the anthology she compiled in 1886, while dying of Hodgkin's disease, she included an undated sonnet that remained unpublished until 1980. Its tone is electric with erotica: "Last night I slept, & when I woke her kiss/still floated on my lips." Although Emerson might not have approved, Whitman would certainly have given it a thumbs-up.

However, the majority of her work centered on something far from sexual; it explored her heritage as a Jew of Sephardic descent. She was proud of her background, in contrast to her father, who tried to assimilate his family into wealthy, Christian society. She was aware that members of her acquaintance referred to her as a "Jewess," and she wrote that she was "perfectly conscious that this contempt and hatred underlies the general tone of the community towards us."

Emma, when not engaged with writing poetry, fending off elderly suitors, or dreaming of her own Sappho, enjoyed a wide circle of friends which included Thomas Wentworth Higginson (an abolitionist minister), Rose Lanthrop (Nathaniel Hawthorne's daughter), Henry James, and Robert Browning. Her activism was ignited in the 1880s, when news broke of anti-Semitic violence in Russia. Pogroms—bloody persecutions named after a Russian word that means to "demolish violently"—drove two thousand Jewish refugees on a monthly basis to New York. They had high hopes for what they called the *goldene medina*—the golden land, a place of hope after centuries of suffering. Not content to vent her ire in ink, she took the streetcar from her lavish brownstone on 57th Street to volunteer at the Hebrew Emigrant Aid Society on East Broadway where she taught the newcomers English. She also paid them visits in their squalid quarters on Ward Island and wrote an exposé about their deplorable living conditions. In her weekly column for *The American Hebrew* she wrote, "Until we are all free/none of us is free." Lazarus served as one of the first high-profile Americans to publicly make the cause for a Jewish state in Palestine. In these crusader years, Jewish themes became her dominant subject. Lazarus incurred the ire of her sisters, who disapproved of her Zionism and her crusade on the behalf of Eastern European Jewish immigrants, who they felt were of inferior stock. After Emma's 1887 death, her family whitewashed her life and portrayed her as a "demure and feminine spinster."

When Lazarus was asked to write a poem to help fund Bartholdi's pedestal, she initially balked, claiming she did not pen poetry made "to order." In addition, she was not particularly fond of France or French society. "Take away the Louvre & the pictures & the statutes," she wrote of Paris, "& I should never wish to see it again." However, in a moment of clarity, she saw a way to link the Russian refugees with the colossal statue destined for New York Harbor and embraced the commission. The resulting sonnet imagined the Statue addressing "ancient lands" to keep "your storied pomp!" Although concern for immigrants was not the Statue's official message, Lazarus' lines resonated, and editor James Russell Lowell wrote he liked it "much better than I like the Statue itself" because it "gives its subject a raison d'être." Lazarus had dramatically recast the meaning of Bartholdi's masterpiece, and her lines served as an invitation to refugees from the Old World to find sanctuary in the New: "Here at our sea-washed, sunset gates shall stand/A mighty woman with a torch, whose flame/ Is the imprisoned lightening, and her name/Mother of Exiles. From her beacon-hand/Glows worldwide welcome. . . ." Politicians were less enthusiastic, and her words were not read at Lady Liberty's 1886 unveiling. Unfortunately, it was not just Emma's poem that was absent. Suffragettes boycotted the event: an enormous female figure would have the power to represent liberty, while her flesh-and-blood counterparts exercised none at the polls. They chartered a boat to circle Liberty Island in order to blast their protests from its deck, but their voices were drowned out by the fanfare.

Emma passed away at age thirty-eight, and the poem she referred to as "her best work" seemed destined to literary ashes; it did not merit a mention in her *New York Times* obituary. It was only resurrected when a friend of hers chanced upon it in a bookstore, and after relentless lobbying from a descendant of Alexander Hamilton, the poem was affixed to a plaque on Ms. Liberty's pedestal. It made Bartholdi's lady "the Mother of Exiles" and her role as beacon for immigrants was launched. The United States would be the haven where newcomers would not just survive, but would also thrive. Tragically, during anti-immigration hysteria the American melting pot has not always followed in her size 879 shoes.

Lady Liberty's beacon refused to go out, even in America's darkest days. Talk show host Jon Stewart, broadcasting a week after the 9/11 attacks, embodied the country's indefatigable spirit. He movingly expressed his feelings, saying, "The view from my apartment was the

World Trade Center. Now it's gone. . . . But you know what the view is now? The Statue of Liberty. The view from the south of Manhattan is the Statue of Liberty. You can't beat that."

CHAPTER 5

Chutzpah (1903)

Hamlet railed against dissembling women saying, "God has given you one face, and you make yourselves another." Yet altering appearance has always been a siren's call, and by listening to this lure, "Madam" not only launched an empire—she also changed the way the world viewed beauty.

At the turn of the twentieth century, only actresses and prostitutes painted their faces, and the woman who altered this paradigm was a study in reinvention. Chaja was the oldest of eight daughters born into a Jewish family on Christmas Day in 1872 in Krakow's Jewish ghetto; the family survived on the meager earnings of the father, Hertzel, a kerosene dealer. His wife, Gitel, understood that girls devoid of dowries depended on appearance and insisted that her children use her concoction of cream, as their flawless complexions was their marital lifeline. Her parents were livid when Chaja refused to be married off to an older, rich man, and as a result, she left home, an extraordinary move in an era when the only thing a woman did was marry and have babies.

Chaja Rubinstein went to live with her uncle's family in Coleraine, an Australian backwater. Before her arrival, she changed her name to Helena, perhaps a nod to the ancient world's femme fatale. Just as one day she would alter the face of beauty, she reimagined a glamorous past. Her squalid home became a country estate; however, her escape from an arranged marriage to an elderly widower rang true. Vertically challenged at 4'10", she always wore the highest heels she could navigate. For two years she worked for her uncle without wages, fending off the advances of another male relative. She left as soon as her command of English was good enough; her adopted language would always carry a marked Yiddish accent. As she moved from one poorly paid job to another, it was hard enough to pay her rent—and borrowing money to start a business was untenable for a woman, even in liberated Australia, where they had won the vote in 1902. The future appeared grim until serendipity stepped in. Her milky skin—which she claimed was the result of a moisturizer created by a Polish doctor, in actuality a parting gift of twelve jars from Gitel—awed the weather-beaten women of the Outback. A financial bloodhound, Rubinstein understood it was not the actual ingredients in the jar that would prove seductive. She dropped hints such as "old family recipe," "secret ingredient," "Hungarian chemist," "evergreen tree from the Carpathian Mountains"—euphemisms for lanolin, the oil produced by sheep, and in Australia she was surrounded by millions of them. Under the tutelage of a chemist, she made her own and christened her product "Valaze": "gift from heaven" in Hungarian. It certainly proved a gift for Helena: she sold vats of it—at an astronomical mark-up with the promise it would deliver what Ponce de Léon had sought. Helena founded her fortune on the philosophy, "There are no ugly women. Only lazy ones."

Within six years, Helena had relocated to Melbourne, with a well-padded purse of millions of dollars and the ambition of Lady Macbeth. She found further commercial success and, in her thirties, romance, when she fell wildly in love for the first time. Born in Poland as Arthur Ameisen, after establishing himself as a journalist in America, he had immigrated to Australia where, because of anti-Semitism, had anglicized his name to Edward William Titus. For their 1908 wedding, Helena gifted Edward her greatest treasure— no, not her virginity, but equal shares in Helena Rubinstein Cosmetics. Titus—who called his wife Madame—had a keen eye for marketing; however, to Helena's horror, hubby also had a keen eye for other women. His philandering began on their honeymoon, when she realized he was a serial seducer. Bordering on stout, his wandering eye fueled her insecurity. She comforted herself with jewelry.

Wanting other worlds to beautify, Helena set sail for Europe. While Rubinstein captured the attention of rich and famous women, bibliophile Edward established the Black Manikin Press, a small publishing company that brought him and Helena into the orbit of the literary avant-garde and led to his affair with Anaïs Nin. Black Manikin published the first edition of *Lady Chatterley's Lover*, as well as Stein, Hemingway, Huxley, and Beckett. Introduced to Marcel Proust—who interrogated Helena for his literary research on the subjects of whether or not a duchess would use rouge and if demimondaines put kohl on their eyes. She later regretted that she had dismissed Proust as "nebbish-looking." Then Helena added, "But then, how could I have known he was going to be so famous?" Colette provided a celebrity endorsement for the Swedish massage at Rubinstein's Paris salon—apparently made all the more satisfying by the use of a vibrator.

With France and London under her ruby-encrusted belt, Madame, leaving her many salons in the manicured hands of a trio of sisters imported from Poland, sailed for New York. There she and Manka, another hastily summoned sister, displayed avant-garde treatment routines to cosmetically starved Manhattanites. After grueling twelve-hour days, she returned home to Edward and her sons, Roy and Horace. Motherhood came second, and she employed nannies so she could get on with her life's mission: beauty and making truckloads of money. Another reason: "Work has been my best beauty treatment! It keeps the wrinkles out of the mind and the spirit. It helps to keep a woman young. It certainly keeps a woman alive!"

Rubinstein's other great passion was art, much of it bought from a young antiques dealer, Christian Dior. Her cluttered residences in New York, Paris, London, and Connecticut were the repositories of priceless paintings. In just one room of her Park Avenue triplex, she had seven Renoirs hung above a fireplace. Other masterpieces were a still life by Frida Kahlo, whom Helena had met on a trip to Mexico and considered "simpatico," and a drawing by Andy Warhol. In mutual admiration the pop artist wore her gift—a ruby and silver ring inlaid with the initials "H. R." Another coup was twelve Picasso sketches, made under duress. After arriving at his door in Provence, she refused to leave until he picked up his pencil.

What Madame lacked in inches, she made up in gems. Her legendary collection of jewels was kept in a filing cabinet, sorted alphabetically: "A" for amethyst, "D" for diamonds, "E" for emeralds, "P" for pearls. . . . Many of these were captured in canvas on a wall of portraits that showcased her as a porcelain-skinned Polish princess. Noticeably missing from the exclusive suite was Edward, who, post-divorce, had discreetly retreated to Paris.

The fact Helena lived at her tony address at all speaks volumes both about the diminutive dragoness and 1940s New York. Denied an apartment at 625 Park Avenue because the owner did not allow Jews, she told her accountants to buy the whole building—whatever the cost. Rubinstein also made a bold decision in keeping her name in an era when anti-Semitism relegated her flagship storefront to the side streets of Fifth Avenue for two decades. Emblazoning Rubinstein on her brand affirmed her religious allegiance—though she was a non-practicing Jew.

In 1938, she—by now in her sixties—married the forty-three-year-old Russian émigré Prince Artchil Gourielli-Tchkonia—both for love and the acquisition of a title, the ultimate coup for the girl from the Krakow ghetto. He said, "Besides Helena, every other is uninteresting" (not to mention, poor). He passed away from a heart attack in 1955; three years later, her son, Horace, died in a car crash.

In 1964, thieves broke into her apartment, posing as deliverymen carrying roses. When they surprised the ninety-one-year-old doyenne in her bed, the keys to her safe that held a million dollars in jewelry were in her purse, buried beneath a mound of papers. She silently extracted the keys and dropped them in her ample cleavage. By the time the thieves spied the purse, it contained only an H. R. compact, five twenty-dollar bills, and a pair of diamond earrings worth forty thousand dollars. These rolled away when the purse was upended, and Madame covered them with a Kleenex. The thieves tied her to a chair with strips from her sheets and fled. When her butler freed her, she calmly instructed him to put the roses in the icebox, in case she had company later that day. She calculated that after paying forty dollars for the flowers, the intruders had just made sixty dollars in profit. However, posthumously, something would finally best Helena. Her empire was ultimately purchased by L'Oréal, a company founded by Eugène Schueller, who had also founded/funded violent anti-Semitic organizations in Nazi-occupied France.

Shortly before her 1955 passing, Helena showed her secretary a piece of paper, yellowed with age. Rubinstein explained, "This is a piece of history. The famous magic formula for my original cream." The secretary expected to see a list of the exotic ingredients that had made her employer one of the richest and most powerful women in the world. In Helena's distinctive handwriting: "vegetable oil, mineral oil, wax."

How could a four feet, ten inches tall Jewish gal rise from Polish poverty to build a cosmetic conglomerate from twelve pots of cream? It's obvious: Chaja had *chutzpah*.

CHAPTER # 6

Do Not Pass Go (1904)

 Nostalgia comes to call with the opening of a box filled with silver trinkets, brightly colored cards, and plastic pieces of real estate. It offers a flight of fancy where, for a time, one could be lord of many manors. If unlucky, we would end up behind bars; if savvy, we would become as wealthy as Rich Uncle Pennybags.

The board games of our yesteryears act as Proustian madeleines, pastimes that perhaps shaped our worldviews. The most prevalent of these was Monopoly, which taught "To the victor belong the spoils." Played by everyone from Jerry Hall and Mick Jagger to Carmela and Tony Soprano, it scratches an itch to wheel and deal that few of us can reach in real life. The game is sufficiently redolent of unbridled capitalism that, in 1959, Fidel Castro ordered the destruction of every Monopoly set in Cuba, while these days Vladimir Putin seems to be the ultimate aficionado. The cardboard board is as famous as the curvaceous Barbie, but its true origin has purposely been relegated to the shadows.

For generations, the story of Monopoly's Depression-era birth delighted fans almost as much as the board game itself. The tale, tucked into the game's box along with the Community Chest and Chance Cards, was that Charles Darrow sold the game to Parker Brothers and lived lavishly ever after. The trouble was that the story is as mythical as George Washington and the cherry tree.

In the case of Monopoly, the term "mother of invention" is not just a nod to the feminine, as its genesis can be traced to a woman. Elizabeth Magie, a Quaker, was born in Macomb, Illinois; her father,

James, was an abolitionist who accompanied President Lincoln as he travelled around Illinois debating politics with Stephen Douglas. Elizabeth stated, "I have often been called a 'chip off the old block,' which I consider quite a compliment, for I am proud of my father for being the kind of an 'old block' that he is." James ran for public office on an anti-monopoly ticket—an election he lost, but his message was not lost on his daughter.

Elizabeth supported herself as a stenographer, barely able to scrape by on her salary of ten dollars a week. To draw attention to the plight of unmarried women being exploited in the workplace, she purchased a newspaper advertisement where she offered herself for sale as a "young woman American slave" to the highest bidder. Due to her notoriety, in 1906 she obtained a job as a journalist. Despite the difficulty of supporting herself without a husband, Magie was reluctant to walk down the aisle. She described marriage as "a germ" and likened it to "a disease." Her philosophy was not just related to the economic ills of capitalist society: "What is love? Nobody knows." She said matrimony was not for her unless she could see her spouse only once every three days. She did not want anyone to interfere with her ability to retreat into her den and spend hours with her books. She commented, "Personally, I love solitude, and were I married I could not enjoy this luxury." Apparently, she met the man who fit this bill; four years later she married Virginian businessman Albert Phillips, who, at age fifty-four, was ten years her senior. The marriage raised eyebrows—a woman who had remained single well beyond the sell-by date and a man becoming the husband of a wife who had publicly expressed skepticism of the institution of marriage. In her spare time, she created a game based on economist Henry George's anti-monopoly beliefs. She felt this venue would convince people of the evils of corporate greed.

Magie's brainchild—the Landlord's Game—featured a path that allowed players to circle the board in contrast to the linear path popular at the time. It included money, railroads, properties, and the three words that have endured for more than a century after Elizabeth scrawled them: "Go to Jail." Its Chance cards had quotations such as John Ruskin's, "It begins to be asked on many sides how the possessors of land became possessed of it," and Andrew Carnegie's, "The greatest astonishment of my life was the discovery that the man who does the work is not the man who gets rich." She created two sets of rules: an anti-monopolist set in which all were rewarded when wealth was created, and a monopolist set in which the goal was to build a fortune by destroying the nest eggs of your opponents. Her dualistic approach was intended to demonstrate that the first set of rules was morally superior. Magie hoped that her brainchild would serve as a rebuke to the land barons of the Gilded Age. The game made its way to Atlantic City Quakers, where they altered the property names from Elizabeth's Manhattan ones to those from their neck of the woods.

The man who received credit for creating Monopoly was a Pennsylvanian named Charles Darrow, who was not an inventor, but an opportunist. During the Depression, Darrow and his wife Esther were introduced to Magie's game by another couple, and a light bulb went off. He asked his friend Franklin Alexander to create illustrations such as Mr. Monopoly—based on J. P. Morgan—and the whistle-blowing cop. Darrow sold the reinvented product to Parker Brothers for seven thousand dollars plus residuals. By 1936, the board game had garnered millions, saving not only Darrow but also the game company from financial ruin. Fortunately for the Darrow descendants, they kept the original game in their possession until 1992, when Malcolm Forbes purchased it for a princely sum. Parker Brothers gave the mother of the invention a onetime payoff of five hundred dollars.

At first, the then-elderly Elizabeth was pleased with the purchase. She hoped the company would turn her "beautiful brainchild" into a popular way of disparaging greedy monopolists. She was infuriated when she discovered they had a different game plan. To add insult to injury, Darrow and the proprietors made sure Magie's name had as little connection as possible to the lucrative blockbuster. When journalists questioned how he had come up with the phenomenally successful game, his stock response was, "It's a freak. Entirely unexpected and illogical." Darrow had monopolized Monopoly. In 1936, amidst the media frenzy surrounding "the inventor" and the nationwide Monopoly craze, Magie lashed out. She gave an interview to *The Washington Post* where she expressed anger at the appropriation. Gray hair tied back in a tightly coiffed bun, she held up the board from The Landlord's Game and Parker Brothers' Monopoly to illustrate their shared DNA. She stated that although the company had the rights to her three-decade-old patent that had passed into public domain, they did not give credit where credit was due. They had kidnapped her child and passed it off as their own. They never righted the wrong. One of Elizabeth's last jobs was at the US Office of Education; here her colleagues knew her as an elderly typist who claimed ownership of Monopoly. She died in 1948, a widow with no children—and an aborted legacy. Her obituary made no mention that she was the mother of Monopoly. In contrast, the Charles Darrow myth persisted as an inspirational parable of rags-to-riches ingenuity, his niche secured as a Depression-era Horatio Alger. Darrow became an industry legend for inventing a story rather than for inventing an economic eureka.

Elizabeth Magie would be pleased with her posthumous recognition. However, she would be gobsmacked at the changes time had wrought. There is now an app for Monopoly, as well as an electronic banking edition introduced in 2006 that features debit cards instead of cash, with tokens including a Segway and a flat-screen TV. She would be equally astounded that her game even played a role in history. In World War II, Monopoly boards, by that point a symbol of capitalism and America, were used to conceal maps sent by the Allies to prisoners of war.

During her lifetime the game had proliferated, selling just over two million copies in its first years of production. Currently, at least one billion people in 111 countries have played Monopoly, with an estimated six billion little green houses manufactured. The iconic board has undergone many face-lifts: it has adopted the streets of almost every major American city, and versions have been branded by financiers (Berkshire Hathaway), sports teams (Chicago Bears), television shows (the Simpsons), automobiles (Corvette), and farm equipment (John Deere). There have been odd sets as well: the Disney Villains, the Walking Dead, and Sun-Maid Raisins. One incarnation that would send the Quaker founder reeling is the bling version created by San Francisco jeweler Sidney Mobell, made of eighteen-karat gold and diamonds and valued at two million. Even more disturbing would be Ghettopoly, whose main "playa" is a far cry from the usual top-hat-wearing mascot. Instead there is a bandana-wearing African American male holding an Uzi and a bottle of liquor. A sample token is a marijuana leaf, while a typical Chance card reads, "You got da whole hood addicted to crack, collect $50."

Monopoly continues to wield its hold; after all, who can resist the endorphin rush of bankrupting friends and family? And for all the capitalists in training, the seed is planted that if they can put into practice the principle of the game, they too can become the contemporary rich Uncle Moneybags, a megalomaniac billionaire who married an Eastern European model and lives in baronial splendor. Its premise can be summed up by Gordon Gekko's famous line in *Wall Street*: "The point is, ladies and gentlemen, that greed, for lack of a better word, is good."

As for Charles Darrow, who misappropriated a Quaker woman's brainchild, the final epitaph could be: "Do Not Pass Go—Do Not Collect $200."

43

CHAPTER 7

Now Abideth Faith, Hope, and Love (1912)

When a Southern woman was none too happy with the way her life's cookie had crumbled, rather than throwing a pity party, she adapted a British institution and made it into an iconic American one. She helped level the gender playing field and allowed girls, rather than wearing their hearts on their sleeves, to instead display their merits.

Ironically, the organization that was a precursor to the Women's Rights Movement began with a lady destined to live the life of a Southern belle. Juliette, nicknamed Daisy, was born in Savannah, the second of six children of William Washington Gordon and Eleanor Lytle Kinzie. In the midst of the fierce fighting in Georgia, while her husband fought for the Confederacy, Eleanor took her children to Chicago, where her family, founders of the city who owned its first house, moved in the highest echelons. When the war ended, the Gordons reunited in their Victorian mansion; that was where Juliette met the victorious and vilified General Sherman and inquired as to the whereabouts of his horns. Ms. Gordon soon became known as "Crazy Daisy" because of her eccentric attitude and her insistence in keeping pace with a nonconformist drummer. In her teens she attended a series of prestigious boarding schools where instruction focused on social graces of upper-class girls. These proved unfulfilling, and her defiant nature resulted in her breaking rules, leading her mother to comment that she was "a pig-headed fool."

As the daughter of wealth and the genteel South, the roadmap of her life after her debutante ball was to embark on the pursuit of obtaining figurines on a white frosted cake. Disinterested in strait-laced suitors, Daisy fell in love with bad boy William Mackay Low—who she nicknamed Billow—a British aristocrat and heir to a vast fortune. In 1886, they married in Savannah; however, their wedding left a tragic legacy. A grain of rice thrown at the departing bride lodged in her ear and compounded an earlier mistreated infection. The doctor, in an attempt to dislodge the rice, punctured her eardrum and caused Daisy to lose most of her hearing.

The Lows settled in England, where they purchased Wellesbourne House in Warwickshire and spent autumns in Scotland, where William pursued his passion for hunting. In London, he introduced his bride to Albert Edward, Prince of Wales, and Daisy curtseyed before Queen Victoria. However, the blue-blood connection wore thin, and Daisy longed for something meaningful to do with her life. However, unable to have children, and with a husband who did not approve of charity work, Daisy became an upper-class social butterfly.

The Low marriage unraveled as Daisy, a strict Episcopalian, did not approve of William's excessive drinking and his second type of hunt—for women. He fell in love with one of them—Anna Bateman—who became his constant public paramour. The intolerable situation prompted Daisy's extended visit to Savannah during the outbreak of the 1898 Spanish American War, where she helped organize a convalescent hospital. Upon her return to England, her husband expected her to share their mansion with his lover, though he magnanimously offered her possession of her own wing. In the midst of the divorce, William passed away, leaving his assets to Anna. Daisy contested the will and was awarded five hundred thousand dollars, as well as ownership of their Savannah Lafayette Ward estate.

At this juncture, the fifty-year-old Juliette Gordon Low, almost deaf, was at an emotional low ebb. Plan A—her role as wife and mother—had gone by the wayside, and she had no Plan B; however, serendipity stepped in. In 1911, at a luncheon party, she sat next to Sir Robert Baden-Powell. She was intrigued when she discovered he had founded the Boy Scouts with the aim of training young boys for military experience. Her interest was further piqued when she discovered his sister Agnes had formed a female version, the Girl Guides. The catalyst for this had been when six thousand girls showed up in makeshift uniforms in 1909 for the first Boy Scout rally, clamoring for inclusion. This encounter led to Low's eureka moment: a similar organization for girls, not to train for warfare but to help develop life skills—a Plan B. Fired with enthusiasm, she started branches in Scotland and London. The effect on its members was so electrifying that she decided to spread her idea to the United States. A year later, she changed the named from Girl Guides, with its connotations of feminine nurturing, to the more adventurous Girl Scouts. Low's personality left a different imprint on her American branch than Agnes had on the British counterpart; Agnes placed a heavy emphasis on domestic skills, while Daisy adopted Boy Scout activities such as athletics, camping, and shooting.

As soon as she returned to Georgia, she called her schoolmistress cousin and said, "Come right over. I've got something for the girls of Savannah, and all of America, and all the world, and we're going to start it tonight!" When Juliette Gordon Low registered her first troop on March 12, it was during an era when few women held jobs, only six states permitted them to vote, and only nineteen allowed them to participate in jury duty. Her movement allowed girls a taste of autonomy and fostered sisterly solidarity. The initial swearing-in took place in the carriage house in the rear of Daisy's home; the first of the eighteen girls was Margaret "Daisy Doots" Gordon, her niece and namesake. The original handbook of 1913 encouraged members to shoot rifles and gave instructions for tying up intruders. They were encouraged to play basketball on outdoor courts shrouded from public view by curtains so that men could not glimpse their bloomers. Although the sisterhood was punctuated with a sense of duty, the overall goal was fun. In this spirit, Low once showed off a pair of shoes during a session with her girls by standing on her head and told spooky stories around the campfire. She was the troop leader with the mostest.

When the Savannah membership swelled, Juliette was convinced her organization should spread to the national level. Juliette dedicated herself heart and soul to her Scouts and was described as having the "force of a hurricane," only stopping for a year to recover from the death of her beloved father. She used her own finances and the resources of friends and family for her organization and, under the guise of her disability, pretended not to hear when people begged off from volunteering or contributing funds.

In 1917, a troop from Muskogee, Oklahoma, sold home-baked cookies in a bid to garner revenue; the idea spread like the proverbial wildfire and the Girl Scouts partnered with commercial companies to produce their wares. This emblematic fundraiser was launched on a massive scale in 1923 by then Girl Scouts President Lou Hoover, who would later become First Lady, and was only interrupted by World War II. Over the past century, Girl Scout cookies have become a ubiquitous annual treat that have generated millions of dollars. Names added to the lexicon of Americana include Thin Mints, Tagalongs, and Trefoils—flavors also available as Lip Smackers.

Once the Girl Scouts had been firmly entrenched in the United States, Daisy promoted overseas participation. In 1920, a parade in New York included six thousand girls of ten nationalities, and the organization had branches from Shanghai to the West Indies. Since that first meeting in a Savannah carriage house, fifty million girls have been devoted alumnae, including Hillary Clinton, Laura Bush, Katie Couric, Gloria Steinem, Mary Tyler Moore, Lucille Ball, Barbara Walters, Venus Williams, and Mariah Carey. Scouts have grown up to be Secretaries of State and scientists, astronauts and actors, teachers and TV anchors, Supreme Court judges and singers—and probably had a hand in inventing s'mores.

Low, who was not a radical like her contemporaries Emma Goldman and Margret Sanger, did not intentionally set out to institute sweeping social changes; nevertheless, her brainchild set the stage for the Women's Movement and helped bridge the gender gap.

Daisy stressed inclusion in her troops, perhaps a nod to her own disability. In the 1947 edition of their handbook, watercolor illustrations showed White, Black, and Asian Scouts, a fact that caused an outcry in the land of Dixie. Dr. Martin Luther King, Jr. called the Girl Scouts "a force of desegregation." Indeed, its liberal attitude has elicited ire: Christians in Texas called for a Girl Scout Cookie boycott because of the organization's support of Planned Parenthood, and there was an outcry over the induction of a transgendered child. On the other hand, the Boy Scouts heard a clarion call to exclude gays all the way to the Supreme Court. Perhaps the reason why men are from Mars and girls are from Venus is the differing visions of Sir Robert and Crazy Daisy.

Juliette Low passed away from breast cancer and an honor guard of her troops escorted her casket to Christ Church. She was laid to rest in her Girl Scout uniform with a note from her organization in her pocket: "You are not only the first Girl Scout, you are the best Girl Scout of them all." On her tombstone is the inscription, "Now abideth faith, hope, and love, but the greatest of these is love."

CHAPTER # 8

The Hand That Rocks the Cradle (1914)

Mothers have always been sacrosanct: the Roman Catholic Church has a cult of the Virgin, beloved nursery rhymes are associated with one named Goose, and Whistler painted a classic portrait of his. Hence, it was only fitting that a day be set aside to honor mothers; however, it came with a bizarre twist.

The genesis of Mother's Day started with a woman from West Virginia, a Sunday school teacher and wife of the Reverend Granville Jarvis, a prominent Methodist minister. During the Civil War, Ann, along with her friend Julia Ward Howe—composer of the "Battle Hymn of the Republic"—formed the Mothers' Friendships Clubs, comprised of both Union and Confederate women, who nursed wounded soldiers, regardless of the color of their uniform. When the war ended, the hatred endured, and to diffuse tensions, Ann showed up in her town square dressed in the gray of the Confederacy with a friend dressed in the blue of the Union. They asked the band to play "Dixie" and the "Star-Spangled Banner" and convinced the soldiers to lay down their arms.

For the remainder of the conflict, Mrs. Jarvis worked tirelessly despite the loss of four of her ten children to disease. The ninth baby was daughter Anna, born in 1864 in a two-story wooden house in Webster and raised in Grafton, where the family moved when she was a year old. Ann was an advocate of female education, and under her encouragement, Anna attended college at Augusta Female Seminary in Staunton, Virginia (now Mary Baldwin College), and then she returned to Grafton where she taught for several years. She left her position to join her brother Claude in Philadelphia and worked with him in his lucrative taxi business. After her father passed away, brother and sister brought their mother to live with them. The day of Ann's funeral on May 9, 1905, at age seventy-two, in tribute the bell of St. Andrews Methodist Church in Grafton pealed seventy-two times.

What helped Anna with her overwhelming grief was her eureka moment, born from a memory that had taken place when she was twelve years old. She had been in her father's church when Mrs. Jarvis gave a Sunday school talk about Biblical mothers that ended with her wish that a day should be set aside in observance of these women. She closed by saying, "I hope that someone, some time, will found a memorial mother's day commemorating her for the matchless service she renders to humanity in every field of life." A year later, on the anniversary of her passing, Anna organized a memorial where she praised the contribution Ann Jarvis made during the Civil War.

Three years later, on May 10, 1908, Jarvis organized another memorial at her church, not just for her own mother, but also for all mothers, which became the first observance of the holiday. Although Anna was not present, she sent a telegram that described the significance of the day as well as providing five hundred white carnations, one for everyone who attended the service. She chose this flower as it had been her mother's favorite, and because of its symbolism. She stated, "Its whiteness is to symbolize the truth, purity, and broad-charity of mother love; its fragrance, her memory, and her prayers. The carnation does not drop its petals, but hugs them to her heart as it dies, and so, too, mothers hug their children to their hearts, their mother love never dying. When I selected the flower, I was remembering my mother's bed of white pinks." The reason for her absence was because she was speaking in Philadelphia at the Wanamaker's Store Auditorium, convincing the crowd that Mother's Day should be adopted on the national level. The idea became her cause cèlèbre.

Anna wrote an avalanche of letters to editors, politicians, and church leaders, and her correspondence grew so voluminous that she purchased the neighboring house to store the correspondence. In 1908, the US Congress rejected a proposal to make the day official, joking that they would also have to proclaim a "Mother-in-law's Day." However, owing to Anna's persistence, by 1911 all the states observed the unofficial holiday, the first being Jarvis' West Virginia. Her diligence finally paid off when her longtime friend, President Woodrow Wilson, signed a proclamation designating Mother's Day to be observed on the second Sunday in May. According to President Wilson, "The American mother is the greatest source of our country's strength and inspiration." A nation divided over women's suffrage could unite over maternal love. Indeed, Jarvis put a feminist slant on the holiday she had fought into existence: "Memorial Day is for Departed fathers, Independence Day is for Patriot Fathers, Thanksgiving Day is for Pilgrim Fathers." Anna Jarvis was pleased with her brainchild and proudly signed each letter, "Mother of Mother's Day."

The thorn on the rose came when Anna grew alarmed at the ensuing commercialization of her holiday, which she considered a holy day. In the early 1920s, she began to resent florists for marketing carnations and raising their prices in May; her ire was also directed at candy companies who upped their advertising for the occasion. In 1932, she broke up a rally of the American War Mothers when they sold carnations, railing they had usurped her trademark flower. Police dragged Anna away, and she spent a brief period in jail, charged with disturbing the peace. She had also crashed a confectioners' convention and chastised them for making millions from her idea. They retaliated by pronouncing her "a crazy old spinster." Her anger also extended to Joyce Hall, who founded his eponymous Hallmark cards and sold thousands of his products geared for the holiday. Jarvis lashed out, saying, "A maudlin, insincere printed card means nothing except that you are too lazy to write to the woman who has done more for you than anyone in the world. And candy! You take a box to Mother—and then eat most of it yourself. A pretty sentiment." She went on to add that those "grafters" who purchased such trifles would "take the coppers off a dead mother's eyes." She organized speaking engagements where she referred to florists, greeting-card manufacturers, and the confectionary industry as charlatans, bandits, pirates, racketeers, and kidnappers. She refused to make money from her holiday that could have proved a cash cow.

In 1934, Miss Jarvis was less than pleased when the United States Postal Service issued a three-cent stamp, designed by Franklin Delano Roosevelt, to commemorate the day. It featured the replica of the painting *Whistler's Mother* along with a superimposed vase of white carnations. Miss Jarvis was vehement in her dislike as she viewed it as a promotion for the floral industry. The iconic maternal image bore the dedication: in memory and in honor of the mothers of America. Jarvis owned the patent to the term Mother's Day and refused its inclusion.

In a nod to irony, while Anna Jarvis had dedicated the first half of her life to launching Mother's Day, she spent her later years trying to rescind the holiday she had birthed. In 1943, Anna organized a petition for its removal, but it and similar efforts were halted when her increasingly erratic behavior led the eighty-year-old to a forced placement in Marshall Square Mental Sanatorium in Pennsylvania. A group called the Floral Exchange paid for her upkeep—either in gratitude for starting their industry's lucrative holiday or to remove the thorn in their side.

Anna Jarvis passed away childless and was interred next to her mother and other family members. No doubt she would roll over in her grave if she knew Mother's Day generates billions in revenue. Since 1979, the wooden home of her birth is listed on the National Register of Historic Places in tribute to the woman who launched an iconic holiday. The honor is understandable as, in the words of

William Ross Wallace's 1865 poem, "The hand that rocks the cradle rules the world."

CHAPTER 9

I Did Invent It (1914)

The bra, once kept tightly under wraps—both literally and figuratively—came out of the closet in the twentieth century. In *The Graduate*, cougar Mrs. Robinson's black lace creation seduced the young Benjamin Braddock. Coo-coo-cachoo indeed. In *Star Wars*, Princess Leia's gold metal garment steamed up the cave of Jabba the Hutt. Victoria's Secret has created a ten-million-dollar, jewel-encrusted treasure that would make for a sweet ransom. These items of lingerie have become iconic, but the woman who launched the modern bra is shrouded in shadow.

Dorothy Parker quipped, "Brevity is the soul of lingerie," and when a socialite put this statement into practice, the underwear industry was never the same. Its designer, Mary Phelps Jacob, nicknamed Polly, later known as Caresse Crosby, was born in 1891 in New York City into a world of power and privilege. She was a descendant of William Bradford, the first governor of the Plymouth Colony. Another illustrious ancestor was General Walter Phelps, who commanded troops in the Civil War at the battle of Antietam. Her great-great-great-great-grandfather invented the steam train. The family divided their time between estates in Manhattan, Connecticut, and New Rochelle. She attended posh schools, and in 1915 was introduced to King George V at a London garden party.

She married fellow blue-blood Richard Peabody, whose family had settled in New Hampshire in 1635, and with whom she had two children. Dick returned from World War I a hero and a shattered alcoholic. Mary lived with her in-laws and a husband whose nocturnal passion concerned an alarm bell above their bed. The shrill ring sounded whenever the emergency bell rang in the station so Peabody could wake, dress in a firefighter's uniform, and wear it while he watched the real firemen fight the flames.

As proof one should never underestimate a debutante with a fashion crisis, twenty-one-year-old Mary was prepping for a society ball when the allure of her couture dress was compromised by the stiff corset peeking out from under her gown. What's a girl to do? Inspired, she told her French maid to bring her two handkerchiefs and some pink ribbon, which she sewed into a makeshift brassiere. Her creation was soft and light and conformed to her body better than the whalebone corset that made a woman look as if she had a uniboob. Mary's invention complimented the style of the time and was less restrictive than the previous Victorian fashions. She described her invention as "delicious," though it still pushed "down one's chest . . . so the truth that virgins had breasts should not be suspected." Never one to shun adulation, Mary was thrilled when friends surrounded her, clamoring to know how she had moved so freely. She obliged their requests to make them their own undergarment. When a stranger offered to purchase one for a dollar, she started a business selling brassieres—a name derived from the old French word for "upper arm." In her application for a patent, she wrote her product was "well adapted to women of different sizes" and "so efficient that it may be worn by persons engaged in violent exercise like tennis."

It was an invention whose time had come. Because of the war, the United States government requested that women stop buying corsets in order to conserve metal. Mary christened her new enterprise the Fashion Form Brassiere Company, located on Washington Street in Boston. With a staff of two, Mrs. Peabody began manufacturing her wireless wonder. However, while she managed to snag a few orders from department stores, her business never took off. This failure was because Mary had fallen hard for a man other than her husband,

and soon nothing other than him held any appeal. Her office space provided cover for their trysts. She sold what she referred to as her sweatshop and her design for fifteen hundred dollars (which would be twenty thousand dollars today), to the Warner Brothers Corset Company of Connecticut; it generated fifteen million dollars over the next three decades.

Harry Cosby, like Richard Peabody, was a war veteran and a heavy drinker. However, the difference was while Richard's nocturnal habit was watching fires, Harry's was causing friction between the sheets. His eccentric nature found a kindred spirit in Mary. He wore black suits and accessorized with black painted fingernails, along with a black gardenia in his lapel. The bottom of his feet were tattooed. He also had a habit of asking his lovers to commit suicide with him. His different drummer personality was not inherited—though his fortune was. His pious mother, Henrietta, founded the Garden Club of America, and his banker father, Stephen, was a former college football star who lived for his Ivy League and Boston society connections. His great Uncle Jack—a.k.a. J. P. Morgan—had the distinction of being the celebrated banker.

The couple met in 1920, when Henrietta invited Mary to an Independence Day beach party. A few hours later, in a Tunnel of Love ride, Harry told Mary he loved her. Soon they were inseparable, oblivious to the blue-blood Boston scandal. In 1922, Mary divorced Peabody and married Harry. Not a fan of the name Mary, Harry suggested she change it to Caresse. In one of her sonnets, she ended with the words, "Forever to be Harry and Caresse."

Two years later, to distance themselves from their wayward son, Harry's parents arranged a bank position for him in Paris. In Europe, the couple helped put the roar in the Roaring Twenties, and in terms of hedonism, Harry and Caresse gave Scott and Zelda serious competition. They held Gatsby-like bacchanals that entailed seven in their gigantic bed; at another soiree, Caresse appeared bare-breasted while Harry wore a necklace of dead pigeons. They dabbled in various Eastern faiths and were equal opportunity users of opiates, with a preference for opium. At other times, the Crosbys drove around France in a green limousine where they, along with their dogs (including a whippet named Clytoris), wore goggles. However, there was a cruel underbelly in their pursuit of pleasure. On holiday in Morocco, they took a thirteen-year-old dancer, Zora, to share their bed: Harry's only known homosexual experience was with an underage boy. Other than this, Harry did not much care for children, which is why Caresse's son and daughter lived at a boarding school.

Though their true vacation was endlessly reinventing their lives, they also had serious pursuits. They operated *The Black Sun Press*, a small publishing house that printed exquisite editions of early extracts from the most anticipated novels such as *Finnegan's Wake* and works by D. H. Lawrence and Ezra Pound. Max Ernst, the surrealist painter, was a close friend of Caresse and provided haunting images. Antiquarian book expert Neil Pearson has stated, "A *Black Sun* edition is the literary equivalent of a Braque or a Picasso painting."

After the Occupation, German troops commandeered the Crosbys' French mill holiday home. To further the indignity, the Nazis painted over a unique curved white wall. Visitors used watercolors to leave their signatures or symbols: D. H. Lawrence drew a phoenix, and Salvador Dali intertwined his name with that of a Pulitzer Prize winning American author. The surrealist used Caresse as a muse, and it is widely accepted she is the subject of his 1934 portrait. Another obliterated name was that of Eva Braun, who left hers alongside that of the Austrian big-game hunter who she had been seeing before she had fallen for the Führer. Caresse lamented that had she known the indignity that would have befallen her "guest book," she would have taken it with her. The comment was not facetious; taking a wall across a country or continent was the kind of over-the-top gesture for which the couple was known.

The Crosbys' mad, bad Bohemian lifestyle, peppered with a rolodex of the cultural elite of the era, ended after the stock market crash. Unwilling to live a life devoid of conspicuous consumption—after Caresse declined to die with him—Harry shot himself and one of his mistresses in an apartment overlooking Central Park. His fellow suicide victim was Josephine Bigelow-Rotch, a young, recently married New Yorker. They had smoked opium and drunk a bottle of whiskey prior to ending their lives.

Harry's death devastated Caresse, but it also served to liberate her from her libertine ways. She started pro-peace movements and campaigned for prisoners of war. However, she continued with her old habit of travelling the world and courting the famous such as T. E. Lawrence, F. Scott Fitzgerald, and Allen Ginsberg. In Paris she fell in with Henry Miller and Anaïs Nin and helped them with their writing of erotica. She eventually returned to the United States, and in 1937 married her third hubby, Selbert Young, eighteen years her junior, a former football player and movie star. They moved to Washington, DC, where she opened an art gallery and started a magazine, *Portfolio*. After the failure of her third walk down the aisle, she spent her final years in Rome, where she planned to launch an artist colony. She passed away in Italy in 1970 from heart disease.

Warner Brothers might have got the better end of the deal, but Caresse held on to her glory. Her proudest boast: "I can't say the brassiere will ever take as great a place in history as the steamboat, but I did invent it."

CHAPTER 10

A Stone Angel (1916)

Larry Flynt, whose pornographic empire forever arm-wrestled the First Amendment, railed, "The church has had its hand on our crotch for more than two thousand years." A tireless crusader also fought for sexual autonomy, but her ends were salvation, not debasement.

In reaction to Donald Trump's campaign against Planned Parenthood, protests erupted over whether to defend or to defund the century-old organization. If the woman who had stirred up this storm had been present, she would no doubt have been pleased; she made a career out of drawing attention to herself on behalf of her Holy Grail.

Margaret Louise was born into a hardscrabble life in 1879 in Corning, New York, the daughter of Irish immigrants. Her father, Michael Hennessy Higgins, was a mason who chiseled monuments on tombstones by day and drank by night. Her mother, Anne, underwent eighteen pregnancies and bore eleven children in twenty-two years; she passed away at age forty-nine from tuberculosis. Determined not to follow in her mother's worn-down footsteps, Margaret left for New York City, where she became active in theater. She aspired to become an actress, but had a change of heart when she discovered this career choice would entail having to divulge her leg measurements.

In 1902 Margaret married William Sanger, an architect by profession and socialist by passion, who was hell-bent on rebelling against his conservative Jewish family. Their Greenwich Village home was filled to overflowing with their three children and the greatest rabble-rousers of the era, such as Emma Goldman. The militant feminism of the Russian

Jewish Emma resonated with the Irish Catholic Margaret, and they shared the philosophy that women had to be emancipated from the reproductive consequences of intercourse. In contrast, the power players believed the only acceptable form of birth control was abstinence. "Can they not use celibacy?" demanded Anthony Comstock, leader of the New York Society for the Suppression of Vice, "Or must they sink to the level of beasts?" His proudest boast was he had destroyed hundreds of tons of "lewd and lascivious material," including sixty thousand "obscene rubber articles," otherwise known as condoms.

Sanger's sexually radical thinking was reinforced through her nursing position in the Lower East Side slums of Manhattan. She took umbrage with the book of Genesis, which exhorted the descendants of Adam and Eve "to be fruitful and multiply"; the tenements manifested the only result of this Biblical injunction as broodmare mothers and neglected children. Many of her patients—old at thirty-five—resorted to self-induced abortions, risking death to end pregnancies they could not avoid. In an era when buying a single condom was criminalized in thirty states, and when priests warned parishioners that preventing contraception was an entry ticket to hell, old wives' tales "to do the trick" proliferated through the slum grapevine.

On a stifling July day in 1912, Margaret was assisting Sadie Sachs, who had attempted to terminate her fourth pregnancy. Sadie begged the doctor for information on how to prevent a fifth; the response: "Tell 'Jake' to sleep on the roof." When Sachs passed away six months later during a second self-induced abortion, Sanger decided her life's crusade was to end "involuntary motherhood." She became a self-appointed evangelist, preaching the separation of sex from procreation. She was prepared to step into the boxing ring, knowing full well her opponents would be powerful: the Catholic Church, the American government, and public opinion.

Although the movies of the era were silent, Ms. Sanger was not, and she published a periodical called *The Woman Rebel*. The term "birth control" first appeared on these pages, under the slogan: "No Gods; No Masters." She also wrote a sex education column entitled "What Every Girl Should Know" for a left-wing newspaper, delivered through the mail. When Comstock banned her editorial on venereal disease, the paper ran an empty space with the title, "What Every Girl Should Know: Nothing, by Order of the US Post Office." Comstock had enough of this thorn in his side and indicted Margaret for disseminating obscenity; her argument that she was exercising her First Amendment rights fell on deaf ears. On the eve of her trial, faced with a prison term of forty-five years, she fled to Europe. Before her escape, she distributed one hundred thousand copies of her birth control pamphlet, *Family Limitation*; she wrote to her friend Upton Sinclair that Comstock now would have something "to really indict me on."

William Sanger was left with the care of the children, not sweetened by the news his wife, in England, had begun ménages à trois or à quatre and had embarked on affairs with novelist H. G. Wells and psychologist Havelock Ellis. A further arrow from the marital quiver struck when an undercover vice officer went to the Sanger home, represented himself to William as an impoverished father, and purchased a copy of *Family Limitation*. At William's trial, he admitted he had broken the law, but he maintained that it was the law itself which was on trial. The judge, a devout Catholic, called William "a menace to society" whose crime violated "not only the laws of the state, but the laws of God." He sentenced Sanger to thirty days in prison. Because of Margaret's efforts, public attitude had changed and the charges against her were dropped a month later. She returned to the States, shortly after her five-year-old daughter Peggy died of pneumonia.

In 1916—four years before women got the right to vote—the indefatigable Sanger opened the first birth control clinic in the United States, behind the curtained windows of a storefront tenement in

61

Brooklyn. Handbills advertising the facility were passed out in English, Yiddish, and Italian. By her side was her sister Ethel Bryne, whose daughter, Olive, would serve as the muse behind the Justice League's Wonder Woman. Hundreds of women lined up for blocks; apparently, the men of New York were not keen on sleeping on the roof. The police raided the clinic ten days and forty-six patients later. Margaret, shouting Irish invectives at the officer, landed in jail. In prison—where she spent a month—she spread the good news of contraception to her fellow inmates. Ethel, also in custody, embarked on an eight-day hunger strike that almost led to her death. Sanger, who would go on to launch the Planned Parenthood Federation of America, founded something far greater than a clinic: she had ignited a movement for women's reproductive freedom.

In 1921, Sanger organized the first American birth control conference at the Plaza Hotel in Manhattan, and her sponsors included Winston Churchill, the Rockefellers, and Theodore Dreiser. When the authorities forbade her to speak in Boston's Ford Hall, she stood silent on the stage, her mouth taped shut, while a Harvard University historian read her prepared statement. Democratic in her choice of audience, she also lectured for the female members of the Ku Klux Klan in New Jersey. Some view this through the lens of Sanger as a proponent of eugenics, especially against African Americans; an alternate perspective is that she only cared about alleviating the anguish of women desperate not to bear children for whom they could not provide. Her philosophy was that quality of care rather than quantity of offspring should comprise a mother's mantra.

Sanger once remarked to a lover that she was "not a peaceful or restful person to know at all." Apparently, William concurred, and the Sanger marriage, after several years of separation, ended in 1921. She confided that she would not remarry, except for money; the following year she wed Noah Slee, seventeen years her senior—a millionaire. He adored her enough to allow her to continue her independent life and liaisons and served as a financial angel for his wife's activism. Slee was the largest individual supporter of the American Birth Control League, and he donated fifty thousand dollars, ten times more than anyone else. In addition, he purchased a five-story townhouse for the clinic. Margaret, as eagerly as she had once courted socialists, took to wooing socialites, writing, "Little can be done without them." Before she became First Lady, Eleanor Roosevelt was a staunch supporter.

When the pill that Margaret helped fund was approved in 1960, she was a widow living in an Arizona nursing home and celebrated by uncorking a bottle of champagne. Her old disagreement with the Roman Catholic Church—and her belief it was time for the rosaries to get off the ovaries—led her to say that if the Catholic Kennedy was elected she would flee the country once more. However, she softened her stance when informed the Senator and Jackie were sympathetic toward the problem of overpopulation. Sanger, who died in 1966 at the age of eighty-seven, had the comfort of knowing that the United States Supreme Court had made its historic 1965 decision in *Griswold v. Connecticut*, giving Constitutional protection to the private use of contraceptives—though with the addendum it applied within the confines of marriage.

Posterity's evaluation of Margaret lies in the murky arena of subjectivity: to those who are of the school of the rhythm method of birth control, she is Satan's handmaiden; for the advocates of the Pill, she is what her father carved on tombstones: a stone angel.

CHAPTER # 11

We Can Do It! (1943)

The feisty feminist Susan B. Anthony is a renowned face in the pantheon of the Women's Rights Movement. Her stirring slogan: "Failure is not an option." Ms. Anthony paved the way for another female icon who, although her personal story is obscure, nonetheless became a face of Americana.

The men who left their imprint on World War II are the stuff of history: the Big Three at Yalta, along with generals like Patton and MacArthur. In contrast, the identities of two of the most readily recognizable women of the war are obscure. One was the nurse in the New York Times Square photograph, locked in a celebratory embrace of a sailor. The other launched a feminist icon.

The genesis of the woman who became an iconic symbol began when Japanese planes, their tails bearing the image of the red sun, initiated the surprise attack on Pearl Harbor. In response, thousands of American men raced to recruitment offices. This situation left a dearth of workers to man the factories; in response, Uncle Sam embarked on a concerted campaign to convince women to leave their homes and pick up the jobs vacated by those who had gone, in the words of the song, "Over There." The massive enlistment entailed a huge shift of the established paradigm: prior to the advent of World War II, the only occupations deemed proper for females were the positions of wives, nurses, teachers, secretaries, or nannies. Respectable matrons did not feel it proper to trade dresses for pants. Hence the government orchestrated a propaganda campaign to convince women to forego their traditional roles as housewives for the positions of riveters: to work with drills instead of frying pans. Millions took up the challenge for patriotic reasons, as well as for the unimaginable lure of economic autonomy. Although the males in the workforce initially protested the influx of estrogen on their turf, necessity triumphed over discrimination. In Chicago, some factory owners refused lucrative defense contracts that would have obligated them to hire "the weaker sex." Those plants that did allow women paid them a third less than their male counterparts.

To counteract male cynicism, and to increase female participation, continual appeals were launched in a variety of venues. Magazines carried headlines such as, "Women, you could hasten victory by working and saving your man." Another slogan: "The more women at work, the sooner we win." This campaign became the estrogen equivalent to the famous World War I British recruiting poster: "Daddy, what did you do in the Great War?"

The genesis of an image that became an integral part of the Americana icon began with a 1942 song, "Rosie the Riveter"; Rosie was the generic name chosen to represent the women who answered the bugle cry of the factories. Artist Norman Rockwell, inspired by the lyrics, painted his rendition of Rosie, who appeared on the cover of the *Saturday Evening Post*. His fictional heroine was portrayed cradling a riveting machine; her penny loafers resting atop a copy of Hitler's infamous book, *Mein Kampf* (*My Struggle*). On her lunchbox is the name Rosie. Sotheby's auctioned the painting in 2002 for almost five million dollars. However, an incident occurred that was to transform the fictionalized Rosie into a real-life one.

In 1943, Hollywood actor Walter Pidgeon arrived at the Ford Motor Company assembly plant, Willow Run Aircraft Factory in Ypsilanti, Michigan, which produced B-29 bombers for the Air Force. His mission was to find an actual female factory worker to appear in a promotional film for war bonds. He noticed a woman whose qualities and appearance made her a candidate: when he discovered her name was the same as the fictional one, he took it as a sign of serendipity. The woman was Rose Will Monroe, a native of Pulaski County, Kentucky, one of nine children. When her husband died in an automobile accident, leaving her with two young daughters, she moved to Michigan to work as a riveter. The wartime short was shown in theaters between features to encourage women to do their part, as well as for all Americans to invest in war bonds.

Rose never capitalized on her Andy Warhol "fifteen minutes of fame"; her aspiration was not notoriety. Rather, Monroe's ambition was to be trained as a female pilot; the government needed pilots to transport aircraft parts around the country. However, she was passed over on the grounds she was a single mother. It was, in the words of Dorothy Parker, "a man's world."

One of the many who saw the film was Pittsburgh artist J. Howard Miller, commissioned by the Westinghouse Company's War Production Coordinating Committee to produce a poster of Rosie the Riveter. Using Rose Monroe as his prototype, he illustrated her wearing a red polka dot bandana; her decidedly feminine facial features made a strong contrast to her bare arm flexing her muscles. In a speech balloon were these words, destined to become ubiquitous: "We Can Do It!" The blue-shirted bombshell had it all: beauty, sex appeal, and attitude. A kick-ass heroine was born. With its dissemination in posters throughout the country, as well as in magazines and newspapers, Rosie's image rivaled the one proclaiming "Uncle Sam Needs You!" The fame of the poster would eventually eclipse the tight-sweater-wearing one of pinup girl Betty Grable—which was, in its fashion, GI standard issue.

Incidentally, another Monroe who found fame on the factory front was nineteen-year-old Norma Jean Dougherty, whose allure caused a photographer to place her, holding a propeller blade, on the cover of the US Army's *Yank Magazine*. Her image helped boost more than enlisted men's morale; it was to eventually boost her into superstardom status when she morphed into Marilyn Monroe.

In 1945 when "Johnny came marching home again" to the chorus of "Hurrah! Hurrah!" the government reversed its former tactics and asked women to return to their "rightful place": their homes. In the space of four years, the Rosies were needed, venerated, and finally sent packing with an honorable discharge. They were expected to revert from Rosies back into roses of the homegrown variety. However, being regulated to the shadows left many of the Rosies less than thrilled. Some felt it was restricting to go back to their former lives; they had proved they could do a "man's job." Having taken a step forward, they were reluctant to take a step back. They had seen America take on the fight against a foreign enemy; women were now ready to take on a fight for what they had come to perceive as their right. In key ways, the entry of these ladies into the workforce had altered the DNA of American society. Many sociologists cite the Rosie the Riveters as the midwives of the modern Women's Movement.

After World War II, Rose Monroe did not go back to a traditional role, although she continued to be a devoted mother. She obtained work as a taxi driver and operator of a beauty salon. She also formed her own construction company in Indiana, Rose Builders, specializing in luxury homes. At the age of fifty, she realized her dream of flying when she obtained her pilot's license. She became a member of the local aeronautics club—its only female member. Her daughter, Mrs. Jarvis, said that her mother was a good pilot and had taught her to fly as well. One can only imagine Ms. Monroe's elation in 1983, when Sally Ride became the first American woman in space.

Ironically, although Rose's achievement led to intense personal satisfaction, it also contributed to complications that impaired her health. In 1978, her small propeller aircraft crashed during takeoff. Her daughter and four other passengers emerged unscathed; however, Rose sustained a severe injury to her kidney and the loss of vision in her left eye. She passed away at age seventy-seven in 1997 in Clarksville, Indiana, when her remaining kidney shut down. She left behind six sisters, two children, nine grandchildren, and thirteen great-grandchildren. Mrs. Jarvis remarked, "Mom happened to be in the right place at the right time." She also added that her parent never believed in government assistance, and that they could not have found a better role model for their riveter than Rose Monroe. A granddaughter described her "as always being ahead of her time." To honor their own, Pulaski County designated a road in 2007 as the Rose Lee Monroe Memorial Highway. Another posthumous honor for the collective female workforce of the war years occurred in 2000, when the Rosie the Riveter World War II Home Front National Historic Park opened in Richmond, California. Two hundred former "Rosies," all wearing red polka dot bandanas, attended the ceremony to receive their belated tribute. The memorial platform bears the quotation, "You must tell your children, putting modesty aside, that without us, without women, there would have been no spring in 1945."

The original Rosie the Riveter poster hangs in the Smithsonian; however, as it has achieved the status of a cultural icon, its image is sacrosanct. It has surpassed its initial intent as a propaganda tool and has become a beacon for women's empowerment. Susan B. Anthony's words to her suffragettes, "Failure is not an option," proved prophetic and paved the way for Rosie's rallying cry to her sisters, "We Can Do It." And do it they did. And that, more than a stretch of a highway named in her honor, is what would have brought the most joy to Ms. Rosie.

CHAPTER # 12

Tiara-Wearing Queen (1946)

Hamlet railed at Ophelia, "God hath given you one face and you make yourselves another." Although the Prince of Denmark was against the art of makeup—what he viewed as female duplicity—the modern-day woman who became Estée Lauder called cosmetics "jars of hope." She pronounced there were no ugly women, just lazy ones.

James Gatz reinvented himself as Jay Gatsby in an attempt to divorce himself from his past, and Josephine Esther Mentzer, who hailed from Queens, used the same ploy. She was one of six children born to Jewish, Eastern European immigrants, and she and her family lived above her father's hardware store. A source of perpetual embarrassment was her parents' thick accents and foreign ways, which set her apart in her mainly Italian neighborhood. She imbibed a love of fashion from her mother, Rose, who always wore gloves; from her father, Max, she learned how to attract customers. During the Christmas season, in a nod to promotion, he gave away gifts of hammers and nails.

An even greater influence on Josephine's life was her uncle John Schotz, who joined the family when he emigrated from Hungary during the First World War. He had been trained as a chemist and concocted cosmetics on the family stove. His feisty niece was his designated saleswoman, and her first customers were friends from Newtown High School who she brought home to try his beauty creams. She later recalled, "I was forever experimenting on myself and on anyone who came in range." Before graduation, she bid farewell to high school and entered the beauty business armed with her uncle's products, her own flawless complexion, and an unquenchable thirst to succeed.

Josephine took the novel tactic of peddling her wares to small beauty salons in her neighborhood. Emboldened, she made her way to the House of Ash Blondes on the Upper West Side. She proved such a dynamic salesperson that its proprietor hired her to run the beauty counter at a new branch. Josephine applied her potions as her customers sat captive under huge metal hair dryers. When their hair was done, Josephine removed the cream and made up the women's faces with her limited selection of home-brewed products. The repertoire included one turquoise eye shadow and one lipstick shade called Duchess Crimson (named after America's fashion idol of the day, the Duchess of Windsor). In most instances, customers would leave with one purchase and one free sample, a nod to Mr. Mentzer's Christmas promotions.

As a teenager Josephine met Joseph Lauter, whose Jewish parents had emigrated from Austria, and the couple wed in 1930. Three years later they had a son, Leonard Allen, but the birth did not prove to be a salve to their marital troubles. In 1939, Josephine obtained a divorce and moved to Florida, where she reportedly had an affair with a married fragrance industry executive. Years later she explained, "I was married very young. You think you missed something out of life. But I found out that I had the sweetest husband in the world." The couple remarried in 1942, and henceforth she referred to their relationship as one of the greatest love stories of all time. Their second son, Ronald, arrived two years later.

Joseph gave up his own business venture, which had not proved lucrative, and the couple joined forces. Josephine's parents had called her Esty after her middle name, Esther, and she decided to christen the company Estée—the accent mark was to associate it with European exotic. Joseph's family name had originally been "Lauder," but an immigration officer had inadvertently altered its spelling. They decided to revert back to its original in order to honor their heritage. Paradoxically, while reclaiming Joseph's history, Estée embellished her own. She claimed to have been raised in a Hapsburg castle, and she described her father as "an elegant, dapper monarchist from Europe." This comment was quite a reinvention for the hardware store owner from Queens, though this outer borough's name (at least) did smack of royalty.

The Lauders only had a handful of products and for distinction they packaged them in a case of greenish blue. Estée, a name which she used personally as well as professionally, went on the road to induce finer stores to feature her merchandise. She would tempt prospective clients with the pitch, "Time is not on your side, but I am!" The greatest coup came when Saks Fifth Avenue agreed to carry her products; it was where the "ladies who lunched" shopped, where customers had the means to say the three most beautiful words in retail: "Charge it please." Estée and Joseph quickly cooked up the creams in their "factory," a converted restaurant, and in two days, Saks sold out. Word spread of the woman who delivered what Ponce de Léon had sought, and soon she was selling to prestigious stores. With her chutzpah and schmoozing, her wares took wing—but interspersed with success there was a painful episode. She was at a salon in New York, where she admired the blouse of an elegant customer and inquired where it had been purchased. The woman replied, "You could never afford it."

The couple hit the jackpot when they marketed a bath oil aimed at the typical matron who could not purchase expensive French perfume. Youth Dew carried a price tag of $8.50, and it catapulted their modest business into the big league. It took the company from a sales volume of $400 to around $5,000 a week. Encouraged when Harrods in London agreed to sell her wares, she was dismayed, but not deterred, when a high-end French shop would not allow Estée Lauder onto its hallowed shelves. In response, Estée arranged for Youth

Dew to spill onto its floor. The inquiries from shoppers concerning the aroma resulted in the blue-green packages receiving a coveted spot. Another stroke of good fortune was Estée's novel practice of giving away free samples and for instituting the concept of "gift with purchase." This ploy became a cosmetic counter staple. When the tactic worked, she sent freebies to high profile women. Princess Grace of Monaco told an interviewer, "Mrs. Lauder is such a nice person. She keeps sending all these things."

With Estée ensconced as the doyenne of beauty, she was photographed with the rich and famous: Princess Diana, Nancy Reagan, Princess Grace, and Begum Inaara Aga Khan. One of her most cherished photographs, of an American divorcee whose wiles had lured a king from his throne, was inscribed: "To Estée, with affection, Wallis, Duchess of Windsor."

With Estée Lauder dominating the beauty industry, its eponymous founder became part of the rich and famous. This feat was partially due to her company's auxiliary lines: Clinique, Origins, Prescriptives, Aramis, and MAC. With a many-splendored bank account, Mrs. Launder accumulated homes as other women did charms on a bracelet: Upper East Side townhouse, Manhattan office with a view of Central Park, oceanfront estate in Palm Beach, London flat, and a villa in the South of France. The fashion horse was always immaculately turned out—five feet and four inches of tooth and claw—in pieces of Paris couturier, often Chanel, purchased six at a time. In 1982, she flexed her economic muscle. Feeling that her ruby and diamond tiara clashed with her turquoise dress, she switched to a gold and diamond crown.

72

When she passed the torch to her sons—the Kennedys of the beauty world—she left them a legacy of billions. Ronald garnered media attention when he purchased the painting of Adele Bloch-Bauer, Klimt's famous *Woman in Gold*, for $135 million. This Viennese Mona Lisa had graced the walls of Austria's Belvedere Museum for over a half-century and now resides in Lauder's Manhattan East Side gallery.

He stated of the gold-flecked masterpiece, "In World War Two there were very few happy endings; this is one of them."

Ms. Lauder, though solicitous of friends, was not above using her lacquered nails as talons against her opponents. She referred to Charles Revson (of Revlon fame) as "My arch and implacable enemy," said that Elizabeth Arden was "Not a nice woman, not a generous woman," and commented that although Helena Rubenstein may have looked like a czarina, "The skin on her neck was less than perfect."

Estée's detractors could be equally lethal. Lee Israel, in his unauthorized biography, *Estée Lauder: Beyond the Magic*, showed an ugly side of the dowager of beauty. He wrote that although she was fabulously wealthy, her uncle John Schotz died in dire straits. He also blamed her for downplaying her Judaism, and he cited an interview where she claimed she was half Italian and convent-bred. He also levied the criticism she was a name-dropper, a social climber, and a user. He quoted an ex-secretary of the Duchess of Windsor who claimed that after the passing of the Duke, with the Duchess shunned and infirm, Mrs. Lauder proved to be a turncoat—albeit one with a designer label. And there was a mention that the Hapsburg castle of her childhood had been located over a hardware store.

It is impossible to know whether the dowager of beauty's mirror reflected the fairest or the foulest of them all. The only truth we can glean is that the girl from Queens, through overweening grit, became the tiara-wearing queen of a cosmetics empire.

CHAPTER # 13

The Puzzle (1951)

 In the heyday of snail mail, a trip to the mailbox was a variation on Russian roulette: the envelopes could contain a love letter, or a bill from an irate creditor. However, a box bearing the name from a certain suburb in upstate New York always held the promise of a personalized gift from a woman who refused to be tied down by the strings of her apron.

Nostalgia beckons when we remember holding a mail-order catalog, wishing that the images could—in fairy tale fashion—materialize. In adolescence, the J. C. Penny "big book" held our back-to-school clothes; in the teen years, the fantasy was that the *Victoria's Secret* glossy would make us angel doppelgangers. Matrons would caress the Ikea catalog, envisioning designer dream homes.

Sometimes great notions have humble beginnings, as was the case with Lillian, born in Leipzig, Germany to father Herman Menasche, a lingerie merchant, and mother Erna. The family enjoyed an affluent lifestyle until Hitler's ascension to power. One of Lilly's earliest memories was hearing anti-Semitic slurs as she walked to school; her brother, Fred, suffered a physical assault. The Nazis appropriated the Menasches' home, and they fled to Amsterdam, where they lived on the same street from the Franks' future secret annex. In 1937, they pulled up roots once more and left for New York City.

Lilly grew up painfully shy, and this trait was exacerbated by the fact that, at age ten, she was a refugee facing the challenges of living in her adopted country without money, relatives, or experience in the local language. Herman started another lingerie business which failed, though he later found modest success manufacturing leather goods. He expected his son to join the business; this hope ended when Fred died in the invasion of Normandy. Lilly attended the City University of New York but left after two years to work with her father. In 1950, she became a stay-at-home wife after marrying Samuel Hochberg, whose family owned a dry goods store in Mount Vernon, New York.

Pregnant with her first son, Lilly was sitting at her yellow Formica kitchen table paging through the women's magazine *Glamour*, when she came up with an idea for supplementing her weekly allowance from hubby. Using $2,000 from her wedding-gift money, she took out a $495.00 ad in the back-to-school issue of *Seventeen Magazine*, offering a personalized handbag for $2.99 and a matching belt for $1.99—products manufactured by Herman's company. Although this was a sizable amount of money to gamble, she felt she had to follow her hunch. She was reinforced by memories of her early immigrant days: "When I came to America, I loved Woolworth and the 5- and 10-cent stores. The things they sold were pretty, usable, and made you happy. I think what turns me on is the pleasure people get from buying things." She was floored when, three months later, she received $32,000 in orders. Bitten by the entrepreneurial bug, she kept working even after giving birth to her son Fred, and after her second son, David, came along five years later. She never mentioned that she had a job outside of motherhood, as this was a social no-no in 1950s America.

Emboldened by the windfall, Lilly, decided to launch a mail-order company, using her first name and Vernon from the town where they lived—Menasche and Hochberg did not have the right ring. It was a risky move as at the time: competitors were the huge catalogs from Sears and Montgomery Ward that carried every kind of merchandise, the era's paper department stores. However, she saw a new retail market niche: unique personalized products.

Step by step, Lillian built her company, mailing an eight-page catalog to 125,000 customers in 1954 that reached $500,000 in sales after four years. Its slogan: "Living well for less." Her husband joined the business, and her father continued to supply leather as well as providing continuous support—in contrast to her mother, always emotionally remote, with whom there existed a sense of rivalry. In her autobiography, *An Eye for Winners: How I Built One of America's Greatest Direct-Mail Businesses*, she wrote of her mother, Erna, "When I was in therapy once, trying to work this out, I went to dinner at a country club, and in the ladies' room there was a woman in the stall next to me together with her mother. Helping her. I said, 'What a daughter.' The therapist said, 'What a mother that her daughter wanted to do that for her.' " Lillian felt that she herself was a good mother, although she rued her own shortcomings: "I just did not learn that loving quality, that touchy-feely thing so important to children." David always called his mother Lillian. She took her sons on a *Roots*-style tour to Leipzig and Amsterdam so they could understand their family's history.

The mainstay of the company remained monogrammed and personalized goods, but the company grew to include tchotchkes (knickknacks and doodads). Lillian Vernon became to the heartland what J. Peterman would later become to Manhattan yuppies. While her customer base was mainly middle-class women, high-end shoppers included Frank Sinatra (monogrammed lint removers), Mia Farrow (children's toys), Princess Caroline of Monaco (a Wild West costume for her daughter), Stephen Spielberg (a tool caddy), and Arnold Schwarzenegger (plastic shoulder shields for suits). Nancy Reagan, Betty White, and Gregory Peck were also devotees. Barbara Bush ordered Lillian Vernon bed linens for the White House, and Hillary Clinton once said that as First Lady of Arkansas, in the 1980s, she would peruse the catalog, thinking "If I just ordered one more thing, my life would finally be in order." Lillian's basement doubled as a warehouse, until the shipment of woks from China became overrun with beetles that had nestled in the boxes. In 1954, with hefty profits, she rented a storefront for a warehouse, and companies such as Max Factor, Elizabeth Arden, Avon, and Revlon engaged her to manufacture custom-designed wares.

In the 1970s, Ms. Vernon, who claimed to be five foot three—maybe in stilettos and including her bouffant hair—began traversing the globe in quest of unusual goods. She became a fixture at trade fairs in Europe, Hong Kong, and Tokyo, and later in China. Her catalogs always began with a letter describing where she was travelling, accompanied by a photograph showing a smiling Lillian in a Chanel suit, red lipstick, and sprayed hair. The part not visible was her steel. She had what she called a "golden gut" for knowing what women wanted—often before they knew. Her products were as diverse as "rescued shards" of Ming vases, fashioned into pendants and bracelets, and the all-pink Lady Tool Kit, complete with hammer, screwdrivers, wrenches, and sometimes a power dill. Other merchandise was geared to achieve a clutter-free home, such as drawer dividers, corner racks, and pullout shelves. Considering how she had to abandon her childhood home, her desire to keep order made perfect sense.

Obsessed with every aspect of her empire, one area she lost interest in was her husband. She said they clashed at work, and she found him lacking "the entrepreneurial spirit." The Hochbergs' disintegrating relationship may have inspired one of the catalog's worst sellers—a pillow with the inscription: "A woman who is looking for a husband has never had one." In 1969, Lillian flew to Mexico to get a divorce. He kept the wholesale end of the business, while she kept her eponymous catalog. (In 1990, she would legally change her own name to Lillian Vernon.) The year after her first divorce, she married Robert Katz, a manufacturer of Lucite products sold in her catalogs, but this also imperfect union ended in 1988, a year after the company went public. Lillian's son, David, entered the family

77

business shortly after and worked there for nineteen years until he and his mother came into conflict over his ascension to the position of chairman. However, the professional disagreement did not harm their relationship, nor did his coming out with his homosexuality. She adored his partner, Tom.

The company apparently sold the right stuff, with a yearly revenue of $300 million and a mailing list seventeen million strong. When the company went public in 1987, it became the first corporation headed by a woman to be listed on the American Stock Exchange. In 1995, President Bill Clinton appointed her chairwoman of the National Women's Business Council. She stated, "I know my customer because I am my customer." She also attributed her success to her fortitude, saying, "I never gave up, and I never let anyone get in my way." The yellow Formica table that had birthed the Lillian Vernon idea held a place of honor in the company headquarters. In 2003, H. Strauss Zelnick's bought the business for $60.5 million. Mrs. Vernon and David Hochberg, who owned 40 percent of the enterprise, received approximately twenty-four million dollars.

In addition to monogrammed items, Lillian also loved to flirt. When she met President Obama, he kissed her on the cheek. Her reaction? "Kiss me on the other cheek too!" A third walk down the aisle came in 1998 with Paolo Martino, a beauty salon owner from a different religious and age demographic than her former husbands. She said, "He's younger than I am. How much I won't tell," and described herself as "the oldest bride in America."

The First Lady of Mail-Order passed away in 2015 at age eighty-eight. One of her quotations could serve as an epitaph: "To me life is a puzzle. At the end of the day all the pieces have to fit."

CHAPTER # 14

Mother Confessors (1955–1956)

 Anyone who subscribes to even basic cable is familiar with the twins best known as the Property Brothers, the gurus of renovation. Possessors of romance-novel good looks and charisma to spare, they are reality TV's shining stars. However, in the past generation, there were twin sisters who dominated newspaper columns and fixed troubles, much as Jonathan and Drew resurrect homes.

The women who launched the advice column into the modern era had lives as extraordinary as any found in their voluminous mail. Esther Pauline Friedman, nicknamed Eppie, and her sister Pauline Esther, nicknamed Popo, were born to Russian Jewish immigrants in Sioux City, Iowa, on Independence Day, 1918. Until they were twelve, they believed all the hoopla surrounding the holiday was in their honor. Their father supported his wife and four daughters by peddling chickens from a wagon and, in a classic New World success story, wound up becoming the proprietor of a chain of movie theaters and burlesque houses. The sisters were so inseparable they shared a bed, played the same instrument (violin), and performed the Andrew Sisters' duets in Yiddish.

When the dimpled dynamic duo graduated from high school in 1936, their yearbook said it all. Next to Popo's picture was the message "Always with Eppie," and next to Eppie's was "Always with Popo." They enrolled in Sioux City's Morningside College, where they wore '50s-style matching raccoon coats and co-wrote a gossip column, "Campus Rat," which carried a single byline. They studied psychology, but as Eppie admitted, in actuality they "majored in boys." On occasion they would attend a party, clad in the same outfit, with a shared date. They dropped out in their junior year, when they married on their birthdays in a fantastic double wedding that included seven hundred guests, three rabbis, a bridal party of twenty-two, and mounted police. To no one's surprise, they wore identical dresses, veils, and hairstyles. Pauline married Morton Phillips, heir to a liquor fortune; Eppie's groom was Jules Lederer, who later founded Budget Rent-a-Car. After a double honeymoon, the twins were forced asunder when they followed their respective spouses to different cities.

In 1955, the Lederers moved to Chicago, where Eppie donned the mantle of an affluent housewife and mother of Margo. She defined herself not as a twin, but as a wife, one so enamored of her role that she had the words "Jules's Wife" stitched into the linings of her fur coats. It was Eppie who initially forged the path that would define both women's lives. She was a fan of an advice column in the *Chicago Sun-Times* called "Ask Ann Landers," and when she discovered its columnist, Ruth Crowley, had died, she entered a competition to become the new Ann. (The name Landers was chosen in tribute to a friend of Crowley's.) The twenty-nine candidates were given a set of identical questions; for her responses, Eppie, a master puppeteer, pulled strings. For one letter concerning legality, she contacted Supreme Court Justice William O. Douglas and for another—dealing with the issue of interfaith marriage—she turned to Reverend Theodore Hesburg, president of the University of Notre Dame. The incredulous editor assumed she was just name-dropping but, after authentication, phoned her and said, "Good morning, Ann Landers."

Eppie, buried under a barrage of letters, asked her twin for help. Pauline, desirous of a life more meaningful than could be derived from mah-jongg, embraced the opportunity. However, after three months, Lederer's editor prohibited her from farming out the advice. Bitten by the writing bug, Pauline decided to follow in her sister's footsteps—as she had followed her into the world seventeen minutes behind—and clad in a black Dior gown and mink, with a chauffeured Cadillac around the corner, Pauline applied to the *San Francisco Chronicle*. The housewife's sole qualification for the advice column: she had always been "a wailing wall without portfolio." The editor was so taken with the responses and chutzpah that she returned home to a ringing telephone. Mrs. Phillips chose her pen name, taking Abigail after the prophetess in the Book of Samuel ("Then David said to Abigail, 'Blessed is your advice and blessed are you.' ") and Van Buren for its old-family, Presidential resonance. She was overjoyed at her new position, but Esther did not share her enthusiasm and cut off relations with her twin for several years. She still viewed her sister as the writer of "Campus Rat." In 1958, *Life Magazine* called their rivalry "the most feverish female feud since Elizabeth sent Mary Queen of Scots to the chopping block." Several years later, they reconciled at an event and ran off to the ladies' room to gossip. For their thirtieth anniversary, they travelled around the world with their husbands and had an audience with another advice dispenser: Pope John Paul II.

The twins, though cast in the same role, penned very different responses to thousands of people seeking succor. Long before the advent of the Internet, and prior to the televised Dr. Ruth, Dr. Laura, and Dr. Phil, the *Dear Abby* column was a forum for the public discussion of private problems and appeared in one thousand newspapers from Brazil to Thailand. Paulina, through her persona, became a beloved cultural icon and was invoked on shows such as *Three's Company*, *Dexter*, and *Mr. Ed*. With her comic yet sympathetic voice, she wrestled the advice column from its weepy Victorian past into a hard-nosed twentieth-century present.

> *Dear Abby,*
> *Are birth control pills deductible?*
> *—Bertie*

Dear Bertie,
Only if they don't work.
—Abby

Although politically left-of-center, she still knew when to bend.

Dear Abby,
Our son was married in February and they had a baby in
August. Can an eight-pound baby be this premature?
—Wanting to Know

Dear Wanting,
The baby was on time. The wedding was late. Forget it.
—Abby

She also willingly expressed views she understood would garner protests. She stated in a 1998 interview, "Whenever I say a kind word about gays, people throw Leviticus, Deuteronomy, and other parts of the Bible to me. It doesn't bother me." In her time away from the world of newsprint, Pauline shared her home with the husband she called her "rock of Gibraltar," two monkeys, her son, Edward Jay, and her daughter, Jeanne, who is currently the voice of *Dear Abby*. One exchange with her reader stated:

Dear Abby,
Between you and me, I think the people who write to you are
either morons or they're just plain stupid.
—Henry

Dear Henry,
Which are you?
—Abby

Pauline's life proved she was neither.

Although her bouffant hair earmarked her as a woman of the 1950s, in 1976 she confided to *People Magazine* that she had recently seen an X-rated movie. She admitted her sister had also wanted to see the film, but she refrained from doing so for fear of being recognized. When Eppie asked how she had got away with it, Pauline responded, "I just put on my dark glasses and my Ann Landers wig and went!"

In contrast to those who wrote for advice, Eppie wrapped herself in the name Mrs. Morton Phillips as snugly as she wrapped herself in her fur coat. In a nod to her line of work, she displayed an antique Italian confessional in her bedroom. She ruled her advice kingdom from one of Chicago's most exclusive buildings on one of its most exclusive blocks, a fourteen-room, 5,500-foot co-op. It boasted unobstructed lake views and featured an entrance hall so vast that Jules dubbed it "the bowling alley." She counted among her friends Cary Grant, Neil Simon, and Henry Winkler, and on her walls hung photographs of the columnist with the famous: Pope Paul VI, Harry Truman, Prince Charles, and Princess Diana. A workaholic, she took to answering letters while in the back seat of her chauffeured Cadillac limousine, which displayed the license plate AL 1955, the date she had begun her column. The Jewish immigrants' daughter from Iowa transformed to such a power player that President Clinton called to ask if the Monica Lewinsky scandal had ruined him. Other friends included Walter Cronkite, Warren Buffet, Barbara Walters, Kirk Douglas, and Helen Hayes. A 1978 World Almanac survey named her the most influential woman in the United States. She was proud of her accomplishments and said, "I would rather have my column on a thousand refrigerator doors than win a Pulitzer." Conservative in her habits—she never drank or smoked—her public expressions of annoyance never got much stranger than "Oh, banana oil!" However, on one occasion she might have uttered one far less reserved. After decades spent advising Nervous in Nevada and Desperate in Denver, she needed her own solace when Jules fell in love with a younger woman and absconded to a new life in England. She broke the news in what Eppie described as her most difficult column: "The lady with all the answers does not know the answer to this one." She used her column as the venue to inform readers that her thirty-six-year marriage was over. She left a third of the page blank in honor of "one of the world's best marriages that didn't make it to the finish line." She received more than thirty-five thousand letters of support.

Eppie, who owned the rights to the Ann Landers' name, stated, "There will never be another Ann Landers." She passed away in 2002 in her lakeview home at age eighty-three from cancer. Her sister had once received the letter a letter asking:

Dear Abby: Do you think about dying much?

No, she wrote in her reply, *It's the last thing I want to do*.

Suffering from Alzheimer's, she followed her twin eleven years later. It was time for the angels to have their own Mother Confessors.

CHAPTER # 15

America's Sweetheart (1959)

 There are many women who lay claim to be the world's most legendary of lovelies: Italy's Sophia Loren, Sweden's Greta Garbo, France's Brigitte Bardot. Yet there is an American beauty who most truly embodies the pronouncement, "Age cannot wither her, nor custom stale, her infinite variety."

In the 1967 film *The Graduate*, Mr. McGuire told Benjamin, "There's a great future in plastics." A woman had understood this a decade earlier, and this knowledge enabled her to launch an empire worth billions and made her daughter's name a slice of Americana.

Ruth Mosko, the youngest of ten children of a Polish blacksmith and his illiterate wife, had been short on playthings during her Denver childhood. She escaped to Hollywood at age nineteen, where she obtained employment as a secretary for Paramount. Her high school boyfriend, Elliot Handler, joined her, and they wed in 1938. There must be something of the sorcerer residing in garages, as they have been where Apple, Amazon, Disney, and a score of other famous companies had their birth. In the same vein, the pink plastic princess originated in one in 1945, when the Handlers founded a toy company along with their friend, Harold "Matt" Matson. Mattel was an eponym derived from the two men's names: Matt and El. Matson did not last long with the ambitious Handlers, and by 1955, the diminutive Jack Ryan took his place.

An iconic doll became a sparkle in Ruth's eye when she observed her daughter, Barbara, dressing paper images of girls with pre-cut cardboard outfits. She turned from a maternal role to an entrepreneurial one when she realized the market was ripe for a teenaged version replete with clothes made of fabric—preferably sequins and satin— and with a nod to womanly attributes. She shared this idea with her husband, who brusquely waved aside her vision with the argument that no mother would buy a toy with breasts. The idea was shelved until the Handlers' Continental vacation that lead to far more than memories enshrined in a scrapbook.

Swiss dolls gave birth to two classics. Mary Godwin was travelling with her lover, Percy, in 1814, when she arrived in Switzerland and stumbled upon some renowned mechanical dolls; two years later, she penned *Frankenstein*. Ruth Handler was travelling in Lucerne a hundred and fifty years later with her husband and two children when her daughter spied a doll which culminated three years later in the world's most famous toy.

The doll Ruth spied in the Swiss window was Bild Lilli, and she was not meant for children. She had originated in Germany in 1952 and was an adult novelty used as gag gifts at bachelor parties, marketed with the phrase that her attire would make her the "star of every bar." She was the possessor of knock-out-your-eye breasts and a platinum blonde ponytail, replete with red puckered lips and heavy blue eye shadow. Ruth purchased three of them, one of which she gave to Barbara. Although a Jewish mother giving her daughter a German sex toy was questionable, her vision was to make her a modern Midas.

When Ruth returned to America, she was determined to make Bild Lili—a deshelled Marlene Dietrich—part of Mattel's repertoire, though less sexual. She felt girls wanted a doll to which they could aspire rather than inspire to look after—such as Betsy Wetsy or Chatty Cathy, the latter of which was a staple of Mattel. For technical assistance, she turned to engineer Jack Ryan, who described Bild Lilli as "looking like a hooker between performances." As his pastime was prostitutes, he based his observation on firsthand experience. His ingenuity created Barbie's flexibility, size, and dimensions; Ruth was behind Barbie's insatiable consumption of clothes. The final product was a blonde beauty whose waist was smaller than Scarlet O'Hara's and whose bust—if it were to be found on an actual woman—would cause her to topple over. Although voluptuous, she has no nipples and only received a belly button in the year 2000. However anatomically improbable, Barbie was celebrated by generations of artists, including Andy Warhol. Adult collectors, with their mantra "Never out of the box," treat her like statues of the Virgin in Catholic communities. Through the force of Ruth's outsized personality, she overcame the prudish resistance of the male executives at Mattel and christened her creation Barbie, after her daughter's nickname. Her parents also called her Babsy and Bobby, so America's favorite doll could have been known by a different moniker.

In 1959, wearing a zebra-striped bathing suit and stiletto heels, Barbie made her debut at the American Toy Fair in New York. She hit the counters at three dollars and walked off them—actually, tottered, given the size of her heels. Her fly-off-the-shelf popularity transformed Mattel into a postwar success story and made the daughter of a blacksmith into a Forbes-worthy matron. By the spring of 1960, Mattel could not keep up with the demand for the jewel in the corporation's crown, although its Japanese factory was producing a hundred thousand a week. Barbie fan clubs mushroomed, and a Hollywood columnist reported that she received more fan mail than Elizabeth Taylor and Audrey Hepburn combined. The statistic says it all: 90 percent of all American girls in the past forty years have owned at least one, and the long-legged beauty is marketed in more than 140 countries. Her brand is estimated in the billions—a little ahead of Armani.

And what of the parents who were the creators of the 1950s valley of the dolls? Jack Ryan took five trips down the aisle, all failures due to his passion for prostitutes, orgies, and cocaine, pastimes funded by his share in Barbie's billions. He purchased a mansion he dubbed the

Castle, once owned by the actor who played the Cisco Kid, and filled it with flesh-and-blood Barbies. His partnership with Ruth culminated in a flurry of lawsuits, and those, along with his multiple divorces, drove him to alcoholism. His marriage to his Bel-Air neighbor, Zsa Zsa Gabor, also unraveled, as the Hungarian sex symbol could not curtail his promiscuous lifestyle. She had been denied entry into the Castle's dungeon, a black torture chamber decorated with black fox fur. When their union dissolved after a year, Ryan remarked, "That marriage cost me $260,000 a bang." In 1989 he suffered a stroke which left him unable to speak or engage in his prurient pursuits; he committed suicide two years later.

In contrast—to paraphrase the Aqua lyric—life was fantastic for Barbie's creator. Not only did she create an empire for the Handlers, Elliot's lucrative Hot Wheels allowed them any number of the real thing. However, while Barbie always landed on her stilettos, in 1970 Ruth's life took a dire turn when she was diagnosed with cancer and had her left breast removed. More *tsuris* (trouble) followed when, five years later, the Handlers were forced out of their positions in the company they had founded when charged with fraud. In 1978, Ruth was indicted for false reporting to the Securities Commission. She pleaded no contest, was fined $57,000, and was sentenced to 2,500 hours of community service.

Ruth Handler, despite her age, refused to become a lady who lunched. She formed a new company, Ruthton Corporation. After her mastectomy, her doctor told her to stuff her empty bra cup with rolled-up stockings. Unimpressed, when she asked a saleswoman in a Beverly Hills department store for an artificial breast, she was handed a surgical bra and instructed to stuff it with a couple of gloves. When Ruth investigated the available prosthetic breasts, she saw they were "a shapeless glob that lay in the bottom of my brassiere. The people in this business are men who don't have to wear these." As a result, Ruth launched her late-in-life venture: the Nearly Me prosthetic, a liquid silicone with foam backing that came in lefts and rights. She explained, "There has never been a shoemaker who made one shoe and forced you to put both your right and left foot in it." She proudly proclaimed her product was so real that "a woman could wear a regular brassiere, stick her chest out, and be proud."

In the 1970s, breast cancer was not the cause of the moment, and even its mention was kept under wraps. Nevertheless, the intrepid Ms. Handler mentioned it *a lot*. She and her sales team fitted women (including First Lady Betty Ford) and helped bring the affliction out of the closet. Indeed, she often performed her "strip act" in which she would take off her blouse—which she did for a *People Magazine* photo shoot. By 1980, the business was a million-dollar one, and she ran it till it was sold to Kimberly-Clark. She said that the business success of Nearly Me, as well as the women who wore her creation, rebuilt her self-esteem. In talking about her two careers, Ruth stated, "I've lived my life from breast to breast."

Ruth retained a gold-plated Barbie in her Century City home, the icon that has sold over a billion models in one hundred and fifty countries. One of these dolls, whose full name is Barbara Millicent Roberts, resides in the Smithsonian, and another became part of the official United States bicentennial time capsule of 1976.

Commercials for Mattel promised, "You can tell it's Mattel, it's swell!" And just as swell is the genealogy of Barbie, who transformed from German sex toy into a life indeed fantastic—as America's most enduring sweetheart.

CHAPTER # 16

La Belle Dame Sans Merci (1962)

"And no birds sing." This was the closing line of British poet John Keats' nineteenth-century poem "La Belle Dame Sans Merci." The reason for the silence of the skies was nature's empathy for a knight, victim of a femme fatale. In postwar America, the skies were also ominously quiet—for a far different reason.

The sea held an allure for Rachel Louise Carson of landlocked Springdale, Pennsylvania, outside of Pittsburgh, in the boom of the Industrial Age. Despite the positive connotation of Springdale's name, from her log cabin window smoke billowed from the stacks of the American Glue Factory that slaughtered horses, much like the one where Boxer from *Animal Farm* met his end. The stench was so rank that, along with the mosquitoes that bred in the Bottoms (the nearby swamp), it prevented residents from sitting on their porches. Her father, Robert, was a ne'er-do-well, and her elder sister, Marian, was obliged to work in the town's power plant. Rachel's mother, Maria, the daughter of a Presbyterian minister, prayed that her own daughter would have better. Her passport out was a one hundred dollar scholarship that enabled her to attend Pennsylvania College for Women. There Rachel went on her first and seemingly only date with a fellow student, Bob Frye, who took her to the annual PCW prom. He did not rate a mention in a letter Carson wrote her friend about the event. However, she had plenty to say about her biology professor, Mary Skinker, who Carson described as "a perfect knockout." Carson was distraught when Skinker left PCW to complete her doctoral studies at Woods Hole, Massachusetts. Missing her mentor, Rachel happened to read Lord Tennyson's "Locksley Hall," one line of which resonated with her: "For the mighty wind arises, roaring seaward, and I go." Although of a scientific bent, Carson took these words as a sign, and she followed Mary until she left her unrequited love for graduate work at John Hopkins University. Rachel helped support her family as the Carsons fared even worse during the Depression.

Rachel became a science editor for the US Fish and Wildlife Service, an agency founded under the New Deal, and she freelanced for *The Reader's Digest*. Driven by her love of the ocean, she wrote on everything from where to go on summer vacation, to the catch of the day, to the life cycle of marine life. She believed people would protect what they loved, so she worked to establish a "sense of wonder" about nature. Carson had once remarked to a friend that she always wanted to write, "but I don't have much imagination. Biology has given me something to write about." Although the sea was the magnet that beckoned, she spent little time on the water, rarely venturing deeper than her ankles.

Carson garnered literary laurels with *Under the Sea* and *The Sea Around Us*, which received the National Book Award. By 1952, she was the author of two bestselling nonfiction books. Miss Carson, shy and reserved, was taken aback by the fame. It took great courage for her to accept a luncheon speaking engagement at the Astor Hotel with fifteen hundred guests in attendance. As part of her lecture, she played a recording of the sounds of the sea, including the clicking of shrimp and the squeaks of dolphins and whales.

The financial success altered her lifestyle; before she had lived with her mother under the ever-present worry about money. She used her royalties to purchase a property on Southport Island, Maine, a remote hideaway with only two hundred and fifty residents where she delighted in her garden, filled with flowers and birds. One of these neighbors, Dorothy Freeman, played a romantic role in Carson's life. However, as Dorothy was married and the two women were extremely private, like the creatures below the surface of the ocean, their relationship remains enigmatic. After all, the term "lovers" is one of infinite possibility. Carson would address envelopes to "Mrs. Stanley Freeman," but her letters referred to Dorothy as "Darling." Both worried that the "craziness" between them might be revealed, and so they penned two different kinds of correspondence: one impersonal, one anything but.

Late '50s America was the era of Walt Disney and Fred Astaire, of Norman Rockwell covers on the Saturday Evening Post and rock 'n' roll, of the Beat poets and the Kennedy campaign—a decade of contentment. However, what fractured the smooth waters was the havoc blighting the environment. No one had a definitive theory—with the exception of the biologist Rachel Carson. For most of 1961, she locked herself in her cottage to complete her book that dealt with the identification of the killer: DDT. She forged ahead, cognizant she was taking on some of the most powerful industrial forces in the world. This battle would have been a daunting task for anyone, let alone a shy single woman of her generation. Her fortitude was all the more remarkable, as during this time Rachel's health deteriorated from breast cancer, and she underwent a mastectomy and radiation therapy. In addition, she was caring for Roger Christie, her orphaned, seven-year-old grandnephew. Despite her clandestine romance with Dorothy, her parenting role, and her illness, Carson felt she never had any choice but to finish *Silent Spring*. In a letter to Dorothy, she quoted President Lincoln: "To sin by silence when they should protest makes cowards of men." In lyrical prose she encapsulated the scientific truth that insecticides "Still the song of the birds and the leaping of fish in the streams, to coat the leaves with a deadly film and to linger on the soil—all this though the intended target may be only a few weeds or insects." Carson said the synthetic killer should not be called "insecticides" but "biocides." *Silent Spring* was also an exposé of capitalism, claiming that the chemical companies cared only about their own balance sheets rather than about the balance of the ecosystem. Rachel settled on the title *Man Against the Earth*; however, at the urging of publisher Paul Brooks, she changed it to *Silent Spring*, which intimated the coming of a perpetual winter if man did not cease his chemical assault on the environment. Previous authors had alluded to the same situation, but none wrote with the eloquence of Carson.

Silent Spring was selected as a Book-of-the-Month Club title, earned Carson a posthumous Presidential Medal of Freedom from Jimmy Carter, and put her face on a seventeen-cent United States postage stamp. Proof positive of its impact was that President Kennedy, beset by weighty matters such as increased Soviet shipping to Cuba, when asked at a press conference whether the government was investigating pesticides, replied, "Yes, and I know that they already are. I think, particularly, of course, since Miss Carson's book." A few weeks later, as the Cuban Missile Crisis unfolded, *Silent Spring* began its ascent to the top of the *New York Times* bestseller list. Supporters compared the book to *Uncle Tom's Cabin*, in that both works reflected the mainstream Protestant thinking of their eras, which demanded personal action to right societal wrongs. Supreme Court Justice William O. Douglas, an ardent naturalist, declared, "We need a Bill of Rights against the twentieth century poisoners of the human race." Two social movements, Greenpeace and Earth Day, are by-products of Carson's seminal work.

Silent Spring hit the affluent chemical industry with the effect of a Biblical plague of locusts, one the corporations wished they could eradicate with a spray of their deadly product. In retaliation they not only targeted her professionally but also claimed she was probably— because of her attack against business—a communist; in a Cold War world, this attack was the ultimate in character assassination. The FBI duly investigated her; the intimidation was a warning not to mess with the boys and their business. The industrialists tried to sue her, *The*

New Yorker (which had serialized her book prior to publication), and her publisher, Houghton Mifflin. When this tactic failed, they ignited a $4,250,000 publicity campaign to tarnish her professionalism. They even tried to cast aspersions on her by painting her as a spinster with an affinity for cats—another unpardonable offense was that "she had overstepped her place as a woman." Her invariable response was to reiterate her fears that man was recklessly gambling with the fate of the earth, and "the obligation to endure gives us the right to know."

A year after the release of her environmental classic, Carson testified before a Senate subcommittee on pesticides. She was fifty-six and dying from cancer, an illness she kept private. Her pelvis was so riddled with fractures that it was nearly impossible for her to walk to her seat at the wooden table before the Congressional panel. To hide her baldness, she wore a dark brown wig. Friends feared she would not live to see the show broadcast.

Silent Spring sold more than two million copies and made a powerful case for the idea that if humankind poisoned nature, nature in turn would poison humankind. If anything, environmental issues have grown larger—and more urgent—since Carson's era. Al Gore also sounded the ecological alarm bell with *An Inconvenient Truth* and was awarded the Nobel Prize. It shaped our contemporary view of global warming, yet Al Gore's book did not galvanize the nation like "the nun of nature" had. The final words of Keats' poem could serve as an epithet for the use of Carson's unhappy detractors: she was indeed *La Belle Dame Sans Merci*.

CHAPTER # 17

A Joyful Noise (1963)

 The dust will never settle on stirring lines from speeches such as "Ain't I a Woman?" "Four score and seven years ago," and "I have nothing to offer but blood, toil, tears and sweat." One iconic quotation would not have been delivered if not for the Queen of Gospel.

Mahala Jackson—nicknamed Halie—was born the granddaughter of a slave and grew up in a three-bedroom New Orleans shack that bordered railroad tracks. Water from the Mississippi was so brackish that cornmeal was used as a filter. From birth she suffered from bowed legs, which a doctor wanted to correct by breaking them so they would heal straight. An aunt who lived with them advised against it; instead, her mother, Charity, applied the down-home cure of rubbing her down with greasy dishwater. Undaunted, the little girl danced for the white woman for whom Charity worked as a maid and laundress. Mahala was the third of six children of Jack, a longshoreman by day, a barber by night, and a clergyman on Sunday. The Jackson residence qualified as a full house, with thirteen people—extended family members, as well as a dog—calling it home.

Charity passed away when Mahala was five, and her care fell to her aunt Mahala, who was called the Duke because of her authoritarian manner. She subscribed to the Biblical injunction "spare the rod and spoil the child," and if young Mahala failed the white-glove test—to check if she had cleaned thoroughly—she received a beating. Motherless and mistreated, she crooned to a doll made of rags and grass and took refuge in the plaintive notes of blues singer Bessie Smith that wafted from her cousin's record player. She also loved the gospel of the Mt. Moriah Baptist Church and said of it, "We Baptists sang real sweet and did beautiful things with our hymns and anthems. When those sanctified people lit into 'I'm So Glad Jesus Lifted Me,' they sang out with a real jubilant expression." Mahala, who never learned to read music, joined in "because I was lonely." Her powerful contralto could fill a cathedral, and the congregation knew her as the little girl with the big voice. School was not her aunt's priority, and Halie left after the eighth grade to work as a cook and washerwoman.

In 1928, sixteen-year-old Mahala departed New Orleans as part of the Great Migration—an exodus of millions of African Americans who fled Jim Crow for the Promised Land of the North. Although freed from government-backed racism, they still faced economic disparity. For the first several years in Chicago, Mahala worked as a maid in a hotel, and she said, "I can still iron a man's shirt in three minutes." Once again, she took solace in music when she sang with the Greater Salem Baptist Church, where her soaring voice "made a joyful noise unto the Lord."

Jackson received her career break in 1929, when she met composer Thomas A. Dorsey, the Father of Gospel, and his composition "Take My Hand, Precious Lord" became her signature song. Seven years later Mahala added the letter "i" to her name and married Isaac "Ike" Lanes Grey Hockenhull. The marriage fell apart when he insisted she accept jobs as a blues singer that offered the greatest pay. However, she believed gospel was God's own music and would sing no other—even when tempted by the lure of a huge paycheck. Isaac was less than pleased, since he needed money to finance his addiction to gambling on horses. Their marriage ended in divorce, as did her second to Sigmund Galloway, both of which did not produce children. She explained her decision, saying, "Blues are the songs of despair. Gospel songs are the songs of hope. When you sing gospel, you have the feeling there is a cure for what's wrong, but when you are through with the blues, you've got nothing to rest on."

Mahalia's meeting with Dorsey was, in the words of *Casablanca*, "the beginning of a beautiful friendship." His music and her voice proved an irresistible combination. Under his patronage, she took part in a cross-country gospel tour that attracted attention in the Black community with songs such as "He's Got the World in His Hands," and "God Gonna Separate the Wheat from the Tares," the latter being her first recording. She sang with such fervor that the combs flew out of her hair, and she moved her listeners to dance and shout. By the 1950s, she had broken into white communities through her records, which sold in the millions, and she performed to a packed house at Carnegie Hall. As she did before every performance, she read selections from her Bible "To give me inner strength." With her wealth she bought a Cadillac that was big enough for her to sleep in when she performed in areas where the only hotels were "Whites Only." She also packed food so that when she toured the segregated South, she would not have to sit in the rear of restaurants. Between tours, Jackson lived in a ranch-style house she bought on Chicago's South Side. There was a racial outcry when she moved into the all-white enclave, and a bullet was fired through a window in lieu of a neighborhood welcoming committee knocking on her door.

News of the Gospel Queen reached a white audience, and requests poured in from Ed Sullivan, Bing Crosby, Red Skelton, Dinah Shore, and Steve Allen. However, just as she refused to sing the blues, she likewise refrained from ever compromising her gospel music. Mahalia turned down an offer for twenty-five thousand dollars from a Los Vegas nightclub despite their assurance no liquor would be served, as it was not a godly venue.

One of the highlights of her career was when she became the first gospel singer to perform at Carnegie Hall. She said, "Think of it, me—a washwoman standing there singing where such persons as

Caruso stood. I've never gotten over it." In 1947, Jackson signed with the Apollo label and recorded "Move On Up a Little Higher," which sold eight million copies. For this accomplishment, she posthumously received a Grammy Hall of Fame Award. The song's success catapulted her career into the stratosphere, and she sang for Presidents Truman, Eisenhower, and Kennedy, as well as for Queen Elizabeth II and Prime Minister Indira Gandhi.

If the legendary gospel vocalist Mahalia Jackson had been somewhere other than the Lincoln Memorial in 1963, her place in history would still have been assured. However, her presence launched one of the world's most iconic speeches, a landmark in the Civil Rights Movement. During the historic March on Washington, to the accompaniment of a Hammond organ, Mahalia sang "I've Been 'Buked, and I've Been Scorned" and "How I Got Over" as her friend Dr. King clapped his hands on his knees and called out to her as she sang. Jackson had a particularly intimate emotional relationship with King, who, when he felt discouraged, would call her for "gospel musical therapy." He had said, "A voice like this one comes not once in a century, but once in a millennium." In front of the assembled crowd of two hundred and fifty thousand, along with millions more watching from home, Bob Dylan, Joan Baez, Marian Anderson, and Peter, Paul and Mary performed, but the consensus was that Jackson's songs had seized the spirit of the day. Rabbi Joachim Prinz, president of the American Jewish Congress, followed her at the microphone and recalled his years in Nazi Berlin: "A great people who had created a great civilization had become a nation of silent onlookers. They remained silent in the face of hate, in the face of brutality, and in the face of mass murder. America must not become a nation of onlookers." Dr. King was next, and as he moved toward his final words, he sensed his speech was failing his vision. He was winding up what would have been a well-received but, by his standards, fairly unremarkable oration when, behind him, Mahalia Jackson cried out,

"Tell 'em about the dream Martin! Tell 'em about the dream!" She had heard him deliver the refrain in Detroit, and it had moved her, and she felt that this time his "Dream" speech would elicit the same response. Her words changed the trajectory of his address, and he put his papers aside and his fingers clenched the lectern. In an instant, he had transformed from a public lecturer into a fiery Baptist minister. In the sea of onlookers were Paul Newman, Sammy Davis, Jr., Sidney Poitier, Harry Belafonte, Josephine Baker, Burt Lancaster, and Charlton Heston. Marlon Brando wandered around brandishing an electric cattle prod, a symbol of police brutality. Through the catalyst of Jackson, Dr. King told of his hope that Black and White people would one day live together equally, punctuating his points with the refrain, "I have a dream." For all of King's meticulous preparation, the part of the speech that would become part of America's legacy was added extemporaneously at the exhortation of Mahalia. Although Martin was well-known before he stepped up to the lectern, after he spoke he landed into the sphere of legend. President Kennedy, who had been watching the televised speech from the White House, remarked, "He's damned good. Damned good." William Sullivan, the FBI's assistant director of domestic intelligence, noted the crowd's reaction and made a recommendation to his Bureau, "We must mark him now as the most dangerous Negro of the future of this nation."

Five years later, an assassin's bullet ended Dr. King's life and Mahalia sang "Precious Lord, Take My Hand" at his interment, the same hymn that Aretha Franklin performed at Mahalia's 1972 funeral. Chicago paid homage, as thousands filed past her mahogany, glass-topped coffin. Together the Baptist King and the Gospel Queen had dedicated their lives to making "A joyful noise."

CHAPTER # 18

Where Rosemary Goes (1968)

The ancient Greek games originated in honor of the gods of Mt. Olympus. After a hiatus of fifteen hundred years, nineteenth-century Frenchman Pierre de Coubertin resurrected the Olympics in order for countries to come together in sports rather than in war. In the twentieth century, an American carried on the tradition of sprinkling the physical with the divine.

Eunice Mary—nicknamed by her family "puny Eunie"—was born in 1921 in Massachusetts, the fifth of nine children of Joseph and Rose Kennedy. At her birth, her father was already accumulating the stratospheric fortune he later supplemented through investments in Hollywood film studios and bootlegging. Rose's faith helped her bear her husband's infidelities—including a long-term affair with Gloria Swanson—and repeated tragedies that befell her children: Joseph died in a bombing mission in World War II, Kathleen perished in a plane crash, John and Robert were victims of assassination, and Rosemary had her life shanghaied.

Joseph expected great things from his children, and an oft-repeated remark in their Cape Cod compound in Hyannis Port was, "We don't want any losers around here. In this family we want winners. Don't come in second or third: that doesn't count. Win." During her father's tenure as ambassador to Britain, Eunice attended a Catholic boarding school and was so devout that it was assumed she would become a nun. She did embark on a holy path—just not in the way anyone envisioned.

Eunice had the prerequisites to be an American princess, but a tiara held little appeal to her. She took to heart her parents' recitation of the Biblical injunction, "Much is expected of those to whom much has been given." Eunice majored in sociology at Stanford, and upon graduation worked as a social worker with female prisoners. Sargent Shriver, Jr. joked that he courted his wife at a federal penitentiary. Her family gave their relationship an enthusiastic thumbs-up. Sargent, a graduate of the Yale Law School, was to become the US ambassador to France, a Democratic vice-presidential candidate, founding director of the Peace Corps, and part owner of the Baltimore Orioles. The couple shared the commonality of religion, and Sargent's well-worn rosary went wherever he did. He venerated the saints, and practically counted his future wife among them. After eight years, she gave in to his entreaties and in 1963 became Mrs. R. Sargent Shriver in a wedding at St. Patrick's Cathedral in Manhattan, with seventeen hundred guests in attendance. Five children and eight Labrador retrievers soon followed.

Older sister Rosemary, born with a mild mental handicap, influenced Eunice's main crusade. In a family of overachievers, her limitations loomed large, a source of consternation for the patrician patriarch. In those days, most families placed those so afflicted in institutions. Though she remained at home, her parents took pains to hide Rosemary's condition. Eunice had "enormous affection for Rosie," and together they swam, sailed, and travelled in Europe. However, in her late teens, Rosemary became, in Eunice's words, "increasingly irritable and difficult." Joseph had his eyes on the prize of the presidency for his sons and felt that the Kennedys' Roman Catholicism was already enough of a political handicap. He feared that an unwed sister could prove the death knell to his aspirations. When his daughter was twenty-three—without consulting any member of his family—Joe arranged for Rosemary's prefrontal lobotomy. The surgeon later explained the procedure by saying that they made an incision in her brain. As he cut, a fellow physician kept Rosemary talking by having her recite the Lord's Prayer and "God Bless America." When she became incoherent, they stopped. The operation ended her outbursts; it also left her in an infantile state. She lived the rest of her years in an institution, mainly staring at its walls. She became the forgotten Kennedy, but not by her older sister and mother. Rose was enraged, and it was the one act for which she never forgave her husband. In an act of *mea culpa*, Joseph created the Joseph P. Kennedy Jr. Foundation, which focused on Catholic charities. Eunice later served as the foundation's vice president and changed its focus to the cause and treatment of mental impairment. The ancient Spartans had abandoned disabled babies on mountaintops; American society was relegating them to notorious "snake pits" no better than contemporary leper colonies. When her brother became President, Eunice had a pulpit from which to preach her advocacy for those without a voice. Her younger sibling Robert, JFK's attorney general, once joked: "President Kennedy used to tell me, 'Let's give Eunice whatever she wants so I can get on with the business of government.' " Eunice was in the Oval Office when John, at her behest, signed a bill to form the first President's Committee on Mental Retardation. Afterward, he handed her his pen. She made her platform so important to JFK, he reportedly left an emergency meeting during the Cuban Missile Crisis to receive the committee's report.

Eunice felt it would be helpful in changing public perceptions if she told the world that the President's sister was developmentally disabled, thereby debunking her family's claim that she was living in a convent. In 1962, she revealed the truth in the *Saturday Evening Post*. Eunice's candor helped move mental disabilities out from behind the iron curtain of prejudice.

Yet her greatest contribution occurred as a result of a phone call. A distraught mother shared how her son had to spend summers alone because no camp would accept a child with limited mental capacity. While other society women would have tackled the problem by writing a check or organizing a charity ball, thereby discharging the duties of her noblesse oblige, Eunice replied, "Come here a month from today." Camp Shriver's grounds were on the family home, Timberland, a huge Civil War-era mansion in Maryland. One of the children's instructors was Mr. Bodybuilder, son-in-law Arnold Schwarzenegger. Word spread, and the camp led to a nationwide campaign for physical fitness for the developmentally disabled. "It didn't hurt to have a brother in the White House," Shriver said of its success. The doctors and experts had been proven wrong. Eunice said of her campers, "They're not accepted in the schools. They're not accepted in play programs. They're just not accepted. We have much to do."

Eunice was thrilled to see how the children thrived with the combination of athletics and camaraderie. Just as Nancy Brinker later founded Susan G. Komen for the Cure in honor of her sister, who had succumbed to cancer, Eunice started an organization in tribute to her own sister—the Special Olympics. Its oath: "Let me win. And if I can't win, let me be brave in the attempt." The inaugural Summer Games were held at Chicago's Soldier Field, just a month after Eunice's brother Robert's assassination at the Ambassador Hotel. In her opening address, Mrs. Shriver said that exceptional children could be exceptional athletes. This mindset was contrary to the zeitgeist of the time, which held that these youngsters should be excluded from physical activity for fear that they might injure themselves. She concluded her speech, "In ancient Rome, the gladiators went into the arena with these words on their lips, 'Let me win. But if I cannot win,

let me be brave in the attempt. Let us begin the Olympics.' " The one thousand athletes outnumbered spectators ten to one. By its fortieth anniversary, three million participants from 181 countries competed, with millions more gathered to watch, cheer, and encourage. Loretta Claiborne, a Special Olympian, said of her mentor, "I think she teaches that no matter who you are, you are no different than the next person. To me, I think she's hope." A special Olympic torch had been lit.

In the years that followed, the Special Olympics expanded to include winter events, and in 2007, the organization took in revenue of $79.9 million. In words far removed from those of her father, "In this family we want winners," Eunice addressed the Fifth Summer Games, in which teams from as far away as Yugoslavia and Samoa participated, saying, "What you are winning by your courageous efforts is far greater than any game. You are winning life itself, and in doing so you give to others a most precious prize—faith in the unlimited possibilities of the human spirit." Evidence of this philosophy was made manifest at the opening ceremony of the 2007 Special Olympic World Summer Games in Shanghai—Eunice's last attendance at her creation, where a crowd of eighty thousand gathered as President Hu Jintao welcomed more than seven thousand athletes to China, a country with a history of severe discrimination against anyone with disabilities.

For her advocacy, President Reagan awarded Eunice the Presidential Medal of Freedom; she became the first living American woman portrayed on a medal, and *Sports Illustrated* anointed her with its first Sportsman of the Year Legacy award. Her portrait, with four Special Olympians, hangs in the National Portrait Gallery; it remains the first painting of someone who is not a President or a First Lady.

The story of the Special Olympics is a tale of two sisters—one tragic, one triumphant. Eunice said of her muse, "If I had never met Rosemary, never knew anything about handicapped children, how would I ever have found out? So where would you find out? Unless you had one in your own family." The lyrics to Edison Lighthouse's 1970 song proved apropos: "Oh, but love grows where my Rosemary goes/And nobody knows like me. . . ."

CHAPTER # 19

Roe v. Roe (1973)

Ironically, although the Thirteen Colonies were christened the United States, certain seismic tremors proved divisive. In the nineteenth century, the Gray was pitted against the Blue; in the twentieth century, there was no love lost between the hawks and the doves; and in the twenty-first century, pussy hats have faced off against the Trumpites. Another tear in the fabric of the Union launched a movement whose tremors still reverberate.

Norma Leah Nelson was born on the very wrong side of the Simmesport, Louisiana, tracks. Like Annie, she was destined to "a hard-knock life," but unlike the fictional redhead, Daddy Warbucks never came to the rescue. Norma's grandmother was a prostitute and fortune-teller, but it is unlikely she foresaw that her granddaughter would become a role model in the Women's Movement. Her mother, Mildred, was an abusive alcoholic who moved with her two children to Texas after her marriage to Olin ended when Norma was thirteen. Part Cajun, part Cherokee Indian, and raised as a Jehovah's Witness, Norma was ten when she stole money from a gas station to run away from home. She ended up in state institutions, ones she described as the highlight of her childhood. Her education came from reform schools until she dropped out in the ninth grade. By age fifteen, a nun and a male relative had sexually assaulted her.

At sixteen, in another attempt to escape, she married an itinerant steel worker, Woody McCorvey, whom she had known for six weeks. The new Mrs. McCorvey became pregnant; thrilled, Norma spent eleven dollars on a Chef Boyardee dinner, some hamburger meat, and a red-and-white plastic tablecloth. She recalled, "I'm fixing this big spaghetti dinner, had a candle on the table, trying to make it real romantic so I could let him know I was going to have a baby." As neither of Woody's previous wives had been pregnant, he wrongly assumed that he was infertile—and that his child bride had been unfaithful. His response: "You're a bitch. You've been sleeping with someone else." Norma recalled, "And then he hit me, from the kitchenette clear into the living room." Norma returned home to raise her unborn child. However, after Melissa's birth, Norma confided in her mother that her sexual preference was for women, and Mildred kicked her out. McCorvey said that in a drunken stupor, Mildred tricked her into signing adoption papers. She explained that she did not want the child raised by a lesbian. Norma acknowledged that while her mother was raising Melissa, she was raising hell.

What followed was years of alcohol and drug abuse, and jobs that ranged from bartender to carnival barker. Looking for love any place she could find it, Norma had affairs with both men and women. After a relationship with a coworker—whom she would only identify as Joe—resulted in a second pregnancy at age nineteen, she relinquished parental rights to the father. In 1969, she had conceived yet again with Carl, a man she had dated for a few months. She said, "I never considered myself a lesbian then. My mother put it into my head I was bisexual. I only ever slept with four or five men, but I got pregnant with three of them." Not wanting to undergo a third unwanted birth, she turned to an illicit abortion mill, only to discover it had been shut down.

Without money to travel to a state where abortion was legal, Norma contacted attorneys Sarah Weddington and Linda Coffee, two lawyers looking for a woman to serve as a plaintiff. At Columbo, a Dallas pizza parlor, the three women met to discuss plans to change the law of the land. Norma signed an affidavit that she did not read and later said that her lawyers did not share the fact that any ruling would come too late for her termination. According to Norma, they were less interested in the predicament of one plaintiff than in the rights of millions.

In the landmark legal ruling *Roe v. Wade*, the Supreme Court ruled that women had the right to the control of their own bodies "free of interference by the State." Jane Roe served as McCorvey's pseudonym to protect her privacy; Wade was the Dallas County district attorney, renowned as the DA in charge of the case against Jack Ruby. The watershed ruling proved a knife in the heart of American unity. The pro-choice group viewed it as a victory for women's rights while the pro-life group felt it the handiwork of the devil. In the ensuing years, images have become embedded on the public—both of posters displaying mangled fetuses, and of a woman standing outside the White House with a message to her current President: Bush keep out of mine.

Lost in the tug-of-war was the woman at the eye of the storm who put her baby up for adoption. She moved in with her lover, immigrant Connie Gonzalez, and the two worked as cleaning ladies. They met when Ms. Gonzalez caught Ms. McCorvey shoplifting groceries from a store where she worked. (She let her keep them.) It was only after a few years together that Norma revealed to her girlfriend she was Jane Roe. The incredulous Connie responded, "Yeah, and I'm the Pope." McCorvey—who had come out of the closet regarding her sexual orientation—also decided to come out to the fact that she was behind the historic ruling. The revelation occurred in 1980, when she became infuriated by a newspaper article that claimed that Jane Roe was not only a fictitious name but also a nonexistent person. Norma took her story to a Dallas TV reporter. The fallout from her confession was that she became the target of egg-throwing vandals and the object of an avalanche of hate mail. The outing ignited a return to the controversial case, and reporters tracked down Mildred in her Dallas trailer park. The antipathy between mother and daughter was readily apparent, and older one groused, "She drank and she took dope and she slept with women. She was a die-hard whore." A solitary tooth rooted in her upper gum, she followed this remark with an obscenity. Mildred stated, "She was wild. Wild. I beat the fuck out of her." The news piqued the interest of NBC, and they consulted with McCorvey for their film *Roe v. Wade*, based on Norma's hard-knock life that led to the historic ruling. As she and Connie watched the movie—Holly Hunter starred as the accidental activist—McCorvey's comments peppered the showing: "That's my necklace! That's my headband!" However, her mood turned sober as she watched the actress enter a pay phone to call her mother with the news that she was pregnant. The response from the other end: "You ever use the word 'No'?" Even more chilling was when anti-choice protestors fired bullets at their house in a pre-dawn attack; Connie covered her lover with her own body. Terrified, she and Connie lived on the move while they searched for an anonymous address. When they finally found a home, Norma hung a dream catcher, an Indian hoop with feathers and ribbons, over her bed and said, "If you have bad dreams, they will be filtered out through the universe to go someplace else." If only. In spite of the trauma that would have flatlined another, the diminutive McCorvey—known as Pixie—never admitted defeat.

After emerging from her cocoon, the woman who had initially chosen not to claim her fifteen minutes of fame appeared at women's rallies in front of a crowd of three hundred thousand in Washington and sat on a speaker's platform with Gloria Steinem, Jane Fonda, and Glenn Close. McCorvey stated, "This issue is the only thing I live for. I live, eat, breathe, think everything about abortion." The spirit of the pro-choice followers was the slogan "It's time for the rosaries to get off our ovaries."

Ms. McCorvey's life took another sharp turn in 1995. While she was working in a Dallas women's clinic, "A Choice for Women," the anti-abortion group Operation Rescue relocated next door. It seemed a deliberate provocation, although the Reverend Phillip Benham, an evangelical minister, attributed it to the hand of God. Its staff adorned its walls with dozens of white crosses tied with pink and blue ribbons, and Benham declared, "At the killing center, at the gates of hell, this is where the church of Jesus Christ needs to be." Their posters of bloody fetuses freaked Norma out, as did the fact that on her smoke breaks, she saw them praying for her soul. Soon Benham and Norma began meeting across protest lines. She attended his church, and within months, McCorvey had accepted Jesus as her Savior. The Reverend baptized her in a swimming pool, making her a born-again Christian. Pro-life activists were jubilant and commented, "The poster child has jumped off the poster." She felt Jesus forgave her for all those dead babies, and now, in a drastic turnabout, she determined to dedicate her life to save them. In 1999, in a nod to irony, Roe testified before the Senate, "I am dedicated to spending the rest of my life undoing the law that bears my name." The famous attorney Gloria Allred—who had gone with her to pro-choice rallies—said of Norma's switch, "It was a career move." The police arrested her when she protested against the appointment of pro-choice jurist Sonia Sotomayor to the Supreme Court. She also made TV ads against Obama saying, "He murders babies." She later converted to Roman Catholicism, which entailed renouncing her lesbianism, and she broke up with her ever-faithful Connie. Given the details of McCorvey's life, the letter "L" could never be put after her given name of Norma—even as norms changed, she was never a "normal" woman.

The restless woman at last found rest when she passed away in 2017 from heart failure. Piper packed quite a punch jousting at windmills, but her greatest battle was *Roe v. Roe*.

CHAPTER # 20

The Queen of Green (1976)

 Kermit the Frog lamented, "It's not easy being green." In contrast, for one lady, being green led to a life of globetrotting, stratospheric wealth, and royal recognition. Her journey from hippie chic to Forbes-worthy woman made her wear the hats both of saint and of corporate bigwig.

During Christmas, visions of sugarplums dance in children's imaginations while their mothers anticipate stocking-stuffers of pineapple facial wash, jojoba moisture cream, and elderflower eye gel. These products were the brainchild of a lady who specialized in breaking the rules. Anita Perilli was born in 1942 in Littlehampton, Sussex, to an Italian-Jewish immigrant family, the third of four children. Her parents, Gilda and Donny, came from Naples to England before the Second World War. The couple divorced when Anita was eight, and Gilda remarried Donny's cousin Henry, with whom she had been in love all along. Henry died a year later from a brain hemorrhage. When Anita was eighteen, her mother revealed that Henry was her biological father; she had been conceived from a passionate extramarital affair. The news delighted Anita, as she had always preferred him to the drunken Donny, who equated rape with intercourse. She attended the local convent school, but her greatest educational moment occurred at age ten, when she read a Penguin book about the Holocaust. She later said this experience kick-started "a sense of outrage and a sense of empathy for the human condition." At age thirteen, she joined in a march for the Campaign for Nuclear Disarmament.

Turned down by drama school, she enrolled in the Bath College of Education in 1962, briefly taught for a time, then worked in Paris clipping newspapers for the *Herald Tribune*, followed by another year in Geneva as an employee of the United Nations. This job was followed by a stint on an Israeli kibbutz where she was expelled for a practical joke. She hit the hippie trail to Tahiti, New Caledonia, Australia, and South Africa. In Johannesburg, she ran afoul of apartheid laws by going to a jazz club on a "black night" that led to her expulsion from the country.

Back in Britain, Anita met Scottish poet Gordon Roddick at Littlehampton's El Cubana nightclub. She was twenty-six and looking, as she put it, for "sympathetic sperm." It took her "four and a half seconds" to know she had found what she was looking for. As for Gordon, he said that the minute he looked at her he was doomed. The couple, together for six years, had daughter Justine before they married in 1970. The ceremony was held in a wedding chapel in Reno, with Anita pregnant with their second child, Samantha. Returning to England, they tried running a picture-framing shop, a restaurant, and a bed and breakfast, all of which floundered. At a low ebb, Gordon announced he wanted to take off on a 5,300 mile, eighteen-month horseback ride from Buenos Aires to New York, in emulation of some Swiss explorer. Most wives would have responded to the news with some manner of husbandcide, moved to a euthanasia-friendly country, or muttered a despairing "Mama mia!" but Anita was not like other women. She turned her attention to the support of her two children during Gordon's gap year. Before his departure, he arranged for a loan for a business his wife was hoping to start because Anita, in a Bob Dylan T-shirt, failed to convince the bank of her credibility.

Digging for inspiration, Anita recalled beauty treatments she had seen on her travels: "In Polynesia I had seen women rubbing cocoa butter on their breasts and bellies and bums. Their skin was like velvet." Roddick opened a small shop in Brighton which she christened "The Body Shop," a name inspired by a cosmetics store she had seen in Berkeley, California, and stocked its shelves with fifteen exotic-sounding skincare products, concocted in her kitchen from "every little ingredient," packaged in recyclable sample bottles to keep costs low. To camouflage the patches of mold, she painted the walls in what would become The Body Shop's trademark dark green. Notoriety ensued when the two neighboring funeral directors objected to its name.

It was not just Ms. Roddick's nature-based concoctions that were different from the creams sold by the reigning cosmetic queens; it was the way she sold her goods. Her wares were displayed alongside photographs of the countries she had visited and the tribal people she met. She used her store as a three-dimensional billboard to advertise the causes near and dear to her heart, from the environment to human rights. In an industry that relies on women feeling badly about their appearance to push products, Roddick made her customers feel good and reminded them they were doing good by helping suppliers from the Third World. The Body Shop enjoyed serendipity, as it opened just as the environmental movement was taking off. This event was long before going green was an international pastime, when the only corporate responsibility was "In Gold We Trust." Anita's message was not that her creams would change her customers' lives, but better someone else's. Her emphasis on the power of one was embodied in slogans throughout her store, such as "If you think you're too small to have an impact, try going to bed with a mosquito." She viewed her nature-based beauty company as being the David to the beauty industry's Goliath.

At the time of her prodigal husband's return—his horse had fallen down a ravine in the Andes halfway through his trek—his wife had opened The Body Shop's second location. Gordon embraced the business, becoming the financial wizard while Anita provided the publicity. Anita remarked of their partnership, "He's the doer,

I'm the dreamer." Within fifteen years, the burgeoning chain had blanketed Britain. After her first US establishment opened in 1988, the hippie entrepreneur had been named Woman of the Year and Queen Elizabeth II's daughter-in-law, Diana, was a loyal follower—Princess Di bestowed upon her the title Dame Commander of the British Empire. Indeed, the Queen, with her tightly coiffed hair and matching suits, was at the other end of the spectrum from the flowing locks and Birkenstock-shod Roddick. To sweeten the pot, by 1990 The Body Shop was valued at eight hundred million pounds, and Anita was listed as the fourth richest woman in England. To many customers, Roddick was a heroine—the tousled-haired Mother Teresa of capitalism. She described herself as a "Ballsy, truth-telling, free-thinking, heart-bleeding, myth-debunking, non-conforming, and hell-raising activist."

However, not everyone was a member of Camp Anita. Roddick's critics said her ethics-over-profits philosophy was merely a publicity stunt. Some charged that although pictures of Anita in the jungle with penis-gourded men looked great in The Body Shop's displays, tribal traditions were destroyed by her company's intrusion. Moreover, her rhetoric about the evils of crass capitalism clashed with her status as the leader of an uber-lucrative multinational corporation with nearly twenty-one hundred outlets in fifty-one countries. Her comment that financiers were "dinosaurs in pinstripes" in actuality applied to her, though in her case the pinstripes were faded jeans. The cries rose to a crescendo when the Roddicks were accused of shortchanging their principles when they sold their empire to L'Oréal for $1.3 billion. The French conglomerate had been given the lowest rating of any cosmetics firm by *Ethical Consumer* magazine because of its widespread use of animal testing for its products. Anita was viewed as a Judas, selling out for far more than thirty pieces of silver. Others called her just plain crazy, a term often levied at people hell-bent on changing the world.

In 2004 Anita was diagnosed with hepatitis C, contracted through a transfusion undergone during Samantha's birth. It had given her cirrhosis of the liver, which resulted in a final burst of activism. She used her dire diagnosis to raise awareness of her disease, expressing outrage that her government was spending forty million pounds to inform the public about the switchover to digital television and only one million pounds on the scourge of hepatitis C. She posted on her Internet blog, "It's a bit of a bummer, but you groan and move on." This activism was in the spirit of the woman who had devoted her life to ethical causes, had dragged the ecological movement into the mainstream, and made saving the planet fashionable. Anita described the sunset of her life as her most exciting period and was pleased that her radicalism had been passed on to her offspring. For years her daughter Samantha was the proprietor of the erotic emporium Coco de Mer, which incorporated The Body Shop's ethical principles: her leather handcuffs were sourced from a Brazilian collective. Anita praised her daughter's moral choice of products—one way to react to your child selling risqué underwear.

Whatever one's views on Dame Roddick, she was a pioneering woman in a man's world, who transformed a cottage industry built on soap, bubble bath, and moral engagement into the Starbucks of cosmetics. Claiming it was obscene to die rich—"shrouds have no pockets"—Anita gave away millions of dollars and lent her name to righting the wrongs of the world. She campaigned against sweatshop labor and protested the imprisonment of two of the Angola Three, Black Panther members held in a Louisiana state prison for a murder for which she believed they had been falsely imprisoned.

Only death could stop the irrepressible Anita, who passed away from a brain hemorrhage in 2007. Posterity will remember her as the Queen of Green.

CHAPTER 21

What Becomes a Legend Most?
(1980)

As Dorothy and her friends walked along the Yellow Brick Road, eerie noises emanated from the forest. Their song echoed their fear: "Lions and tigers and bears, oh my!" Unlike the girl from Kansas, a woman from Britain does not fear animals; animosity is reserved for the two-footed.

There are white-meat people and there are dark-meat people; some prefer the thigh, others, the breast. In 2011, *The New York Times*, in their "Dining & Wine" section, highlighted another group of gourmets: those whose palate favors chicken skin, especially in tacos. Its visual showed a chicken arranged in a classic pinup pose: legs crossed, wing resting on thigh. The accompanying quotation: "Everyone knows deep down that they are closet chicken skin lovers." Well, not everyone. Ingrid Newkirk commented the headless fowl smacked of necrophilia.

Ingrid Ward, who grew up in Surrey, England, was never lonely, as her family kept cats, chipmunks, mongooses, and exotic birds. Sean, her dog, was both surrogate sibling and best friend. When Ingrid was eight, her father's engineering position took the family to New Delhi. Before leaving, her parents told her that Sean died during a visit to the vet. The truth did not come out till later: her dog had been euthanatized, as he was too old to withstand the trip. Ingrid's take was that "they would never have done that to a child." A year later, she saw a scene that left her with an indelible memory: an emaciated bullock was struggling to pull a heavy cart up a hill. As the animal faltered, its angry owner lifted the animal's tail and stuck a pole up its rectum, jolting it forward. Ingrid recounted, "I ran out of the house and grabbed the stick away from the man. I knew then that something had to be done." Ingrid attended boarding school in the Himalayas, which she recalled as cold showers and abusive nuns. During vacations, she helped her mother, a social worker, tend to those afflicted with leprosy.

When she was eighteen, the Wards relocated to Florida, where Ingrid met Steve Newkirk, a race car driver. He introduced her to Formula One racing, for which she developed a lifelong passion. She told *The New Yorker*, "It's sex. The first time you hear them rev their engines, my God! That noise goes straight up my spine!" They married the following year and moved to Poolesville, Maryland, where Ingrid studied to be a stockbroker. The trajectory of her life changed when a neighbor moved, abandoning over a dozen cats. Ingrid brought them to the local shelter where a woman said, "Come in the back, and we'll put them down." Ingrid misinterpreted the euphemism, and when she discovered they had been killed, she blew the whistle on the inhumane shelter. She became an animal protection officer for the District of Columbia and was DC's first pound master, named "Washingtonian of the Year." At this time, she decided to bid *adieu* to meat and pronounced, "My test is if it screams and runs away when you go after it, don't eat it." She still longs for its taste, and said if liver were permissible she would indulge, and she would even eat roadkill if she could.

In 1980, Ingrid met Alex Pacheco, who gave her a copy of philosopher Peter Singer's book *Animal Liberation*, which opposed "speciesism" and advocated the idea that all creatures deserved equal rights. They formed PETA—People for the Ethical Treatment of Animals—with the core message that animals are not ours to eat, wear, experiment on, or use for entertainment. Newkirk feels that the idea that humans should have more rights than animals is a "supremist perversion" and compares a leather belt to "one of those Nazi lampshades" made from human skin. PETA was fated not just to affect the possessors of fur and feathers. Steve Newkirk found himself married to an animal activist who put the four-footed before those with two legs—including him. The marriage went further south with Ingrid's repeated arrests for acts of civil disobedience. The icing on the marital cake was that they regularly received dead animals in their mailbox from those whom Ingrid had enraged. The couple divorced in 1980; there was no custody fight, as Ms. Newkirk had undergone sterilization at age twenty-two; she believed it wrong to reproduce when there were orphans in the world.

PETA consisted of what Newkirk later called "five people in a basement," its tenants drawn up at her kitchen table. Soon an event took place that transformed PETA into a force to be reckoned with—one with three hundred employees, three million members, and an annual budget of twenty-five million dollars. In 1981, the group's investigation of the abuse of experimental monkeys in a Maryland laboratory resulted in the first police raid on any American lab. The Silver Spring Monkeys, as the case became known, turned the group into a worldwide organization, one both beloved and reviled. Their action led to an amendment of the Animal Welfare Act and became the first animal rights case heard in the Supreme Court. It also turned Newkirk into a self-proclaimed publicity slut.

PETA's best-known campaign plays the sex card by having the beautiful and famous appear in a state of undress on billboards. Models such as Naomi Campbell, Christy Turlington, Cindy Crawford, and actresses Kim Basinger, Pamela Anderson, and Eva Mendes have obliged. The billboard's classic caption: "I'd rather go naked than wear fur." A variation on this theme is a model holding a rabbit: "Try telling him it's just a little fur trim." On occasion a male does the honor, such as Tommy Lee's tatted bod: "Ink, Not Mink." Paul McCartney is a huge supporter, though he has yet to shed clothes for the cause.

Ingrid, at age sixty-seven, bared all in protest of the Bacon and Beer Classic. She stripped down in a meat market in Covent Garden, London, where she paid a few pounds to the butcher to allow her to pose while dangling from a meat hook between pig carcasses. She said that she was freezing and that the looks on the butchers' faces were incredulous. PETA plastered Newkirk's pork photo-op on a billboard truck that circled the New York Mets' stadium. She liked the fact that her flesh was the same color as the pigs', as it highlighted the common denominator of man and "beast." Newkirk's point was that it is bizarre to kill animals for a sandwich, saying, "Why are we so obsessed with bacon and not obsessed with saving the lives of smart and sensitive animals?" A tactic directed against Nordstrom—which has a policy of taking back anything for any reason—led a Seattle member to return a dead fox. In 2015, PETA called for dentist Walter Palmer "to be charged, tried, and if found guilty preferably hanged" for his murder of Cecil the Lion.

Turning their attention to the famously fur-wearing personality who inspired *The Devil Wears Prada*, PETA deposited a dead raccoon on Anna Wintour's soup as she dined at the Four Seasons in Manhattan. And who could forget the Victoria's Secret fashion show infiltrated by PETA, who deemed one of its "angels" diabolical? As Gisele Bündchen sashayed down the runway, clad in a beaded bra and black panties, several PETA members leaped onto the stage with signs reading "Fur Scum." Gisele had aroused the animal activists' anger when she became the spokesperson for fur designer Blackglama. No doubt Kim Kardashian, victim of a flour bombing in Paris for her furry fashions, could relate to the brouhaha. The shock and awe tactics bore fruit as designers such as Ralph Lauren, Donna Karan, and Calvin Klein, along with stores such as Banana Republic, Forever 21, and J. Crew, stopped selling fur and its related products.

PETA also bears arms against the consumption of animal products and distributed Unhappy Meals at McDonalds, complete with gory toys. Their 2000 poster showed a cow's severed, bloody head above the words: "Do you want fries with that? McCruelty to go." The group disagrees with the Colonel's slogan that its fried chicken is "finger-lickin' good" as evidenced by their website: kentuckfriedcruelty.com. Whenever someone knocks veggie burgers, Ingrid's response is, "So you prefer the decomposing corpses of slaughtered animals?" In a nod to live theater in London, Newkirk sat at a dinner table outside the Fortnum & Mason food store with a foie gras feeding funnel rammed into her bloodied mouth. In response to those who say her outlandish tactics alienate people from the PETA cause, Newkirk responds with a quotation from a Texan politician which has an unintended animal rights twist: "There's nothing in the middle of the road but yellow lines and dead armadillos."

After a near-death experience in a plane mishap in 2009, the rebel with a cause wants to continue her activism post-grave. In her will, she divvies up parts of her body: the "meat" of her body to be used for a human barbeque, her skin to be made into a leather product, and her liver to be vacuum sealed and shipped to France, a nod to the nation's indulgence of foie gras. The document also instructs "a little piece of her heart" to be buried by the Ferrari pits where Formula One racer Michael Schumacher won the German Grand Prix.

Newkirk established an eight-acre sanctuary in Norfolk, Virginia, replete with a two-million-dollar building that could have been designed by Dr. Doolittle. In its reception area, there is a quotation from Leonardo da Vinci which states, "The day will come when men such as I will look upon the murder of animals the way they now look upon the murder of men." In her years as an activist, Newkirk has made powerful friends and an equal number of powerful enemies. The answer as to whether she is an archangel or an arch-devil lies in Blackglama's classic question: "What becomes a legend most?"

CHAPTER # 22

The Mantra (1983)

Fashion is an exacting taskmaster, and its modern dictate is that women need to be svelte: the Old Masters depiction of fleshy females has been replaced with gaunt-eyed Twiggy. The obsession with thinness led to a modern-age guru whose name became a household one.

During the Great Depression, in 1932, the sixth and last child, Genevieve, was born to James Yoric Guidroz and Gertrude Acosta of Berwick, Louisiana, a small town a hundred miles south of New Orleans. The greatest gift they gave their children was the philosophy that work was "not a dirty four-letter word." Although Gertrude and James divorced after thirty-five years of marriage, their love for one another persisted: when Gertrude died from cancer, James was by her side.

During Christmas, 1952, Genevieve, who went by the name Jenny, went to New Orleans to visit her brother Bobby and his wife, Mabel, who introduced her to their neighbor Robert Bourcq. Mabel warned her sister-in-law about harboring romantic illusions about Bobby, a confirmed bachelor. Jenny viewed it as a challenge; she never took well to the words "You can't do it." After dating for a year, Bobby and Jenny married in a small church on her twenty-second birthday. Their first daughter, Denise Patricia, was born the following year, followed three years later by Michelle Rae. Jenny's second pregnancy proved difficult; to counteract nausea, she overate and packed on fifty pounds. In a 1990 magazine article, she stated, "I used to look in the mirror and cry. I would just cry and say, 'What did you do to yourself?' " To fight her weight, which had never before been an issue, she joined the Silhouette American Gym. When she had shed thirty pounds, the manager took notice and offered her a job selling memberships. During this period, it dawned on her what was not obvious in the 1960s: "I began to realize that there was nothing out there telling people that they should eat this kind of food as healthy or avoid that kind of food as unhealthy. I was sure there were a lot of people just like me that want someone to tell them what to do." She left to work for her sister Elsie, who had opened her own gym, Slim Figures. One day she answered the phone, "Slim Figures. May I help you?" Sid Craig laughed and answered, "Hi, Slim." The person on the other end was going to impact her life and make her future married name a world-renowned eponym.

Sidney Harvey Craig, born in Vancouver, British Columbia, and raised in Los Angeles, attended California State University in Fresno, where he majored in business and psychology. After graduation, he, along with partners, established a chain of women's fitness salons called Body Contour. In 1970, Jenny began working with him, and when he offered her a position in Chicago, she was faced with a crossroads. Life with Bobby was miserable, and she viewed the transfer as a chance to break away from a soul-sucking relationship. In 1975, Jenny took the plunge and with her two daughters drove to her new job. In the Windy City, she met Sid for dinner; when he inquired as to the whereabouts of her hubby, she explained that she was in the middle of a divorce. He replied that he had separated from his wife, Irene, with whom he had three children. Before he returned to his home in California, he invited her to visit; it was the start of their cross-country relationship. They married in 1978 in Las Vegas, followed by a reception at Caesars Palace. Despite their different religions—she was Catholic and he was Jewish—their union was one of unity and love. She said of her husband, "Sid is a very lovable character. He has the charisma of a Jack Kennedy, the intelligence of an Alan Greenspan, the creative mind of a Steven Spielberg, and the humor of a Jackie Mason, along with the good looks of a Clark Gable." To add to the mix, he was also soon to have the wealth of Midas.

In 1981, Sid and Jenny realized the need to incorporate nutrition into Body Contour; however, when they approached their partners, they refused to accept their ideas. Convinced of their vision, the Craigs sold their company, which had grown to a two-hundred-store chain, in a deal that netted the couple $3.5 million. Although Jenny and Sid were fifty, they were of the mindset that retirement would not sit well with them. As their buyout included a two-year non-competition clause that prevented them from opening up another fitness company in the United States, Sid and Jenny departed for Australia. When they arrived, it was apparent that Australia was a ripe market for their business: there was no similar concept, and there were a lot of overweight people. Sid suggested they christen their business "Jenny Craig" because he felt that by using a person's name, customers would more readily identify with the business than if they were to use a generic name such as "Weight Loss, Inc." In addition, since Jenny was going to act as spokeswoman, the eponym made further sense. From its onset, the weight loss center was a runaway success; the only main snafu occurred during a training program, when Jenny asked a student, "What would you say if a client walked in and said she only wanted to lose a couple of inches in her fanny?" Jenny was confused when the room exploded with laughter—in Australia, "fanny" refers to female genitalia. It was during this time the couple had the eureka moment that was to lead to the thinning of the world: to offer packaged frozen meals which could be purchased at their centers. They understood that the pitfalls of dieting were especially dangerous when people embark on diets, when they become overly preoccupied with food—thus defeating their purpose. The Craigs decided that if they provided the meals, it would let their clients focus less on food.

By the time the Craigs took their leave of the Land Down Under, fifty Jenny Craig centers were part of the continent's landscape.

With the ten million dollars generated annually from their Australian enterprise, Jenny, who admits to having a black belt in shopping, could have once more opted for a life of leisure; however, she and Sid still did not want to embark on that route. Armed with their frozen food idea, they opened up twelve Jenny Craig centers in Los Angeles. The Cajun girl succeeded beyond her wildest dreams; Jenny Craig grew to include six hundred worldwide locations that generate three hundred and fifty million dollars annually.

With their vast fortune, Jenny and Sid lived *la dolce vita*: they purchased the 237-acre Rancho del Rayo, in Rancho Santa Fe, California. Their horse, Candy Ride, won a one-million-dollar purse at the Del Mar Racetrack. A longtime goal of Sid's was to win the Kentucky Derby; to that end, Jenny bought her husband a $2.5 million present for his sixtieth birthday: a thoroughbred named Dr. Devious. The colt finished seventh in the Kentucky Derby and won the Epsom Derby in England. Sid's classic car collection showcased vehicles that had once belonged to President Franklin D. Roosevelt, Dean Martin, and Al Capone. Other perks of their life included a second home in Aspen, a private jet, partnership in the Phoenix Suns of the NBA, and making the acquaintance of famous film stars, five US Presidents, and Queen Elizabeth II. In addition to having fabulous wealth and a famous brand, Sid and Jenny never lost their mutual devotion. She said of her husband, "I've learned that everyone has a soul mate somewhere, and if we're lucky enough to find them to share our life with, then we are more fortunate than most. I thank God every day for allowing me to find mine. Sid has enriched my life in more ways than I can count." Tragically, misfortune was to intrude on their charmed lives.

In 1995, Jenny fell asleep on her couch and was startled awake by a loud noise from her television. Her head shot up, resulting in her lower jaw locking over her upper one with such force she had to literally pry her teeth apart. The next few years were endless rounds of pain and doctors; however, with perseverance, she was able to overcome her affliction. She told Larry King, "Why should I dwell on the one negative in my life? We can't afford to squander one day with self-pity—life is too short—we must enjoy each and every day in order to avoid regrets of lost happiness or adventures missed." During her illness, she was no longer able to be the voice of her empire and instituted what has become her company's standard practice of using celebrities as thinspirations: Monica Lewinsky, Kirstie Alley, Queen Latifah, Sarah Ferguson, and Jason Alexander. In 1995, the Craigs sold Jenny Craig to Nestlé for six hundred million dollars.

With the fortune won from weight lost, Jenny purchased real estate, which she has recently put up for sale with hefty price tags. The octogenarian diet magnate listed her Del Mar, California, oceanfront property, its zip code is one of America's priciest, for nine million dollars. It sold for considerably less (six million dollars) to Michelle and Dwayne Weinger—Jenny's daughter and son-in-law. Another fortunate daughter is Bill Gates' teenaged daughter Jennifer, who jumps horses competitively. He purchased the Craigs' Rancho Santa Fe horse farm for nearly nine million dollars. Not a bad real estate year for the woman who was formerly Genevieve, a divorced single mother.

The greatest tragedy of Jenny's life was the loss of her beloved Sid in 2008. What pulled her through the morass of widowhood was her indomitable spirit. As she said in her autobiography, "My only regret is that I don't have seventy more years to enjoy the unimaginable wonders of the future." The diet queen, like Lady Simpson, lived by the mantra "You can never be too rich or too thin."

CHAPTER # 23

The Beast (1985)

The attire of the 2011 Pussy Riot punk rock group was not a fashionista statement, but a feminist one: Crayola-colored balaclavas and bright-hued leggings. The adoption of masks stemmed from a desire for anonymity during protests against the repressive regime of President—to them a.k.a. Dictator—Vladimir Putin. The Russian dissidents followed in the footsteps of an earlier American women's group who, although they adopted black clothes and alternative headcoverings, shared sisterly solidarity.

New Yorkers expect the unexpected, and this came to pass when the city awoke to hundreds of posters plastered on walls, kiosks, and construction site fences. The action was not a novel event; what set it apart was that the posters were dedicated to data. They proclaimed, "These Galleries Show No More Than 10% of Women Artists or None at All" and named names. They were signed "The Conscience of the Art World." The message was the F word: *Feminism*. This display threw an unwelcome spotlight on the oh-so-progressive Manhattan art scene. Who were these vigilantes who dared swipe at an august institution?

The protest movement was birthed after the Museum of Modern Art held an exhibition in which only thirteen of the 169 artists featured were female, even though it was purported to be the definitive showing of contemporary painting and sculpture. A group of friends felt this fact was a stick-in-the-throat statistic in the twentieth century, a throwback to a history that discouraged women from expressing themselves on canvas. The girls went ape over this gender injustice and decided to turn angst into action.

The band of sisters picketed the Museum of Modern Art and were ignored. It was not as if New Yorkers had never seen a posse of pissed-off ladies. A gimmick was needed, and bikinis, thongs, and stilettos were not their style. They decided to garner attention by wearing ski masks, in keeping with their role as urban guerillas. When one of them misspelled guerilla as gorilla, they felt it was serendipitous and agreed on simian masks. This tactic would not only garner the requisite notice, it would also protect against professional counterattacks, as many of them worked in galleries. The costumes all bore varying facial features, similar to the characters in "The Masks" episode of *The Twilight Zone*. While Russian Communist revolutionaries assumed pseudonyms—Lenin took his name from a river in Siberia, "Stalin" translates to "man of steel"—the Guerrilla Girls wore tags displaying the names of pioneering, deceased female artists: Frida Kahlo, Kathe Kollwitz, and Diane Arbus. Kahlo—whose gorilla visage sports glittery pink lipstick—highly recommends this modus operandi and explained, "If you're in a situation where you're a little afraid to speak up, put a mask on. You won't believe what comes out of your mouth." A variation of *in vino veritas*.

When the public took notice—and how could they remain oblivious to a number of black-clad, smart-talking apes?—the method as message became more refined. Instead of bearing statistics, the simian clique designed posters which showcased arresting images and thought-provoking captions laced with humor. In the 1990s, an iconic image was of a Manhattan bus muddying Carrie Bradshaw's dress; in 1989, New York buses displayed the artistry of the Guerrilla Girls. A nude courtesan reclined on plush, red fabric. Half of her right breast was visible, while her left foot rested on her right calf. She was a parody of the "Grande Odalisque"—seductively lounging in the Louvre since 1814. But where was her come hither look? Under the head of a gorilla. Above her body hovered the slogan: "Do women have to be naked to get into the Met Museum?" The caption was a satirical nod to the fact that while only 5 percent of the museum's canvases bore a woman's name, 85 percent of the female figures were nude. It was enough to drive the Guerrilla Girls to pelt the walls with a certain yellow, phallic-shaped fruit. Skewering this skewed ratio caused the requisite shame; it also proved that art is not gender-blind. After all, when was the last time you heard someone mention an important "male artist?"

The initial reaction to the Guerrilla Girls, who named and shamed major museums, was to brand them as rabble-rousers. A critic dubbed them "quota queens" and art dealer Mary Boone described their campaigns as being "an excuse for the failure of talent." However, they found loyal listeners, one of whom was Gloria Steinem—she stated of her hirsute sisters, "I think they're the perfect protest group because they have humor." Other fans include Yoko Ono, the Russian protest band Pussy Riot, and—fittingly, considering their appearance—Jane Goodall. A shot of adrenaline for their cause was when *New York Times* columnist Roberta Smith, who was among the list of critics singled out in one poster for not covering more female artists, acknowledged the error of her ways. Touché.

Over time, their activism expanded to other arenas that had ties to misogyny, and they rattled Hollywood cages long before others took up their causes. In 2002, the Guerrillas made posters about the number of male Oscar winners compared to their female counterparts and placed a billboard near the Kodak Theatre during the 2002 Academy Awards: "The Anatomically Correct Oscar. He's white & male, just like the guys who win!" Its visual was of a portly white male and around him were captions: "Only 3 percent of the Acting awards have gone to people of color"; "Best Director has never been awarded to a woman." (They must have pounded their chests eight years later, when Kathryn Bigelow won the award for Best Director, breaking an eighty-two-year-old Hollywood glass ceiling.) In Montreal, the Guerrilla Girls left behind their own variation on the mark of Zorro—a collage of sexist language through history. Pablo Picasso: "There are only two types of women—goddesses and doormats." Eminem: "You were supposed to love me now bleed, bitch, bleed." Frank Sinatra: "A well-balanced girl is the one who has an empty head and a full sweater."

In addition to the provocative posters, the Guerillas have left their fingerprints on comic books, stickers, videos, billboards, museum bathrooms, and magazines. The feminist masked avengers likewise lecture at colleges, where their early grassroots fights are part of women's studies and art history classes at which sexist audience members are likely to be pelted with bananas.

The Guerrilla Girls have been welcomed into the mainstream and are now beloved by the very institutions they spent three decades fighting. Their works have become collectors' items and have been displayed at major museums such as the Tate Modern, the Whitney Museum of American Art, and, ironically, the Museum of Modern Art. The New York Public Library not only owns A. A. Milne's original Pooh Bear and Christopher Robin's other friends, it also possesses Guerrilla Girl posters. Their work is exhibited internationally, and people from Iceland, Paris, and Sarajevo have had guerrilla sightings; the GGs receive thousands of letters expressing gratitude for their activism each year, with return addresses ranging from Thailand to Brazil. The art world has leveled the gender playing field, and the girls have been a catalyst for that change. If you had X-ray vision, no doubt their smiles would be visible under hirsute Playtex.

As with many celebrities, the ladies have penned their collective memoirs. Their first book, 1995's *Confessions of the Guerrilla Girls*, covered their founding and the first ten years of their existence, starting with the birth of their "maskulinity" as member Ms. Kollwitz puts it. Their second book, the 1998 *The Guerrilla Girls' Bedside Companion*

to the History of Western Art, deconstructed the "stale, male, pale, Yale" perspective on art history. A perk of being a Guerrilla Girl is that they went on a ten-city tour in 2004 for their third book, *Bitches, Bimbos and Ballbreakers*, that scrutinizes female stereotypes.

As veteran artists who refused to be ignored, they were the guests of honor at their thirtieth anniversary party at a New York gallery. They posed and preened in all their hairy glory while they sipped prosecco through straws (their gorilla lips would not allow much more). Guests gazed at the walls lined with a retrospective of their posters protesting elitism and bias, their *cause cèlèbre*. They also convened on the West Coast, where they surveyed the Los Angeles County Museum of Art. Strolling amidst the Chagalls, Magrittes, and Kandinskys, they ran a tally. "That's nine out of nine 'WMs' in this room," remarked the hairy persona of Zora Neale Hurston, using a shorthand abbreviation for "White Males." This dire statistic was offset somewhat when a father explained to his daughter, terrified by the presence of the gorillas in their midst, "They're doing this so that you can grow up and be anything you want."

The main manifesto of the masked ladies is to tell women that the fault for their oppression does not lie in their stars, but because they are underlings. The male, white establishment is reluctant to cede their centuries-long power. The guerrilla gals are the real-world counterparts of Tom Joad in *The Grapes of Wrath*, who proclaimed, "I'll be aroun' in the dark. . . . Whenever there is a fight so hungry people can eat, I'll be there. Whenever there is a cop beatin' up a guy, I'll be there. And when our folk eat the stuff they raise an' live in the houses they build—why, I'll be there." Perhaps one day New Yorkers will wake up to the ultimate estrogen bomb. They would behold Beauty astride the spire of the Empire State Building, her face bearing the visage of a gorilla—and at her foot, the supine body of the Beast.

CHAPTER # 24

The Woman in Pink (1992)

 Traditionally, pink has been the go-to color for girls as well as Barbie's preferred hue, and it merited a mention in a Molly Ringwald film. In the last decade of the twentieth century, pink became a ubiquitous shade, evocative of an equal opportunity slayer.

The genesis of an icon began with the 1972 Tony Orlando song: a man wrote his wife that if she wanted him back, she was to "Tie a Yellow Ribbon Round the Ole Oak Tree" of their home. When he approached, he did not see one—he saw one hundred. Seven years later, in a nod to the hit single, Penny Laingen fastened her own around the tree in her yard, in a prayer that her husband Bruce, an Iranian hostage, would be released. In the 1980s, the yellow ribbon became a sign of solidarity for the soldiers fighting in the Gulf War. AIDS activists wanted something for the boys dying back home, and changed its color to red. And the ribbon was destined to undergo yet another metamorphosis.

Evelyn, the woman who would place pink alongside October's autumnal colors, was born in 1936 in Vienna, the only child of Ernest and Mimi Hausner. Her father lived in Poland and Berlin and settled in Austria with his wife, the daughter of a Viennese lumber merchant. Ernest owned a profitable lingerie shop; post-Anschluss, as a Jewish-owned business, it carried an expiration date. After Kristallnacht, a Nazi officer announced that he would take a partnership in the lingerie shop. Understanding the ramifications, the Hausners fled to the border, trading family silver for exit visas. They first went to

Belgium, then to England. To their horror, Britain did not prove to be a sanctuary. At the outbreak of war, its government, fearing German spies, arrested Mimi and interred her on the Isle of Man. Evelyn later recalled how the separation from her mother—and the Blitz—proved traumatic. Her father was able to secure Mimi's release, and the Hausners sailed to New York. Mimi woke Evelyn to show her the Statue of Liberty, that famous woman who promised the American Dream. In their competitive immigrant community, Ernest worked as a diamond cutter for several years before establishing Lamay, a dress shop in Manhattan which he would eventually expand to include five more stores.

Evelyn enrolled at Hunter College, working between semesters at a Barnes & Noble. At age eighteen, on a blind date, she met Leonard, a naval officer and the elder son of Estée Lauder. She agreed to a second date, although she set her heart on snagging a lawyer. Estée, who liked the girl, whom she saw as a younger version of herself, asked Evelyn to be the hostess for her son's birthday party. "So I stayed," Evelyn recalled. "What could I do? She was like a steamroller." The romance almost ended before it began, and she recalled, "My father loved him, and I was at the stage where anything my father approved of, I didn't—so that killed it for a while." In hindsight, her father did know best, and Evelyn and Leonard married four years later with a reception at the Plaza Hotel. On her wedding day, Estée told her daughter-in-law, "Now that you are going to be Mrs. Lauder, you can't go in the street without wearing your makeup." Evelyn quit her job as a Harlem public school teacher and joined her husband at the fledging cosmetics company launched by his mother in 1946. In the early days of her marriage, she would return to their apartment to find that Estée had rearranged all the furniture. Evelyn recalled that Estée "Would put the furniture one way. When she left, I moved it right back. Then she'd come a couple of days later and move it her way again. I'd move it right back. Finally, she walked in one day and

131

said, 'I guess I ought to leave it alone.' I just replied, 'It might be nice.' " It was furniture as power play. Despite having her dynamo mother-in-law as a boss, Evelyn held her own. She explained, "I was very strong. Having had a childhood like the one I had, I was much more tough than a lot of people. I was one of the few people who spoke my mind to Estée."

At this juncture there were only six Lauder products—a red lipstick, creams, lotions, and Youth Dew bath oil fragrance—and sales of less than one million dollars a year. These were the days when Evelyn would answer the phone in different voices to convince callers that the company was far larger than in reality. While Estée was the namesake and head honcho, it was Evelyn who helped transform the eponymous cosmetics company into an international empire and made her its Crown Princess. She partially accomplished this feat by coming up with classics such as cheek color in the form of colored pressed powder and lip gloss in a lipstick tube rather than a pot. As the firm continued to rise, it acquired satellites such as Clinique— named by Evelyn—Origins, Prescriptive, and Aramis. Success arrived when the company sold their products directly to beauty salons and department stores.

Through the Lauders' acumen, the family-owned company became a two–billion-dollar enterprise, and the once penniless refugee was among the Fortune 400; Evelyn became a socialite around whom Manhattan society orbited. In 2008, she merited inclusion in the *Vanity Fair* International Best-Dressed List. However, under her understated designer clothes lay a will of steel. The secret to her svelte figure lies in her quotation, "Whenever a waiter asks me if I'd like dessert, I tell him, 'I can't. I'm suffering from a condition called Fatonmythighs.' If you say it fast it sounds downright medical." Her penthouse on Fifth Avenue held a significant collection of modern art, including works by Picasso. Despite her high profile in society, Evelyn was extremely private and shared only the most cursory details regarding her sons,

William and Gary. She shunned public intrusion on the couple's homes in Manhattan and Aspen, as well as their rustic retreat in upstate New York where Evelyn—an accomplished cook—prepared German food for family and friends.

Even the most charmed existence was no armor against the slings and arrows of the breast cancer with which she was diagnosed in 1989. With her characteristic grit, Evelyn was determined that she would spend her days living with—rather than dying from—the disease. Through it she also found her life's great crusade as a warrior against the scourge ravaging her body. She raised a good part of the $13.6 million for the construction of the Evelyn H. Lauder Breast Center at the Memorial Sloan Kettering Cancer Center, which opened in October 1999. In addition, she arranged for another five million dollars to endow its clinical research branch. That might have been enough for most, but it was just the end of Phase One for Mrs. Lauder. Two years later, she set up the Breast Cancer Research Foundation, which generates funds for eight medical institutions around the country. Leonard, the company's chief executive, underwrote the cost of registering the foundation in every state. To date it has generated upwards of three hundred and fifty million dollars. Although a tireless campaigner, she was always reluctant to discuss her own condition. "My situation doesn't really matter," she told a reporter in 1995 in a voice that brooded no further probing. "The fact that I'm an activist is what's important."

Rival makeup mogul Charles Revson claimed, "In the factory we make cosmetics. In the store we sell hope." And hope was what Evelyn did her best to bequeath to fellow victims of cancer. In her long career as an executive, she worked with many shades and hues, but pink was the color that changed her life. In partnership with Alexandra Penney, then editor-in-chief at *Self* magazine, Ms. Lauder created the pink ribbon campaign aimed at breast cancer awareness. It began with Evelyn and Leonard financing millions of pink bows that were handed out to women at Estée Lauder department store makeup counters along with breast self-examination information cards. This giveaway grew into fundraising projects that led to Congress designating October as Breast Cancer Awareness Month. Evelyn said of the icon she launched, "There had been no publicity about breast cancer, but a confluence of events—the pink ribbon, the color, the press, partnering with Elizabeth Hurley, having Estée Lauder as an advertiser in magazines and persuading so many of my friends who are health and beauty editors to do stories about breast health—got people talking." A flight attendant noticed the pink ribbon on Lauder's lapel and mentioned that she knew what it represented. Lauder remarked, "From there, it became ubiquitous." Unsurprisingly, a new shade of lipstick, Pink Ribbon, debuted and generated one hundred and twenty thousand dollars in its first year.

Mrs. Lauder earned a Guinness World Record by starting a tradition whereby historic landmarks are illuminated in pink lights during the month of October to focus attention on the killer. Each year prominent sites around the world participate—including Niagara Falls, the Tower of London, and the Leaning Tower of Pisa. For her indefatigable efforts, she received the Carnegie Medal of Philanthropy. Evelyn's relentless energy was only slowed in 2007 when she developed the ovarian cancer which would lead to her death in 2011. Fifteen hundred people attended her funeral, and the Empire State Building was bathed in pink to mark her passing.

In 2006, Ronald purchased Gustav Klimt's portrait of Adele Bloch-Bauer for $135 million. No doubt its subject—a Jewish, Viennese woman—holds a personal connection. The masterpiece had long been engaged in a legal tug-of-war between Adele's niece and an Austrian museum. It is the crown jewel of Ronald's Manhattan art gallery. As priceless as the painting of the *Woman in Gold*, dearer still is the memory of his sister-in-law—the woman of pink.

CHAPTER # 25

The Golden One (1995)

 In the 1968 film *Funny Girl*, after bagging bad boy Nicky Arnstein, Fanny Brice waxes poetic: "Sadie, Sadie, married lady/See what's on my hand/There's nothing quite as touching/As a simple wedding band." In a similar ode to matrimony, in the 1971 movie *Fiddler on the Roof*, Tevye's daughters run through the field of their Russian shtetl, their song mirroring their dream: "Matchmaker, matchmaker, make me a match/Find me a find, catch me a catch. . ." In the mid-'90s, the path to becoming an altar girl was marked out on a new roadmap.

The Irish wag George Bernard Shaw observed, "We men chase women until they catch us"; however, the wrinkle in that adage was the question of how women are to conduct that chase? Enter Ellen Fein and Sherrie Schneider, two BFFs from New York. Their bestselling how-to tome originated with a group of friends who met regularly at a Chinese restaurant on the Upper East Side to share dating diaries. Their fear of becoming old maids had been intensified by a *Newsweek* article which declared that single women over forty were more likely to be killed by terrorism than to get married, an observation which prompted nationwide hysteria. Suddenly, any heterosexual male without felonies was considered matrimonial material. What added fuel to the fire of desperation was the relentless ticking of their biological clocks.

Ellen was at a loss as to why she and her friends had unadorned ring fingers, a fact that deeply saddened them, not to mention their mothers. They were professional women: she was an accountant, Sherrie a magazine writer, and the other posse members were management consultants and Wall Street executives—yet none could get, let alone keep, a guy. Moreover, Ms. Fein knew she was arm-candy, what with her straight, long blonde hair and svelte figure, which were often showcased to perfection with a black micro-miniskirt, high heels, and dangling gold earrings ("They scream *Va-va-va-voom*!"). To remedy the dreary situation, Ellen and Sherrie put their blonde and brunette heads together to come up with a plan of attack, one worthy of a Napoleonic campaign.

They pointed their manicured fingers at the Sexual Revolution and the Women's Movement, where passivity had become as quaint as hoop skirts and corsets. Daring ladies went after what they wanted, both in the professional and dating arena and—gasp!—asked men out. Fein and Schneider viewed this behavior as the heart of the problem and felt that the only occasion where women should approach men was at a Sadie Hawkins dance. They deemed appearing desperate worse than going on a date with a run in one's stocking. The males of the species, they reasoned, were hardwired to be the aggressors, and when women took on the role of hunter, their prey was emasculated.

The two friends came up with The List: thirty-five rules of dos and don'ts for shedding spinsterhood. The main commandment was the premise at the core of a Jane Austen novel, "man pursues woman." Premature intercourse was sexual suicide; rather than sealing the deal, it would only lead a "wham, bam, thank you, ma'am" before the potential bridegroom took off, leaving skid marks in his mad dash to freedom. Their plan of attack was a throwback to Grandmother's words of wisdom, "A man will never buy the cow if he gets the milk for free." Light kissing was permitted on the first date, but intimacy must be ladled out in miserly doses. It was also mandatory to stay in the hard-to-get arena: the authors would as soon stick pins in their eyes as accept a Saturday night date after Wednesday. In the quest for Mr. Right, ladies should invest in manicures, pedicures, and facials, and, if biology proved unkind, nose jobs. Hair should be kept long (men love Rapunzel locks), and lipstick was a must, even on a jog. On dates, it was de rigueur to wear black sheer pantyhose and to hike up one's skirt, an erotic entrée.

In a nod to sisterly solidarity, as well as financial remuneration, the friends decided to submit their bible to the publishing world. Their credential at the time? They had both attained the "Mrs." status. The book was entitled *The Rules: Time-tested Secrets for Capturing the Heart of Mr. Right* and was released, of course, on February 14. Its cover was adorned with pink ribbons, and in its middle sparkled the Holy Grail: a diamond ring. For the paltry sum of $5.99, devotees would have men prostrating themselves in front of Rules Girls' shiny high heels. Adherence to The Rules would lead to heaven on earth: a home in the suburbs, a relieved mother, and half of Mr. Right's assets. What marriage-minded gal could resist such a marketing ploy? Apparently not many, as it became a bestseller with women lunging for copies much as a later generation would grab *Fifty Shades of Grey*. *The Rules* sold two million copies in twenty-seven languages and shot to the top of the *New York Times* bestseller list. Their book appeared on the most rational of ladies' bookshelves, tucked away between *The Brothers Karamazov* and Zadie Smith. There was even a Rules lipstick shade. The book polarized the nation: *Elle* magazine described it as "one of the best self-help books of all time," while *Jezebel* pronounced it "sexist garbage." Alas, those damn detractors.

Jay Leno had a field day, Oprah's audience went ballistic, and critics railed that the feminist movement had been set back fifty years by an outmoded code of courtship which implied that men would make idiots of themselves to woo demure femme fatales. Women's libbers cried out that bra-burning had been in vain. Ellen and Sherrie appeared on talk shows where they faced off with firing squads of furious feminists. However, the Rules originators laughed all the way to the bank; indeed, they had huge revenues to deposit. Not only did they rake in the green from royalties, film rights were sold for two hundred and fifty thousand dollars, and they also profited from readers who flocked to forty-five-dollar-a-person seminars and dished out two hundred and fifty dollars an hour for phone consultations. Faced with one clueless Hollywood executive's question, "Can I send my limo to pick up my boyfriend?" they responded with a resounding "No way!" Devotees organized Rules Girl support groups that met wherever singletons lived. Scores had converted to the ranks of Rules Girls after asking men for their phone numbers, invited them to NBA playoffs, showered them with Cartier cufflinks, and slept with them on the first date (violation of Rule No. 15), only to face devastation when their suitors sailed off into the murky waters of the uncommitted. Perhaps the appeal of the dating mantra tapped into the stories women were read to as girls: of Prince Charming coming to the rescue, Mr. Darcy, or Heathcliff.

Given their success, no one was overly surprised when the dynamic duo released the 2007 *The Rules for Marriage: Time-tested Secrets for Making Your Marriage Work*. Its cover displayed pink roses; in its center were matching wedding bands. The fly in the publishing ointment was that it coincided with the divorce of Mrs. Fein, a mother of two, from Paul Feingertz, her pharmacist husband of sixteen years. What a messy media moment, although it no doubt provided sufficient schadenfreude for their critics. Stephen Gassman, who represented Ellen, was also the lawyer for John Gotti's daughter Victoria in divorce proceedings against reputed Gambino family mobster Carmine Agnelio. The heavy-hitting choice of attorney flew in the face of Rule No. 41: Divorce with Dignity. However, in the spirit of a Rules Girl, Ellen brushed away her tears—making sure it did not smudge her mascara—and plunged back into the fray.

In 2001, Ellen went with five girlfriends to a singles weekend at Club Getaway, a sleepaway camp for adults in Connecticut. On the dance floor, she spied Lance Houpt; since she was interested in him, she did not initiate conversation or make eye contact. That would be against The Rules. He invited her for a paddleboat ride, an activity that fueled her infatuation, so for the rest of the weekend she avoided him even more. This coyness is in keeping with the Rules' Commandment: Thou shalt not call a man. He called her two days later and asked her out for Saturday night. She counted to four—because shouting "Yes!" screams desperation—before accepting his invitation. Three years later, Rabbi Ronald Broden conducted their intimate wedding.

Since a crusader's work is never done, in 2012, Ellen and the still-on-her-first-husband Sherrie, released *Not Your Mother's Rules: The New Secrets for Dating*. The authors felt it timely, as the Internet provided even more ways to "unwittingly mess up your dating life." The book is a guide for younger women in the digital age, where sex and cyberspace collide, to help them navigate potential online relationship waters. Some online rules: "Never friend him first. If he friends you, wait at least five weeks to accept his request. Don't write on his Wall, don't message him, don't appear as if you check Facebook too often." After all, a Rules Girl must appear busy, even if she is at home watching reruns of *Friends*.

Fein and Schneider launched a cultural phenomenon; however, the premise of their philosophy is disingenuous. It instructs obsessive women on how to pretend they are not obsessive. And what happens to a marriage when Dr. Jekyll turns into Mrs. Hyde and the demure girlfriend turns into the motor-mouth wife? The well-intentioned Long Island friends are a high-heeled version of Old West snake-oil saleswomen peddling the emotional equivalent of a miracle cream banishing fat. In the end, the only rule in love—as in life—is the Golden One.

CHAPTER # 26

Wanna Have Fun (1997)

The image of the zany old woman generally evokes a smile, a nod to those not diminished by time. She is celebrated in the 1955 book *Auntie Mame*, the 1971 film *Harold and Maude*, and the 1980s television show *The Golden Girls*. Yet, for the most part, she is rendered invisible by the contemporary youth-obsessed culture. In protest, a lady launched a campaign that proves the twilight years are not about disappearing into the shadowland.

A fragment from an ancient poem tells of a Greek woman who smashed her mirror because she could no longer see what she once was, and she would not see what she had become. Having drunk from the Fountain of Age, a matron can relate to *The Three Little Pigs* who swear on "the hairs of their chinny chin chins." She has to endure seeing male eyes pass over her and direct their gaze onto a lady who is a stranger to celluloid. This mindset goes a long way in explaining why the Queen organized a hit on Snow White.

Buried in the heart of an adult woman remains the little girl who wobbled in her mother's pumps and played dress-up, sipped pretend tea from miniature china cups, and shared giggles with friends. Alas, as childhood slipped away, the carefree days disappeared, replaced with wife-mother duties. How many of these gals dream of recapturing those halcyon hours? Because of the convergence of a poem and hat, it became possible to call back yesterday, to once again indulge in dress-up, to once again laugh with friends. And this escape can be undertaken as if she had nary a care in the world or if her hair be fifty shades of gray. This new breed can be seen—dressed to the nines, laughing with abandon in singular attire. Just who are these exuberant dames? The birth of the breed started by happenstance.

In 1997, on a whim, a greeting-card illustrator from Fullerton, California, Sue Ellen Cooper, bought a $7.50 red hat at a Tucson, Arizona, thrift store. The hat ended up in her closet until her good friend, Linda Murphy, was turning fifty-five. Sue Ellen was puzzling over what might be a creative gift to mark the fearful milestone, when she recalled the British writer Jenny Joseph's 1961 poem "Warning." It opens with the lines, "When I am an old woman I shall wear purple/ With a red hat which doesn't go and doesn't suit me." Its speaker explains that she is going to do all the madcap things in her twilight years to compensate for the sobriety of her youth. Cooper framed a copy of the poem and gave it to her friend along with a red chapeau. Its implicit message: to see the half-century anniversary not as a cause for mourning but for celebration. Mutual friends were so taken by the spirit of the poem and the vivacity of the hat, they requested the same when their big five-zero rolled around. Sue Ellen agreed as a "reminder to be eccentric and silly." Cooper thought her group ought to emulate the verse even further and buy purple outfits to accompany their cherry-hued headgear. A year later, the women donned their clashing ensembles and painted the town red on their visit to an Orange County, California, tearoom. Instead of finding themselves invisible—a usual occurrence for females in their age bracket—they were the focus of curious stares. Sue Ellen said, "We had more fun than we ever expected to have and decided to keep on doing it. All of that just sort of stimulated a return to a childlike attitude of play that I was surprised we all have buried in there."

In middle age, Cooper had wrestled with ways to retain her individuality. She recalled that as a stay-at-home mom to her children, Andrea and Shane, she once decided to give herself a gift—now, she would give herself the time to indulge in her passion for art. However, this luxury proved elusive in light of obligations. After her recent raucous outing, she remembered her earlier craving for playtime and realized that rather than the single night of dress-up, it could become a regular ritual. The Red Hat Society was born. The women attended events—a sea of poppies, often accentuated with boas and fake diamonds. Membership grew, and as it became unwieldy to go out *en masse*, Cooper encouraged the ladies to form their own Red Hat Society. Murphy inspired its second chapter when, visiting friends in Florida, she talked about going out with her Fullerton friends "in full regalia." The Floridian Golden Girls were enchanted and incorporated an eight-woman chapter.

For the first year and a half, the organization remained a local attraction, until a feature article appeared in the July 2000 issue of *Romantic Homes* magazine covering the bicoastal sister chapters that gave the Red Hatters their first appearance in the spotlight. The Associated Press likewise circulated a California newspaper story, and Cooper & Co. were inundated with requests for assistance in starting societies. The movement caught on like the proverbial wildfire, and groups with spicy names cropped up wherever women wanted to let their pigment-free hair down. American branches include the Scarlet Harlots, Hell's Belles, and the Red Hot Chili Peppers. One is known by the acronym Purple COWS: creative, outgoing, wise, and sexy. The sisterhood across the sea followed suit: Daft Old Bats, Brighton Belles, and the Red Hot Flashes. Their retort to the British stiff upper lip? "Not bloody likely." Their perspective is that fifty is the new eight, and they age in Benjamin Button fashion, boogying to the sounds of the Rolling Stones' "Honky Tonk Woman." Play dates run the gamut, from bingo to belly dancing, from high tea to hijinks, even including sightseeing on motorized Segway scooters. The proliferation of hats the color of matador capes is now worldwide. There are forty thousand R. H. chapters dotting the globe—far afield from Fullerton—in Australia, Cuba, and Qatar. In the embryo stage, Sue Ellen vowed to get a red hat tattoo if the number of chapters ever reached ten thousand. When it hit five figures, she submitted to the needle, and the logo is now displayed on her back.

Ms. Cooper calls her chapters a "disorganization" rather than an "organization," and the one rule is that there are no rules. Members meet as often as they like, and are governed by a designated leader, the Queen Bee, and her court. Valentine Shaw, fifty-nine, who heads the British branch of the Rose Hips includes an e-mail female (who informs everyone about gatherings), a mistress of anxiety (who takes on other people's problems so they don't have to), and an anti-parliamentarian (who enforces the "no rules" rule). Virginia proclaims, "Our inhibitions are gone, gone, gone." Arline Lillibrige, another participant of this branch, has a business card which proclaims, Matriarchs UNITE: There's Fun After Fifty. Little did Mrs. Cooper dream that her impulse buy would eventually become an international symbol of sisterly solidarity which has evolved into the world's largest women's social group. Sue Ellen, who uses the exaggerated title Exalted Queen Mother, said of the phenomena, "I was not trying to start a fire. I was trying to entertain myself and friends and do something to make our lives more fun." Proof of her brainchild's iconic stature is that Mrs. Cooper's original red fedora and purple boa were inaugurated into the Smithsonian. Other indications that the society has penetrated into mainstream culture was its parody in the *Simpsons* episode "The Last of the Red Hat Mamas," and it featured in a question on TV's *Jeopardy*. In *Rules of Engagement*, Russell Dunbar gets stranded on a cruise ship filled with Red Hatters; he booked his ticket after misreading "Red Hat Ladies" as "Red-Hot Ladies."

The headquarters—which Cooper jokes is "hat-quartered in Fullerton"—prides itself on not only having no rules, but also in not having minutes or meetings. *Laissez-faire* rules; after a lifetime of commitments, they would have it no other way. Participation in the society has a minimum age requirement of fifty. However, younger women can join. They are referred to as "pink-hatters" and wear the corresponding colored hats and lavender clothing. Their attire proclaims to the world that they are not yet ready for the rocking chair and the knitting needles.

In a nod to the irony file, Ms. Cooper, who formed her group to steal time for herself, created a crimson tide that keeps idle hours at bay. The Red Hat Society, Inc. has expanded to sixty employees, including her husband Allen, her daughter Andrea, and her son-in-law Matt—who all maintain their website, which receives thirty thousand visitors per day, edit its magazine, organize conventions, and design red and purple merchandise. Sue Ellen says that the stress pays off because her work gives the one million members the encouragement to go for the gusto.

Most people tend to look upon these ladies, who are not "going quietly into that good night," with a bemusement bordering on the benign. Hence, when Paula Span wrote a 2008 *New York Times* article entitled "Hatless, and Aging on My Own Terms," criticizing the colorful clique, many looked upon her in the same way they would upon someone setting fire to an orphanage. Span argued that it was the realm of teenagers to declare non-conformity in unison, and that this is what the uniform of the red and purple was doing. She added that it was tricky enough for women who had used up a large portion of their allotted three score years and ten to be taken seriously, and acting like madcap adolescents was not helping their silvery status. Perhaps Ms. Span was anticipating power pantsuits? Her umbrage can be understood, given the bedrock of the Judeo-Christian society that blamed Eve for eating the apple that led to giving birth in pain as women's lot. However, in their twilight years, it is perfectly fine for women to carve out a fun-filled niche and to grow old disgracefully. After years of paying their dues, older women—in the words of Cyndi Lauper—"Just wanna have fun."

CHAPTER # 27

One Butt at a Time (2000)

 To historians, the Battle of the Bulge is a chapter in the story of World War II; to others, it is a fight against ever-expanding waistlines. And, to an enterprising lady, it presented opportunity. Her slimming of America made her a modern Midas, with a fortune built on body issues.

Ralph Waldo Emerson observed, "Build a better mousetrap and the world will beat a path to your door." Sara Blakely, the woman who launched a Spandex mousetrap, was born in 1971 and raised in a home near the ocean in Clearwater, Florida, with her younger brother, Ford.

Her mother was a watercolor artist, and her father was a personal injury attorney renowned for his work on *Mays v. Wigg*, a trial involving two babies swapped at birth. It was a high-profile case, and Sara recalled that when she was at her dad's office the phone would ring; at the other end would be journalists such as Diane Sawyer.

In the fairy tale, Sleeping Beauty was gifted with many attributes, and the same applied to Sara, who possessed beauty, brains, and wealth. She also had an enterprising spirit; like Tom Sawyer whitewashing his fence, Blakely convinced friends to complete her chores by turning it into a competition. In high school, Sara managed to be both a cheerleader as well as a member of the debating team. However, even in the Sunshine State, clouds make their appearance: her parents divorced when she was in her teens, and the same year she witnessed one of her closest friends being run over by a car. Sara said of the trauma, "I think that when you witness death at age sixteen, there's a sense of urgency about life. I think about mortality a lot. I find it motivating. It can be any time that your number's up." Sara also has a sense of humor, which she explains as being something she developed growing up in a beach town as a young woman able to pass the pencil test.

Sara graduated from Florida State University with a degree in communications, but was sidelined from following in her father's lawyerly footsteps when she twice bombed her LSATs. She tried her hand as a stand-up comedienne, and then took a job at Disney World. At five foot six, she was too short to be Goofy and became a greeter whose uniform included a hat with mouse ears. She was humiliated when, dressed as a rodent, she encountered former classmates. In response to their patronizing glances, she would just nod and escort them to their rides. She was later to learn that living well is indeed the best revenge.

After a few months, Blakely exited the Magic Kingdom and became a door-to-door saleswoman for a fax company. Although a top earner, Sara was not overly enthused about schlepping chunky office equipment in subtropical heat. She recalled of these inglorious years, "I woke up one day and thought, 'I'm in the wrong movie. Call in the director! What happened? This is not my life.' " However, lacking a trust fund or a wealthy husband, she continued to schlepp—until her eureka moment arrived.

On an evening in 1998, Sara was going to a summer party and

wanted to debut a pair of white slacks. The problem was that although her size-two body looked svelte in the garment, she was not thrilled with the faux pas of the dreaded VPL—visible panty line. She felt that other attendees need not be privy as to whether her underpants were bikini, thong, or granny. Unable to purchase any product that would give her a smooth look, she made her own: she took a pair of control top tights and cut off the feet so the nylon would not interfere with her strappy open-toed sandals. Although this makeshift method worked on an aesthetic level, it fell short on comfort, as the material rode up her leg. Suddenly a light bulb went off: undergarments that would both smooth and slenderize.

Sara felt she had stumbled upon a market niche and figured no one had ever gone broke overestimating the heartfelt panic that the average woman feels about her body. Over the ages individuals have cashed in on this panic. In the nineteenth century, females were compressed into fainting hourglass shapes. Mammy lacing Scarlett's corset ever tighter dramatized this style statement. Sara felt that ladies would shell out the green for merchandise which would combat the effects of gravity on sagging breasts and droopy butts.

Sara relocated to Atlanta with her nine-to-five job and invested two years of nights and weekends into her dream, as well as five thousand dollars in savings. With no knowledge of how to launch a business, Blakely also researched the technical aspects of breaking into the male-controlled lingerie world. At first, she did not share with anyone what she was working on, believing that she did not need validation from friends or family. She explained, "I think that ideas are really vulnerable in their infancy." She also remarked that if she had listened to the naysayers, she would still be selling fax machines door-to-door. She remembers being asked the kiss-of-death question: "Sweetie, if it's such a good idea, why hasn't somebody else done it?"

With the shapewear and the distinctive packaging in place, Blakely came up with the name Spanx, which she found more intriguing than Spandex. She became aware of the name's sexual innuendo when Spanx's website first went live and her mother accidentally directed patrons to Spanks.com—a porn site. Although Spanx were not made of a natural fiber such as cotton or silk, artificial materials had worked wonders for Wonder Woman and had a slimming quality. The next step was to promote her brainchild, and she managed to find a Dallas-based Neiman Marcus buyer who agreed to a brief meeting. When she failed to elicit enthusiasm, the ever-enterprising Blakely told the woman to follow her to the bathroom, where she used the white pants as a before and after. An order was immediately placed for seven stores. However, it took someone with a well-documented battle with weight to give Blakely her proverbial break. Sara quit her day job right after she got a call that America's chat show high priestess had chosen to anoint Spanx as her favorite product of the year 2000. Acting on Oprah's thumbs-up, thousands of viewers scooped up Spanx and gave glowing testimony that their thighs had seen the glory. Sara also succeeded in taking lingerie out of the closet and made the erstwhile unmentionables so mentionable that even stars such as Gwyneth Paltrow admit that they have been Spanxed. Unlike traditional girdles, the product is sassy, something that made housewives all over the world feel like they could have a cameo in *Fifty Shades of Grey*. The product caused the biggest wave in lingerie circles since 1913, when Mary Jacobs had stitched together some silk handkerchiefs and launched the modern bra. *Ka-ching*. Sara became America's first female self-made billionaire.

The white trousers that started it all now reside in a display case at the Spanx headquarters in Atlanta. Every day, 189 employees walk past them as they work on products such as the Slim Cognito high-waisted shaper, Boostie-Yay! bodysuit, and the Bra-llelujah! The genesis of the latter name came about when it was test-worn on women who started singing "Hallelujah" and raised their hands in a "praise be" gesture. Spanx is now sold in sixty countries, from Sri Lanka to Peru, and has become a red carpet mainstay. In fact, the body-controllers are the bedrock for most of the Kardashian-Jenner women's skin-tight looks. The world's most powerful pantsuit aficionado is also a fan. Sara said she met Hillary Clinton at an event, and the Senator made a point of telling Blakely she is a fan. The irony of Spanx is that its inventor does not really need them, because she still retains her svelte figure. However, luckily for her, most of her sisterhood have a little extra junk in their trunks—and elsewhere. Her genius lay in the fact that while most women were trying to hide their extra gut, she trusted hers. The business she created has expanded as quickly as some waistlines, and she has branched out with products for men; after all, why leave out half the population? The male line offers brands such as Manx and Mirdles, and there are any number of testimonials that state that the compression garments "really help with back pain." Yeah, that's why we all wear them.

On the romantic front, Sara also hit the jackpot. While working her way onto the Forbes list, she met Jesse Itzler at a celebrity poker tournament in Las Vegas where Bill Gates and Warren Buffet were also guests. Over dinner, she fessed up that she made more money than he did. However, it did not prove an impediment to their romance. Indeed, if Itzler had a problem with dating a beautiful billionaire who was also part owner of the Atlanta Hawks basketball team, his nearest and dearest would have had to take out a conservatorship. They were married in Boca Grande, Florida, where Olivia Newton-John gave a surprise performance. The couple has four children, and they divide their time between six multi-million-dollar properties. Not bad for a former mouse-hat-wearing Disney greeter. Spandex has been good to Sara, whose empire's slogan is "Changing the world one butt at a time."

CHAPTER # 28

Huff and Puff (2005)

The press barons of yore were alpha males whose giant shadows shaped the way the world received its news: men like Joseph Pulitzer, William Randolph Hearst, and Harold Ross. In the twenty-first century, this glass ceiling was shattered with an infusion of estrogen when a Greek colossus emerged to stand astride the shores of media.

In the 1980s, Helen Gurley Brown had taken a giant footstep when she assumed the reins as editor of *Cosmopolitan* magazine. She had not only shown that a woman could excel in a traditionally male position, she also created a new demographic. Before Helen took her place atop the masthead, *Cosmopolitan* had been targeting married suburbanites preoccupied with raising the perfect child and making the perfect Jell-O salad. She changed it into a how-to-guide for bagging a billionaire, as she felt becoming a trophy wife was, after all, the Holy Grail.

Her successor was the Athens-born Arianna Stassinopoulos in 1950. Her father, Constantine, was a journalist; her mother, Elli, immigrated to Greece from Russia after the Russian Revolution. Her parents met at a sanatorium after World War II, where Constantine was recovering from his two-year incarceration in German concentration camps and Elli was recovering from tuberculosis. She had been told that because of her illness she would never have children, yet at their wedding she was visibly pregnant. Despite Constantine's name, which calls to mind the word "constant," his eyes wandered to women other than his wife. Eleven-year-old Arianna encouraged her mother to leave, saying, "You're not happy and you should be." Elli found an apartment where she lived with Arianna and her younger daughter, Agapi. One of her favorite sayings to her children was that their education would be their dowry.

At age sixteen, Arianna saw a magazine picture of Cambridge University, and her mother, an advocate of the idea that "dreams do not just have to be for sleeping," encouraged her impossible dream. Everyone else told her she was being ridiculous, as her English—and funds—were limited. She ended up with a partial scholarship, and Elli supplied the rest by borrowing from her brothers and selling her jewelry and family carpets. In 1969, Arianna traded the shores of the Aegean for the halls of British academia, where she lived in one room with a heater which she fed with shillings. Her arrival coincided with the apogee of the hippie movement, when Carnaby Street was at its most hedonistic. The strait-laced and serious Arianna never partook of rock 'n' roll, and refused even a puff of marijuana. She also felt alienated by her fellow classmates, who were not comfortable with the almost six-foot Greek girl who was neither from their country or their class. As an outlet, she joined the debating club and became immediately smitten. Her less-than-charitable peers referred to the newcomer who sat entranced at the debates as Starryanna Comeacropppalos. Despite her heavy accent, she became its president.

A pivotal event in Arianna's life occurred in 1971, when she appeared on the BBC classical music quiz show *Face the Music*. One of the other panelists was Bernard Levin, the lionized leading columnist for the London *Times*. By the end of the taping, he had invited her to dinner. He was twice her age and half her size and not of her faith—he was Jewish—but she was gaga. She recalled, "All I remember is that I spent the week prepping, getting myself up to the date on Northern Ireland, the latest developments in the Soviet Union, and the latest Wagner recordings." Her homework paid off, and the two became a couple with Levin in the role of Svengali. She stated of the man whom she called the big love of her life, "He used to say that going to bed with him was a liberal education." Not exactly the education her mother had in mind, but he proved to be a brilliant Henry Higgins.

Arianna graduated from Cambridge with a MA in economics in 1972, and the former debater, perennially seduced by the written word, wrote *The Female Woman*, a direct rebuttal of Germaine Greer's *The Female Eunuch*. Its premise was that the Women's Movement denigrated marriage and motherhood. To promote her first literary endeavor, her publisher scheduled an appearance with Barbara Walters. The twenty-three-year-old was not fazed, since she had never heard of either the *Today Show* or its famous host. In London, she became a journalist and published articles in the British editions of *Vogue* and *Cosmopolitan*, as well as maintaining a column in the *Daily Mail* and *The Spectator*. She also threw herself into the London social swirl, attending every party of any distinction, usually on the arm of Levin. Although the two were soul mates, the fly in their romantic bubble was that he was a committed bachelor and Arianna longed for commitment. Following her own youthful advice to her mother, "You're not happy and you should be," Arianna ultimately broke off their ten-year relationship.

In 1980, Arianna came to New York to promote her third book, a bestselling biography on Maria Callas. As it turned out, the author, even more than her book, became the toast of the Big Apple. Encouraged by her success and wanting to put distance between her and Levin, she remained in the States. Soon she was hosting grand parties at her East Side duplex for the glitterati, including Barbara Walters, Henry Kissinger, Ann Getty, Dr. Salk, and Dan Rather. There were also dinners at the Reagan White House and grand charity balls where Arianna, clad in designer gowns and Bulgari jewels, appeared with trophy dates such as California Governor Jerry Brown and garnered space in the gossip columns. The Upper East Side socialite was described

as "the most upwardly mobile Greek since Icarus." Yet she was not
without her detractors; a Los Angeles magazine once referred to her as
"the Sir Edmund Hillary of social climbers." Despite the heady social
milieu, in 1984, mother in tow, she relocated to Los Angeles to join
her sister and finish her fifth book; its subject was Pablo Picasso.

At age thirty-five, Arianna was desperate to clasp the brass
ring of marriage and motherhood. The heiress Ann Getty assisted
in that endeavor by providing a list of eligible men. She arranged an
introduction at her San Francisco mansion to Roy Michael Huffington,
Jr., who was thirty-eight, handsome, tall, and so reclusive that only
five people had his home telephone number. He was also co-owner,
along with his sister, of Huffco, a Texas oil company founded by
their billionaire father. Arianna and Michael were married in New
York six months later, in a spectacular wedding for which matchmaker
Getty footed the bill. Gracing the bride's earlobes were vast diamond
earrings on loan from Princess Michael of Kent. The guest list of five
hundred was comprised of the crème de la crème of Manhattan and
Los Angeles. Barbara Walters was a bridesmaid. The power couple
moved to Washington, where her husband pursued a political career
masterminded by his wife, whom critics referred to as a "right-wing
Lady Macbeth." His aspirations culminated in an unsuccessful Senate
bid to the personal tune of thirty million dollars.

After a stillbirth, the couple had daughters Christina and Isabella.
However, the girl from the country that gave birth to drama was
destined to have more than her fair share. Several years into their
marriage, Michael confided he had engaged in adulterous affairs—with
men. It was not a deal breaker; however, after he outed himself in an
interview in *Esquire*, the couple agreed to a divorce. Arianna claimed
that she did not know of his homosexual inclinations, but others say
she had been blinded by his bling. A friend remarked, "Honey, when
they fixed me up with Michael in Houston, I knew he was gay at

shrimp cocktails, and Arianna's smarter than I am." Arianna's closing comment? "I don't believe in marriage, just really good divorces."

After undergoing a transition to the political left, Arianna made an unsuccessful bid to be elected governor of California—the Greek lost to Austrian Arnold Schwarzenegger. In 2005, Arianna launched the *Huffington Post*, which started as a political blog before branching out to other venues, many of which lie along the gossip grapevine. Approximately two thousand unpaid bloggers contribute—she is undoubtedly the world's most accomplished networker—including friends such as Norman Mailer, Walter Cronkite, Larry David, and Nora Ephron. *Vanity Fair* described its debut as "the biggest burst of star power to ever hit the blogosphere." However, upon its debut, the verdict was harsh. *LA Weekly* wrote, "Her blog is such a bomb that it's the movie equivalent of *Ishtar* and *Heaven's Gate* rolled into one." Many of the vitriolic barbs seemed to be aimed at its founder; *the Boston Herald* sniped at its founder, calling her "a woman who changed her politics like Jennifer Lopez switches husbands"; another denounced her as "an intellectual lap dancer." Despite—or because of—the huge amount of controversy, the site took off and receives millions of hits per month.

Arianna, who set up her online news agency on a shoestring, sold it to AOL for $315 million and still retains full editorial control. In addition to her many-splendored bank accounts—from billionaire ex and the Huffington Post, LaHuff is on speed dial on her several Blackberries—with the world's most famous: Barack Obama, Oprah, and the Dalai Lama.

Whatever one's perspective on LaHuff, opponents beware: as with the big bad wolf in the classic child's tale, if angered—with the help of her bloggers, she can huff and puff. . . .

CHAPTER # 29

Back Seat Betty (2006)

In his song "Two Outta Three Ain't Bad," Meatloaf sang, "But there ain't no Coup de Ville hiding at the bottom/Of a Cracker Jack box." Be that as it may, a man paid four dollars at a Pennsylvania thrift shop for a picture frame that hid a copy of the Declaration of Independence—sold for $2.4 million. Teri Horton popped into a Salvation Army in San Bernardino to find a gift for a depressed friend; she was unable to fit the five-dollar painting through her trailer's door, and Terri kept the purportedly fifty-million-dollar Jackson Pollock. Salvation indeed. A patron of a Midwest flea market purchased a golden egg that—true to its name—led to a price tag of thirty-three million dollars. In the same vein, a woman, like the lady in *Rumpelstiltskin*, turned a bargain store find into pure gold.

A self-described Nasty Gal was born in San Diego in 1984, raised in the Greek Orthodox faith. Sophia Amoruso said of her Good Friday, 4/20 birth (the same day and month as Hitler), "Before you think this is some kind of omen, let me assure you that the only thing I smoke is my competition." After a psychiatrist diagnosed her with depression and ADD, she joked about her first job at Subway, saying that she got OCD on the BLT. An early possessor of a work ethic, she set up a lemonade stand at age nine, read books about start-ups before she was in braces, and worked in bookstores and records shops. Sophia and high school did not mesh; it made her feel like a zombie, and she opted for home schooling. Her home ended with her parents' divorce, and she moved into a Sacramento apartment that she shared with musicians. On her arm, she got a tattoo of the Virgin Records logo. Her room was a closet under the stairs that rented for sixty dollars a month; her boyfriend lived in a tree house. She had become an anti-capitalist crusader, allergic to responsibility, and survived on dumpster-diving for unopened food. Nevertheless, Sophia retained a remnant of her earlier entrepreneurial streak, and in 2002 sold her first online item: a book she had stolen. After being detained at a store for shoplifting shower-curtain rings, she quit stealing cold turkey. With her passion for fashion, she would have soon tired of jailhouse stripes. She toyed with the idea of attending photography school but was deterred by accruing debt. After being diagnosed with a hernia, she took a job that provided health insurance and worked checking IDs at an art school in San Francisco.

Adrift at age twenty-two, guided by the book *Starting an eBay Company for Dummies*, she opened a cyber-shop selling vintage designer items she found rummaging at Goodwill. She always loved the clothes of yesteryear and bought her first at age thirteen, a persimmon-red pair of disco pants she debuted at a roller rink. She named her business Nasty Gal, but because the domain was already taken by a porn site, Amoruso christened it Nasty Gal Vintage. Its motto: "Nasty Gals do it better"; Sophia's personal proverb: "Only the paranoid survive".

One of the first items Amoruso posted was a Chanel jacket purchased at a Salvation Army for eight dollars that she flipped for one thousand dollars. She found Yves Saint Laurent clothing on the cheap by Googling misspellings of the designer's name, reasoning that anyone who spelled it as Eve Saint Laurent was oblivious to its value. The Nasty Gal line did not cater to mom jeans; it carried edgy threads for millennials who eschewed the everywoman clothes from the malls of America. Inspired by success, Sophia shelved her Peter Pan duds for entrepreneurial shoes.

Amoruso anticipated the power of social media and started a Myspace page that garnered sixty thousand "friends" by connecting with *Nylon*, the music and fashion magazine. Her one-of-a-kind chic couture ignited bidding wars among shoppers from Australia to Britain. Booted off eBay for promoting her own web page, she switched to Facebook. She tantalized fans with inventory from shrunken motorcycle jackets to high-end vintage Versace, as well as provocative company creations such as the "Lita," a lace-up platform boot with a five-inch heel. Outfits were modeled by friends who, like herself, were recipients of the genetic lottery, and Sophia paid them with a salary of burgers. Amoruso also encouraged her customers to post pictures of themselves, thereby making her site interactive.

With skyrocketing sales, the thirty-year-old e-commerce golden gal was ready for a glass and mortar locale and moved to a sixty-five-thousand-square foot Los Angeles headquarters—where twentysomething Nasty Gal employees in mesh crop tops, leggings, and platform shoes stood out from the paralegals—followed by a branch in Santa Monica. The Council of Fashion Designers of America inducted Ms. Amoruso into its hallowed halls, and in an impressive vintage rags-to-riches tale, the former dumpster-diver had a staff of three hundred and fifty employees and one million fans on Facebook and Instagram. She bought a white Porsche with cash, remodeled her dream home, and landed on the Forbes list of America's richest Self-Made Women, estimating her fortune at two hundred and eighty million dollars, putting her ahead of Beyoncé and Taylor Swift. *Business Insider* dubbed her "the sexist CEO alive," and a *New York Times* article stated, "If ever there were a Cinderella of tech, Sophia Amoruso might be it." In keeping with her fairy tale life, and in a nod to the Amor of her last name, Sophia was in love with musician Joel Jarek DeGaff and stated that she hoped never to have to date again. In the words of Eliza Dolittle, everything was "loverly."

Following in the elegant footsteps of Sheryl Sandberg—and predating Ivanka Trump's *Women Who Work: Rewriting the Rules for Success*—Sophia penned *#GIRLBOSS*, a *Lean In* for misfits, published by Penguin in 2014. The commonality between the two self-help books is the message that bosses should have breasts, but the two authors, other than being dynamos, could not be further afield. *The New York Times* stated, "#*GIRLBOSS* is a DIY success manual aimed at women more prone to be voted "Most Unique" than "Most Likely to Succeed." Typical business how-to tomes are not written by former dumpster-diving, anti-capitalist shoplifters, but then again, Amoruso is not a typical CEO. On its cover is Sophia, hands on hips, a superhero in shoulder pads. #*GIRLBOSS* is part memoir—the author details how she learned that credit cards can be the devil (think mall lingerie), part millennial woman manifesto. It espouses when to follow the rules and when to rewrite them. Sophia also offers three pieces of advice: "Don't ever grow up. Don't become a bore. Don't ever let The Man get to you." She also says, "For the girls who have never bought a business book, I think this can be the gateway drug." Her book rose into the ranks of bestseller lists, and through the auspices of Charlize Theron, became *Girlboss*, a Netflix series. The critics were not kind. The *New York Post* declared *Girlboss* a feminist fraud, saying, "If you want to watch a show about feminism, hold out for *The Handmaid's Tale*. The outfits might not be quite as cool, but the message will resonate a lot more."

A hashtag does not a feminist make, a truth that became apparent when Nasty Gal Incorporated had a nasty habit of firing pregnant employees. Lawsuits from the mamas-to-be joined one by the Hells Angels for trademark infringement. Company morale plummeted when Amoruso, once personally involved in every aspect of Nasty Gal, became more celebrity than CEO. Once she had entrenched her company with the Netflix production and book tour for #*Girlboss*, as well as the #Girlboss Foundation (a laudable organization that provides grant funding to up-and-coming female entrepreneurs), Amoruso relinquished hands-on control. In 2014, Sheree Waterson became the new CEO; she hailed from Lululemon, which had fired her in the wake of See-Through-Pantsgate, for which she was held responsible. Employees viewed her as their resident "devil wearing Prada," and it was under her reign that the firings and resignations occurred. Nasty Gal laid off former accountant Farrah Saberi while she was suffering from kidney failure. At a company meeting, Sophia stated that the reason they were let go was because they were "mean girls." The flurry of bad press greatly undermined the girl boss's feminist creed.

In addition to her entrepreneurial woes, Sophia's marriage— once featured in *Martha Stewart Weddings*—dissolved. Joel told her—despite an ironclad pre-nup—that they were not right for one another. She became the lady screaming into a pillow at the Beverley Hills Hotel, unable to eat, chain-smoking in a bathrobe, and wearing a baseball cap, flanked by her three now fatherless poodles. She was also dealing with Nasty Gal's purchase by the aptly named (in this case) British company Boohoo, which had bought her company in a twenty-million-dollar takeover that staved off bankruptcy.

Sophia was in Australia promoting her second book, *Nasty Galaxy*, at a networking brunch, where she was to speak in front of a thousand women. She stated, "When the death knell of your company is the breaking headline and you're literally under a spotlight, what do you do? I showed up." The opening scene of *Girlboss* has her character saying, "Adulthood is where dreams go to die." Sophia, who has found her new love—thank you Facebook!—and launched a new business, shows that this is not always the case.

Amoruso christened her company "Nasty Gal" after the sexy singer and style icon Betty Davis' 1975 album. Her husband, Miles Davis, composed a song in his wife's honor, which bore a title both redolent with a sexual innuendo and the opposite of Ms. Amoruso, a gal always in the driver's seat: "Back Seat Betty."

CHAPTER # 30

#MeToo (2007)

 A common expression from the mouths of babes—desperate not to miss out on any fun—is "Me too!" Tragically, these two words, which are associated with childhood innocence, were destined to undergo a dire metamorphosis.

For those perusing their Facebook posts in October 2017—amidst the pics of food, puppies, and travel shots—a hashtag proliferated. It consisted of two words, but they packed a powerful punch: #MeToo. They had been inspired by actress Alyssa Milano. The catalyst for her tweet was the scores of women who denounced powerful film director Harvey Weinstein as master manipulator of the casting couch. Milano wrote, "If all the women who have been sexually harassed or assaulted wrote 'Me too' as a status, we might give people a sense of the magnitude of the problem." In a mere three days, the words became a battle-cry. The exposé moved beyond one man and the imbalance of power in the Hollywood hierarchy. Time Magazine featured a black-and-white photograph of Weinstein and to the left, in red, its "J'accuse!": producer predator pariah. Its message was that the days of the Big Boy's impunity was no more.

Caroline Crido-Perez wrote of the crime that had been forced from its closet, "It's done by friends, colleagues, 'good guys' who care about the environment and children and even feminism." Immediately those who had been victims of abuse took to social media; their clarion call was the desire to illustrate the preponderance of this societal ill. Facebook reported that within forty-eight hours, 4.7 million people around the world had engaged in the conversation in the United States, Europe, the Middle East, and beyond. The French used #BalanceTonPorc; the Spanish, #YoTambien. The chilling hashtag had been retweeted forty-eight million times. However, the phrase well predated the fall of 2017 and had not begun with the actress.

In 1997, Harlem-born Tarana Burke was working at an Alabama organization that ran a camp for young people living in marginalized communities. A thirteen-year-old in attendance named Heaven trusted Tarana enough to let down her angry demeanor and confided that she had been the victim of sexual violence from her mother's boyfriend. Tarana recalled of her response to being cast in the role of mother confessor, "I was horrified by her words, the emotions welling inside of me ran the gamut, and I listened until I literally could not take it anymore . . . which turned out to be less than five minutes." In the middle of the pain-filled narrative, Burke cut her off and directed the youngster to another female counselor who could "help her better." Burke rued the fact that she will never forget the look on Heaven's face, an expression of pain that the person she had turned to had dismissed her. Tarana stated, "I think about her all the time. The shock of being rejected, the pain of opening a wound only to have it abruptly forced closed again—it was all on her face." The youngster never returned to the camp, and Tarana has no idea whatever happened to Heaven. Burke closed her painful reminiscence by stating, "I watched her put her mask back on and go back into the world like she was all alone."

The reason why Tarana refused to offer solace was not indifference; it was because she herself was too emotionally raw to offer succor—she had likewise been a victim of sexual abuse. A friend of her mother's raped her when she was six, and a neighborhood teenager molested her on and off for three years. As an adult she was once more the victim of rape by an acquaintance while they were on their first date.

The painful episode when she let down the child left a lasting legacy and "sat in her spirit for a long time." Her epiphany was that she could have provided a salve to the young girl's soul, had she been able to offer empathy. Burke expressed her remorse: "I could not muster the energy to tell her that I understood, that I connected, that I could feel her pain." If she could have turned back the hands of time, she would have whispered, "Me too."

Determined to be the voice for those who had none, Tarana sought advice from a local rape crisis center. The response was they would only work with girls who had been referred by the local police after they had filed an official report. If Heaven had trouble confiding in her, how would the thirteen-year-old ever have the courage to trust someone in uniform to levy a complaint against an adult?

Ten years after the encounter, Ms. Burke created Just Be Inc., a nonprofit organization dedicated to helping victims of sexual assault. Its purpose is to teach survivors to speak out and dispel the shame and secrecy that surrounds sexual violence. Burke explained, "The work is really about survivors talking to each other and saying, 'I see you. I support you. I get it.' " She sought out the resources that had not been available a decade earlier. Her creation's mission statement is "Empowerment Through Empathy." Tarana also gave her movement a name: "Me Too."

Burke travelled the country from Philly to Atlanta, from Tuskegee University to Alabama State, presenting two-hour-long workshops to seventh- and eighth-grade students. Having learned the sad lesson from her failure with Heaven, Tarana was candid about her own experience with sexual assault. At the close of each session, she showed photographs of Black celebrities—Mary J. Blige, Missy Elliott, Queen Latifah, Gabrielle Union, Fantasia, and Oprah—each of whom had endured abuse and surmounted their scars to soar. Her message was that the culture of capitulation—the "boys will be boys" mindset—had to go the way of the dodo.

When #MeToo ignited a media firestorm, some African American women were upset that the decade-long effort by Ms. Burke, who is Black, had not received such support over the years and had only gone viral when prominent white feminists championed the cause. In response to the misappropriation they, along with Latino and other women of color, started alternate campaigns such as #WhatWereYouWearing and #YouOKSis. April Reign, a digital media strategist and the lady behind #OscarSoWhite began to organize support around the hashtag #WOCAffirmation (Women of Color Affirmation). Its purpose was sisterly solidarity in what they viewed as the disparity in how women of color were treated when they reported their stories of abuse to police. Ms. Reign stated that Black females "are demanded to be silent and erased like with Tarana."

Ms. Burke was also taken aback when she saw the name of her organization—and her brainchild—proliferate, and she remarked, "Initially I panicked. I felt a sense of dread, because something that was part of my life's work was going to be co-opted and taken from me." As it transpired, Ms. Milano, who had been unaware of its previous usage, quickly acted to rectify this and gave credit where credit was due. Two days after she had sent out the #MeToo tweet, she reached out to Tarana and expressed hope that they, united in purpose, could collaborate. The actress appeared on *Good Morning America*, where she credited Ms. Burke as the woman behind the famous phrase. In her interview, she stated, "What the #MeToo campaign really does, and what Tarana Burke has really enabled us to do, is put the focus back on the victims." In response, Ms. Burke said that it would be selfish of her to lay claim to #MeToo as something that she owns. She expressed her view, "It is bigger than me and bigger than Alyssa Milano. Neither one of us should be centered in this work. This is about survivors." The current online home for Burke's organization is metoo.support, a new, sleek, black-and-fuchsia home page emblazoned with the words "Because you are not alone" splayed across the top.

After Milano's public acknowledgment, Burke (now a resident of the Bronx) has expressed her gratitude for the watershed response to the tweet that galvanized survivors and garnered empathy. The yesteryear of blaming the survivor had reached a dead end. The current zeitgeist has been the Red Queen's own "Off with their heads!" and this time it referred to both anatomical parts. Weinstein and Co. were found guilty by the jury of their peers.

However, Burke does not want the movement to end with a hashtag. That, she said, leaves too many survivors with nowhere to put the raw feelings unearthed by those two powerful words. She argues that after disclosure must come healing and that this is possible now that the public is not adopting the stance of the three proverbial monkeys: hearing, speaking, and seeing no evil does not make the evil go away.

Burke shared that when she was growing up in Queens, two weeks before her first Holy Communion, the neighborhood boys made her a part of their roughhousing. Her shirt ripped and it could have been much worse, but one of the boy's mothers intervened. She warned Tarana that girls shouldn't go looking for trouble. Tarana quit going out to play; she said she felt dirty. The episode was pushed to the back of her mind until the arrival of the viral hashtag, after which she stated, "Last week I was reminded why I feel skittish around groups of men—even ones I know. #MeToo."

CHAPTER # 31

Our Gallup Poll (2009)

 We all remember that certain teacher who, for better or worse, left us with a lasting legacy. And then there were our unofficial mentors who imparted how babies made their debut: stork delivery, cabbage patch finds, the birds and the bees. A self-proclaimed "rampant feminist" launched a website to separate the wheat from the chaff.

Cindy Gallop did not set out to become a sex evangelist. Born in England in 1960, the eldest of four girls of a Malaysian Chinese mother and a British teacher father, she described her childhood self as "chronically insecure." She grew up in Brunei ("a great deal more boring than it sounds") and returned to Britain to study English at Oxford. There she indulged her passion for theater and, after graduation, worked for several theaters. However, she "got fed up with working every hour and earning chicken feed." She felt she might have the requisite chutzpah to make it in the corporate world—"and I thought it was time to sell out and go into advertising." She joined the publicity firm Bartle Bogle Hegarty in London where, despite overt sexism, quickly rose in the ranks and in 1998 found herself in charge of the company's Manhattan branch. Gallop stood out in the Big Apple, partially due to her wardrobe of black leather and tight dresses, drawing fashion inspiration from characters such as Lisbeth Salander from *The Girl With the Dragon Tattoo*.

Her parents had never given her "the talk," and Cindy clung to virginity till age twenty-one. She made up for being a sexual late bloomer and became a card-carrying cougar when her firm pitched an online dating site, and, wanting to experience the product firsthand, Cindy posted a profile. She said the majority of responses came from younger men, and Ms. Gallop never looked back. No doubt this Mrs. Robinson proved popular: attractive, uninhibited, and the owner of quite the crib—a cavernous 3,800 square foot "black apartment" in New York City's fashionable Chelsea neighborhood, patterned to emulate a Shanghai nightclub. It had originally served as the site of the locker room of the first YMCA in the Unites States, which explains the fact that at her parties, the strapping young men who pass the hors d'oeuvres wear small white towels printed with the YMCA logo as their uniform. The pad's décor consisted of animal prints, paintings, Gucci stilettos, and Chinese lacquer. The unique dwelling garnered fame when it was featured in The Notorious B.I.G.'s music video for his song "Nasty Girl." It was also the venue for multiple beddings that would lead to Gallop launching a unique enterprise.

On Cindy's forty-fifth birthday it was time to try something new, and in what she called "my own personal midlife crisis" she resigned her position at BBH. Her something new was the website *If We Ran the World*: its message was to encourage people to make small changes that would fuel larger action. Her own contribution stemmed from her relationships with younger men. She felt that while their stamina and her experience made a winning combination, she had observed a disturbing trend: the boudoir moves of most of her lovers seemed drawn entirely from pornography. She noticed that they were asking her to do things they had seen online and stated, "I was experiencing what happens when two things converge—when today's total freedom of access to hardcore porn online meets our society's total reluctance to talk openly and honestly about sex. It results in porn becoming, by default, sex education."

In 2009, Cindy took her findings to a TED conference; her four-minute presentation quickly became one of its most talked-about videos, and for good reason: "I'm the only TED speaker to utter the words 'c*m on my face' six times.' " In the role of evangelist, she explained, "As a mature, experienced, confident older woman I have no problem realizing that a certain amount of re-education, rehabilitation, and reorientation have to take place." She shared her concern that men, women, and children, via porn, are receiving an unrealistic, violent, and misogynistic vision of sex—something that can only lead to extremely damaging relationships. Ms. Gallop then unveiled her website, *Make Love Not Porn*, which compares what it calls the "porn world" with the "real word" of sex. Its aim is to provide viewers with the chance to see what it really looks like when people have sex as opposed to scripted scenes, so they can garner greater insight into what their partner really wants. Gallop expressed the thinking behind her website: "Nobody ever brings us up to behave well in bed, but they should. When we take the shame out of talking about sex we also end sexual harassment, sexual abuse, sexual violence—all areas where the perpetrators rely on shame to ensure their victims will never speak up—then we are fundamentally empowering women and girls."

Initially the site was mostly text, but in the spirit of "a picture is worth a thousand words" she took it up a notch and launched *MakeLoveNotPorn.tv*—a YouTube for erotically unshrinking violets. It consists of streaming videos of real people engaging in non-performance sex, hence devoid of insta-orgasms and showing a variety of size demographics. Thus, the men are not actors with Schwarzenegger bodies and the women are not Megan Foxes possessed of athletic moves—generally the realm of prepubescent Romanian gymnasts. Cindy does not see the difference between sharing pictures of romantic dinners during a weekend in Paris and what one does behind closed hotel doors. She claims that what her site is doing is in keeping with sharing other milestones on social media which were once considered for-your-eyes-only: naked selfies, childbirth, live liposuction. . . and then there are the rest of us who post pics of dinners and brunches.

On the entrepreneurial end, the videos are user-generated, so people submit a video of themselves getting busy and pay a non-refundable fee of five dollars to have Gallop and Co. check out their, er, work. Successful candidates are posted on the site, where users can pay five dollars to rent one for three weeks, during which they are free to view the video as often as they like. Fifty percent of the proceeds go to the cyber couple—affectionately dubbed by Gallop as "Make Love Not Porn stars." She adopted the rent-and-stream model instead of providing downloads so that if those featured in the videos no longer want their home videos on the Internet, they are immediately removed. In contrast to mainstream pornography, the videos come across as sweet, playful, and human. In one episode, Lily LaBeau and Danny Wylde, professional pornographic actors who are a couple in real life, partake in a coupling, showing their lovemaking outside of work.

Shortly after its launch, nineteen thousand users signed up for invitations, with would-be viewers coming from countries such as China, Iraq, and Afghanistan. Gizmodo's blog declared it "what the Internet has been waiting for." Cindy said, "It's not about performing for the camera. We're looking for the comical, the messy, the ridiculous. We're looking for the real."

Cindy views *MLNP.tv* as filling a niche market, as porn lacks socially acceptable navigation, a situation she hopes to change, one video at a time. She feels it unfortunate that a number of her female pornographer friends are making innovative films without receiving sufficient traffic or income because "no one can f**king find them." This problem was illustrated when Emma Watson called for feminist alternatives to pornography in a discussion with Gloria Steinem. She had no idea of the vast number of authentic lovemaking videos that no one had ever told her about—after all, there is no Yelp for porn. Gallop contends that her brainchild is vastly different from the traditional, as it is so much more than "masturbation material." The mission of her website is to make it easier to have discussions about sex, and to take it out of the subterranean closet.

The fly in the ointment of "feminist pornography"—a term she does not view as an oxymoron—was that investors were scared off by its explicit content. Undaunted, Gallop launched All The Sky Holdings—a nod to Chairman Mao's statement that "women hold up half the sky"—the goal of which is to fund her business as well as those of other women entrepreneurs. Though the world of raising venture capital is new to Gallop, this did not prove an impediment; she said, "I haven't the faintest idea how you start a fund, but I'm going to."

Cindy stated that the current political climate—"an utter fucking nightmare"—reinforces her mission. She commented ruefully, "The fact that we now live in a country where grabbing women by the pussy is presidentially endorsed is actually a good thing for my business, because it means that all of this has to come into the open." Gallop might be insinuating that this misogyny might have had its genesis from women featured in traditional pornography being reduced to sexual objects, playthings for pleasure.

What started as a "tiny, clunky website"—which bears a name playing on the '60s slogan "Make Love Not War"—now boasts upwards of four hundred thousand global members and over eight hundred videos, featuring more than one hundred video participants. Ms. Gallop's hope is to bring real-life sex into the mainstream, and she believes that there will come a time when no one will feel ashamed of having a nude photograph or a sex tape of themselves floating around in cyberspace. Cindy's hope is for a societal seismic shift in our relationship with pornography, so that it will no longer be the object of condemnation—though millions partake—but will rather be accepted in an authentic forum. A litmus test for liberalism may well be how one rates Ms. Gallop's views on one's personal Gallup poll.

CHAPTER # 32

That's All That I Remember (2013)

A proverb states that "mighty oaks from little acorns grow," and this was the case with a hashtag heard round the world. Its seed was planted on a fateful Florida night, when a chance encounter led to the convergence of the Titanic and the iceberg.

Alicia Schwartz grew up in Marin County, the daughter of an African American mother and a Jewish stepfather. She showed an interest in activism in middle school, when she worked to make information about contraception available in Bay Area schools. Her youthful aspiration was to be an architect; she liked the idea of "figuring out how to create something from nothing." At age twenty-three, Alicia told her parents she was queer; being an inter-racial, inter-religious couple themselves, they did not judge. In 2003, she met Malachi Garza, a twenty-four-year-old trans male activist who she married five years later.

Alicia was with her husband at an Oakland, California, bar when a hot-button verdict came down: George Zimmerman had been found not guilty in the shooting death of seventeen-year-old Trayvon Martin. The decision resonated, as Garza's brother was of similar height, build, and race, and it could have been him—Skittles, not gun, in hand. President Obama echoed this sentiment, "That could've been my son."

Alicia logged on to Facebook and wrote an impassioned online message, "essentially a love note to Black people," and posted it on her page: "I continue to be surprised at how little Black lives matter." She ended with the words, "Black people, I love you. Our lives matter." Garza's close friend Patrisse Cullors, a community organizer for prison reform, read the post in a motel room three hundred miles up Interstate 5. The friends had met in 2003 and had danced together till 4 a.m. They took to calling each other Twin, as both were Black, lesbian, California-born freedom-fighters. Another commonality was that Patrisse would also later marry a transgender partner. They shared the message using the hashtag #BlackLivesMatter. Determined to transform words into action, they reached out to Opal Tometi, an activist for immigrants' rights. The trio set up Tumblr and Twitter accounts and encouraged users to share stories of why #BlackLivesMatter. A rallying cry was born.

The turning point in its transition from online post to twenty-first century force arrived the following summer, when police officer Darren Wilson shot and killed eighteen-year-old Michael Brown in Ferguson, Missouri. In protest marches, hundreds chanted the words believed to be Brown's last: "Hands up, don't shoot!" Watching the drama unfold on TV, Garza felt a sense of déjà vu of Treyvon's slaying. Along with Cullors and Tometi, she organized a "freedom ride" to Ferguson under the auspices of the #BlackLivesMatter campaign. More than six hundred people signed up from eighteen different cities across America. When they reached Ferguson, Alicia was astonished to see her own phrase mirrored back at her on posters, shouted by hundreds.

When a grand jury announced that Wilson would face no indictment in Brown's death, a group of protestors shouting "Black lives matter!" shut down a local shopping mall. After a spate of further deaths of unarmed Black men, the phrase became ubiquitous, appearing on T-shirts, mugs, and badges. Hillary Clinton invoked it at a New York City human rights gala, and it was referenced in an episode of *Law & Order*. Over the next three weeks, #BlackLivesMatter appeared on Twitter twelve million times, making it the third biggest "social hashtag" in the ten years of the online platform's history. The hashtag grew exponentially after the shooting of nine people in a church in Charleston by white supremacist Dylan Roof. This crime carried chilling echoes of the 1963 bombing of the Baptist Church in Birmingham, where racists murdered four Black girls. Dr. King said they had been killed "by monstrous men whose leaders fed them the stale bread of hatred and the spoiled meat of racism." In reaction to Roof's massacre, Bree Newsome climbed the flagpole outside the statehouse in Columbia, South Carolina, and removed the Confederate flag. Her action was tweeted and retweeted under the famous hashtag. At a eulogy for the victims, President Obama paid tribute to Black churches for being a place where children were "taught that they matter."

There are now over forty-two Black Lives Matter Global chapters across the United States and one in Toronto, Canada, which have tens of thousands of supporters. Well-known advocates are Lady Gaga and Serena Williams, who wrote, "To those of you involved in equity movements like Black Lives Matter I say this: 'Keep it up.' " Beyoncé brought the slogan into the nation's living rooms with her Super Bowl halftime performance.

A heartfelt Facebook post spawned a wave of a new civil rights movement. It is exemplified by the action taken by Garza, fueled by grief and fury, by righteous rage against injustice and institutionalized racism. However, the organization is not your grandfather's civil rights movement. Rather than led by the rhetoric of male activists—Dr. King, Malcolm X, Stokely Carmichael—females are at its forefront. In addition to protesting racism and unlawful killings, BLM groups have taken on sexism, homophobia, and transphobia. These protests are in keeping with Dr. King's precept, "Injustice anywhere is a threat to justice everywhere."

It is perhaps inevitable, as a movement gains in scope and visibility, that a stumbling block appears. Alicia talks of how other, well-meaning groups have tried to adapt the slogan to "All Lives Matter." Alicia's response? "The reality, of course, is that they do, but we live in a world where some lives matter more than others. 'All Lives Matter' effectively neutralizes the fact that it's Black people who are fighting for their lives right now." The movement is not asserting that their members' lives are more precious than white lives. They are merely seeking to illustrate an indisputable fact—that the lives of Black citizens in America historically have not mattered, and have been discounted and devalued. The slogan is meant to illustrate the disparity that Black people in America are nearly eight times more likely to die of homicide than white people. An analogy is one would not disparage a breast cancer campaign by arguing that all cancers matter. Mark Zuckerberg, reacting to the video streamed live on Facebook of Philando Castile being shot in his car by a police officer in St. Paul, Minnesota, with his girlfriend and her daughter inches away, erected a giant sign reading "Black Lives Matter" at his Menlo Park headquarters. The tech titan reprimanded employees for repeatedly altering it to "All Lives Matter." Ben & Jerry's chimed in on this divisive topic with a letter to customers saying, "All lives do matter. But all lives will not matter until Black lives matter . . . we'll be working hard on that, and ask you to as well." In a *Vanity Fair* article, L-Man S. Viney wrote, "Do all lives matter? Of course! But we will continue to say Black Lives Matter until African Americans' lives are given the same value as the lives of people from other countries, our police officers, your property, a lion named Cecil, and a gorilla named Harambe."

The trio felt vindicated by the fact that they had succeeded in arousing the conscience of a country which had now become sympathetic to its cause after years of highly publicized police shootings. The watershed moment occurred in Dallas, when Micah Johnson intentionally murdered white police officers in an act of what he felt was justifiable retribution. Immediately there was a backlash from those who demonized the BLM movement for inspiring his deadly attack. In response, the leaders of the movement put out formal statements that vehemently described the attacker as a lone gunman, unconnected to their cause. Consequently, the #BlackLivesMatter was joined by #BlueLivesMatter, a rival reference to police officers. The BLM refused to pause their protests, even though a negative spotlight had now been turned on their movement.

In Oakland, Alicia reflects on how much has happened since her original Facebook post, the hashtag that launched a thousand protests. She reflects that although progress has indeed been made, there is yet further terrain left to travel. The trio of Garza, Cullors, and Tometi are earning their place in history—a notable turn of events, since too many Black women have been little more than footnotes in civil rights textbooks. An eloquent tribute was penned by actress Uzo Aduba in *Glamour* magazine: "The courage heard in their voices mirrors the size of some of history's greatest giants; the sharp echoes of Rosa Parks, the custodian of dignity. . . . The power of this lady-led legacy continues to ripple through today's Black Lives Matter Movement in the form of a simple cry breathing out 'Enough is enough.' " In a sense, Alicia has become an architect. Not by building a house, but by building a movement born out of a love letter.

The pain of African Americans is encapsulated by a 1925 poem, "Incident," by Countee Cullen. It recounts the story of an eight-year-old tourist whose smile is returned with the word "n****r." It concluded, "I saw the whole of Baltimore/From May until December/Of all the things that happened there/That's all that I remember."

CHAPTER # 33

The Seven of Us Can't Do (2013)

 Certain books have left their imprint on the face of the world; their authors were godlike in determining the destiny of humanity. Karl Marx's *Communist Manifesto* changed the sociopolitical landscape, Sigmund Freud's *On the Interpretation of Dreams* shed light on the subconscious, and Charles Darwin's *On the Origin of the Species* rattled religion's cage. These nineteenth-century men were the power players whose pages became the dice of destiny. A twenty-first century woman likewise launched a movement through her words.

Dorothy Parker observed, "It's a man's world"; her flippant remark held a treasury of truth. Even post-women's-lib females and males did not stand on an even playing field: one became the teachers, the other the principals; one became the nurses, the others, the doctors; one became the worker bees, the others, the CEOs. It was time to Lean In.

Florida served as hostess to designer Lillian Pulitzer, Attorney General Janet Reno, crime writer Patricia Cornwell—and modern-day "how to succeed in business" guru Sheryl Sandberg. In the Sandberg family, brains were not in short supply: Sheryl's father Joel is an optometrist, while her mother Adele has a PhD and worked as a college French teacher before giving up her career to raise three children. When not at rallies to free Soviet Jewry—a cause to which her parents were committed—Sheryl bossed around her two younger siblings, David and Michelle. At North Miami Senior Beach High School, Sheryl was at the top of her class, even though a girl with brains was not the type asked to prom. In addition to being the resident Brainiac, she was a member of the National Honor Society. Even as a teen, Sheryl was already leaning in. In a nod to being well-rounded, Sandberg was also an aerobics instructor and wore blue eye shadow, a '80s-inspired silver leotard, leg warmers, and a shiny headband. Social life revolved around her group of several girlfriends, with whom she still remains close—a yearbook photograph captures the clique, their faces turned toward beckoning futures.

Sheryl earned her undergraduate and MBA from Harvard and set her sights on Silicon Valley, with an eye to joining the technology boom. Armed with a knack for dealing with difficult, socially awkward males, she helped grow first Google and then Facebook into the titans of the Internet. From her salaries and shares in the two companies, she accumulated a fortune hovering at a billion dollars. This astronomical feat was accomplished while sporting perfectly coiffed hair, Prada-shod feet, and a figure immune from the middle-age spread: her go-to snack is snap peas. She also married her second husband, Dave Goldberg, CEO of SurveyMonkey, with whom she had a son and daughter. His sudden death while they vacationed in Mexico left Sheryl in a state of profound grief.

Nevertheless, the life of a superstar mommy holds the same vicissitudes as other mothers face. For example, head lice come with the territory of parenting, but when Sandberg discovered her kids had them, they were all flying to a business conference on the corporate jet of the CEO of eBay. To help lighten one's burden on the domestic front, Sheryl claims that it is essential to marry the right kind of guy, specifically one who is respectful of his wife's career and willing to split household tasks and parenting fifty-fifty. It is hard enough to find a straight, employed man without felonies, let alone land one who is into dad duty and is his lady's number one fan.

It would seem that Mrs. Sandberg, being Chief Operating Officer of Facebook and a widowed mother of two, would scarcely have time to shower, let alone write a tome on how to succeed in business, but as a member of some more evolved species, she penned *Lean In: Women, Work, and the Will to Lead.* It has been described as a "feminist manifesto," urging women—in Marxian speak—to throw off their chains. She quotes a saying pinned to a wall in Facebook corporate office: "What would you do if you weren't afraid?" Her impetus was her displeasure that the top of the entrepreneurial hierarchy had a dearth of estrogen, and she decided to create a female counterpart to "the old boys' network." Its message, which led to a national discussion, was that women could lean into—as opposed to away from—the pinnacles of power. The book's central metaphor is that women can view the upward climb not as a ladder, but as a jungle gym: there are many different paths to reach the top, some of which might temporarily lead sideways or even downward at times. Like all truly inspired notions, *Lean In* engendered a flood of controversy and an equal number of devotees and detractors.

In Camp Sandberg are those who feel that the alpha female is the embodiment of the Madeleine Albright quotation, "There's a special place in hell for women who don't help other women" and view her work as a gospel that leads to the Promised Land of economic equity. Naysayers assert that a substitute title could be *The Elitist's Guide for Working Women.* These detractors feel Sandberg placed the blame on female shoulders for their inability to crack the glass ceiling. Joanne Bamberger, writing in *USA Today*, accused Sandberg of "inflaming working mothers' guilt over not acting with more ambition" and argued that her premise "just requires women to pull themselves up by their Louboutin straps." Perhaps the column that resonated the most was Rosa Brooks' *Washington Post* article, "Recline, Don't Lean In (Why I Hate Sheryl Sandberg)." She explains her animosity does not stem from Sheryl's stratospheric wealth or meticulously coiffed hair; rather, it is because *Lean In* makes women feel like self-sabotaging slackers if they are not simultaneously the perfect employee and mom of the month. Sometimes, she proposes, it is OK to just lounge on a hammock, one hand holding a schmaltzy novel while the other holds a glass of wine. What she says ladies really require—in Seinfeldian speak—is a "festivus for the rest of us," the denizens of suds in the city. Brooks ends her article, "Women of the world, recline!" The common denominator of these anti-Lean Ins is that every woman is not of Ms. Sandberg's ilk—someone who wakes up with thirty items on her to-do list and checks them all off before darkness draws its curtain. Of course, what enables her to do so—besides her superhuman resolve—is a support circle of employees who congregate in her nine-thousand-square-foot mansion.

Beyond the endless debate of whether or not the Facebook bigwig is good or bad for feminism, the legacy of Sandberg's movement does not rest on book sales or a forthcoming movie. It is defined by Lean In circles: clusters of women who meet on a monthly basis and keep one another focused on the prize: how to navigate the twin demands of work and motherhood. The philosophy is that these circles are far more beneficial than friends getting together to discuss a book—Rachel Thomas, president of Leanin.org, describes it as "A book club with a purpose"—one that is more uplifting than to see a film or stuff bills into the briefs of scantily clad men. Of course, with Sandberg at the helm, the organization is far from slapdash. All funds are funneled back into the foundation, and its website has videos that explore such issues as how to negotiate—a Hydra's head for many women, raised to accept rather than decide. When a member expresses self-doubt, Lean In sisters squash it as being a spider in the way of success. The organization also provides detailed kits for all facets of Lean In circles. Lean In has caught on like the proverbial wildfire, with upwards of fourteen thousand dotting the globe; Sandberg has visited circles in Beijing, Istanbul, Minneapolis, and Miami. For many, the element of personal contact holds the most appeal. Linda Brandt, a forty-three-year-old group leader from Minnesota, stated, "It's like Girl Scouts for adults." Melissa Lloyd, who chairs a Brooklyn branch, says that her group has grown so large that it has been dubbed "A Circle Grows in Brooklyn." One of the most positive attributes of Lean In circles is that it saves wives from complaining to significant others, and, because it is a group of acquaintances as opposed to friends, conversation stays in the realm of the professional.

Showing that "what's good for the goose is good for the gander," men also buy into the philosophy. When Sandberg spoke to a packed audience in Washington, she asked the males to raise their hands and quipped that they would all get laid that night. It was a comment garnered to generate laughs, but Sheryl is earnest about bringing men into the fold. In her follow up book, *Lean In for Graduates*, Sandberg states, "It's time to man up and Lean In." Erica Zimmerman is looking for a partner, and she used the Lean In mantra as a dating litmus test. If she mentions her support group and the guy seems interested, she concludes he is a feminist. If he raises his eyebrows or makes a snarky comment, her response is "Check, please." Hopefully, the gender prejudices of yesteryear will diminish with the next generation.

In the North Miami Senior Beach High School yearbook for 1987, Cheryl and her BFFs took out a full-page spread. It featured a photograph of the posse alongside modified lyrics of Kenny Rogers' 1981 song "Through the Years." In retrospect, it is a metaphor for Lean In: "Can't imagine anything we've missed/Can't imagine anything the seven of us can't do. . . ."

CHAPTER # 34

Monsters Ink (2014)

Once the province of sailors, gang members, and prison inmates, tattoos have migrated out of the backwater of alternative culture and into the mainstream. Tattoos enable flesh to serve as a scrapbook to showcase the people, places, and pets one holds dear. Yet the ink carries sinister shadows—the branding of slaves on the plantations, or of prisoners at Auschwitz. Tattoos also hold a present terror, a testimony of mankind at his most depraved.

Tattoo parlors proliferate in most urban centers where devotees can inscribe souvenirs onto their flesh: of a newborn, honeymoon locale, or a deceased loved one. Some provide nods to humor. Johnny Depp inked Winona forever on his forearm; post-split, he altered it to read wino forever. However, ink can be nefarious, especially when displaying a barcode.

Jennifer Kempton's long day's journey into night began in 1959 in Columbus, Ohio. She was a victim of rape at age twelve at the hands of her older brother's friend, and, in her early teens, predictably looked for love in very wrong places. Drawn to bad boys, she fell for one whom she believed was her Prince Charming. Shortly into their relationship, Salem said he loved her, but added that if they were going to stay together, they had to enjoy the same things. He got her hooked on heroin as a means of control. Their apartment, the Bottoms, had rooms rented to drug dealers, and Salem expected Jennifer to earn money to finance their narcotics addiction. He arranged a job at a local strip club where he said she could earn three to five hundred dollars a night giving massages. She had to dole out far more than rubdowns, and this service evolved into solicitation ads on Craigslist. Matters became even grimmer when Salem began physically abusing her during her pregnancy. It was also in the Bottoms where he branded her above her groin with the words Property of Salem. According to Jennifer, "To me, what happened there was that I was taken apart as a person, and since then I've been trying to put myself back together." Assailants kidnapped her and took her to a hotel in Akron, where her captors raped her and forced her to have sex with a steady stream of men for ten days. When they returned her to Columbus, her boyfriend's response was to slap her, telling her to get back to business. Desperate for drugs, he sold her to a local gang.

Her pimp's first order of business was to brand her on the side of her neck with a crudely etched black crown bearing his gang's insignia and its name: King Munch. Branding is so prevalent in this criminal subculture that often they employ their own resident tattoo artist. One gang, the Bar Code Pimps, ink this graphic on their sex slaves.

In 2013, Kempton was held captive by one of her tricks and was repeatedly raped and sodomized with a butcher knife for two hours. With no other place to go, she returned to her slave-owners. They handed her three paper towels and told her to clean herself up and get back out. Drowning in horror, she tied a filthy bed sheet around her neck and tried to hang herself. When it broke, rather than view her aborted suicide as yet another failure, she underwent a religious epiphany. She recalled, "God came to me and spoke to me and He said I have a purpose for you and it's not to die in the basement of a crack house." After six years of enslavement, including giving birth on a stranger's floor, Jennifer escaped, knowing full well the beatings, torture, and possibly murder that would ensue if she were recaptured.

After eighteen months in drug rehab, Kempton vowed to turn her life around; for a woman suffering from post-traumatic stress disorder, this goal was a gargantuan undertaking. The first task was employment, but no one was chomping at the bit to employ an ex-junkie prostitute sporting gang insignia. Jennifer eventually found work at Freedom a la Carte, a box lunch and catering kitchen that employs sex-trafficking survivors. Although reunited with her grandmother with whom she lived, the obstacle on her road to wellness were her tattoos, which Jennifer called psychological enslavement. Every time she took a shower or glanced into the mirror, she was pulled back into the morass. She said, "You begin to wonder whether you'll ever be anything but the person those tattoos say you are." After eight months of saving, Jennifer was able to go to the Among the Living tattoo parlor to cover up one of her four horrific souvenirs; "Property of Salem" was no more. In its place was a heart-shaped lock with key, symbolic of God unlocking her chains. Another cover-up tattoo was of an elaborate cross with the words "Love" and "I Cor 13:4–13." The reference is to Paul's famous words on love, which begin, "Love is patient, love is kind" and which close, "And now these three remain: faith, hope, and love. But the greatest of these is love." She then met an anti-sex-trafficking activist who funded the erasure of the remaining brandings. A flower—a medley of yellow, pink, and green—camouflaged the King Munch and crown on her neck, and her back now bore the words I believe again. This kindness led to Jennifer's realization that she herself would be the instrument of paying it forward, that this would be her reason for not becoming a statistic of suicide.

Jennifer stated that the feeling of freedom and empowerment she experienced from reclaiming her body was life-changing. It also led to her launching Survivor's Ink, an organization dedicated to funding the camouflage of tattoos which keep victims in emotional bondage. It raises money through fundraisers at churches, universities, and community events. To qualify, women must be survivors of sex trafficking, bear a tattoo associated with exploitation, and have been involved in a recovery program for at least six months. An integral part of the program is veteran tattoo artist Charles "Chuck" Waldo.

He was so appalled that people were using his beloved tattoo art to brand women that he performs all Survivor's Ink's work for free, charging only for the price of the ink and the rental of space in his shop. His volunteer work is a form of mea culpa after a life of bank robberies, jail, and "other very bad shit," as he puts it. Survivor's Ink pays from $50 to $80 for cover-up tattoos that would normally cost from $425 to $500. Jennifer reviews every application, and asks the applicant to specify the sorts of images she would like to cover her scars. The most prevalent requests are for hands locked in prayer, a flower to represent that they can still bloom, and a butterfly to signify the metamorphosis from larvae into symbols of beauty.

From her treatment program, Jennifer knew she was not supposed to venture back into old territory that could trigger drug cravings. However, in her role in Survivor's Ink, she went back to the streets of darkness to bring victims to the light. There she would relay her mantra, "You can make it out, dammit, like I did, like I know you can." She repeated the words of encouragement she wished someone had cared enough to tell her. However, Survivor's Ink is about more than redesigning tattoos; it is about giving the hopeless hope. Jennifer described herself and the women she helped as a sisterhood. She stated, "We stand and unite as one, as the Survivor's Ink Women. We stand up against these men and tell them they can't hurt us, you can't hurt us anymore." During the procedures, Jennifer and her scholarship recipients held each other and cried. The organization's mission statement is to help, one tattoo at a time—a big 'eff off to traffickers everywhere.

Kempton's charity thrust her into the spotlight, and she became a familiar figure at anti-trafficking conferences, heralded for her bravery and eloquence. She spoke about her foundation and its position that sex slave survivors would very likely not make it on their own. It is difficult to obtain gainful employment with lengthy rap sheets for solicitation in a society that views them as criminal junkies. In interviews with the media, she explained the need for jobs, education, and to be reunited with their children. She said of what they all have to endure, "Once we escape there is a whole new hell."

Kempton's dream was to have Survivor's Ink become an international charity that would appear the world over. Andrea, one of the first Survivor's Ink clients, claimed that her new reworked tattoo changed her self-perception. Thanks to the organization, instead of her former owner's initials on her chest, she now sports a flower with her daughter's name in its center. For Jennifer, the work she performed through Survivor's Ink was therapy, as it provided her a sense of purpose; her message was for those who are not on the streets to never judge those who are.

In an interview for *The Guardian*, the reporter asked where she would have been, had she been raised in a loving, abuse-free household. She replied, "I'd be in the frickin' White House!" as she lit up another cigarette and pumped her fist into the air. But fate had a different plan. She hit rock bottom after giving up her third child, a daughter, for adoption.

In 2017, Jennifer Kempton passed away from an accidental drug overdose. Her legacy proves the exception to Marc Antony's eulogy for Julius Caesar: "The evil that men do lives after them; the good is oft interred with their bones." Heartfelt tributes poured in from the women for whom Jennifer had arranged the disguise of scarlet letters, giving thanks to the woman who had given her all to confront the real Monsters, Inc.

CHAPTER # 35

Mr. Darcy (2014)

 In the olden, un-golden days, marriages were made not in heaven, but sometimes they served as matters of convenience. Blue-blooded women were political pawns; Jewish girls were at the mercy of the shadchan. Parental concern centered on dowries, not trivialities such as mutual affection or commonalities. In our more enlightened clime, finding one's life partner hinges on free will, but the desire to find one's soul mate leads to the nonaromatic scent of desperation, the relentless ticking of the biological clock. What's a lonely heart to do?

Jane Austen's novel *Pride and Prejudice* famously begins, "It is a truth universally acknowledged that a single man in possession of a good fortune must be in want of a wife." Alas, this observation is fifty shades of wishful thinking, and that is why the $2.4 billion online dating industry has exploded. Only shipwrecked survivors marooned on deserted islands are oblivious to Match.com, JDate, Christian Mingle—or the website for marital cheaters, Ashley Madison. Although these modern matchmakers have led to love, more often than not they translate to looking for love in all the wrong places. Enter Bumble.

Whitney Wolfe is a five-foot-six blonde (five-foot-ten when sporting suede Manolo Blahnik pumps) who looks like she was raised under the California sun, although she was born in 1990 in a small town outside Salt Lake City, Utah. Her father, Michael, was a property developer; his wife, Kelly, was a stay-at-home mother to her two daughters. When Whitney was eleven, her father took a sabbatical and moved the family to Paris, where she attended an international school with the children of diplomats and royalty. Upon her return to small-town USA, she stood out—but not in a positive way. Classmates mocked her for her clothes, which were fashionable in France but outlandish in the heartland. At age nineteen, a student at Southern Methodist University, Whitney demonstrated her entrepreneurial and altruistic streak when she established her first business, designing and selling bamboo tote bags to raise money in the aftermath of the catastrophic BP oil spill in the Gulf of Mexico. The bags attracted the attention of actresses Denise Richards, Nicole Ritchie, and Kate Bosworth, with proceeds being earmarked for the Ocean Futures Society. She also volunteered in orphanages in Southeast Asia; the trip inspired her to start a travel website.

Ms. Wolfe did not set out to change the dating game. She was twenty-three, unemployed, and living with her divorced mother in Montecito, California, when she met two wealthy Jewish men of Persian descent: Sean Rad and Justin Matteen. (Whitney is Jewish on her father's side.) The three, along with Jonathan Badeen and three other men, all in their twenties, upended the way single people connect with their smartphone app: Tinder. With fifty million users per day—from diverse places such as Rome, London, and Rio de Janeiro—the company has evolved into a three-billion-dollar enterprise. Downloading its app was the equivalent of having a 24/7 singles' bar in one's pocket. During Tinder's nascent rise, Whitney and Justin began dating; however, it ended, according to Wolfe, because he became verbally controlling and abusive. After she put the brakes on their relationship, Justin acted as if "hell hath no fury like a man scorned." His texts became peppered with words like "slut" and "whore." Whitney reported this abuse to Rad, whose response was that if she did not back down, he would terminate her employment. He also tried to strip her of her cofounder status, because having a woman at the helm made the company "look like a joke." Wolfe resigned, but she did not go quietly. She filed a lawsuit claiming sexual harassment and sexual discrimination. The resulting legal showdown—played out in the public eye—was malicious and illustrated the challenges women face in a notoriously bro-friendly tech culture. Overnight she became Silicon Valley's Gone Girl. Tinder's parent company admitted no wrongdoing, but awarded her a settlement of one million dollars and corporation stock.

One would think that, given the public fallout of her messy departure and with a well-padded bank account, Whitney would open up a Parisian bookshop or act on her youthful aspiration of owning a travel agency. However, based on the cruelty she experienced at school and in the workplace, Whitney planned to create Merci, an app for teenage girls to share photos and converse, a chat room where users would leave compliments rather than comments. Her plan changed when Andrey Andreev, a London-based Russian cofounder of the European dating behemoth Badoo, a multibillion dollar social network, suggested that Merci's ethos could be used in the turbulent world of online romance. A feminist version of Tinder was born.

Due to humanity's universal habit of passing aesthetic judgment on others, Bumble operates on the same smartphone dynamic as Tinder: a profile pic is posted, and users swipe right for "yes," left for "no, thank you." A match is made if the interest is mutual. Yet there is one major difference that distinguishes Bumble from its competitors—only women can initiate the online messaging. An addendum is that the ladies have to reach out within twenty-four hours or the match disappears. After all, if Cinderella had played too coy, her carriage would have turned into a pumpkin and her cover would have been blown. This innovative dynamic lets women be the hunters, not the hunted.

Whitney always felt that there was something amiss in society's social network, with its ingrained—and she believes antiquated—notion that the only time it is permissible for the ladies to make the first move is at a Sadie Hawkins dance. To Whitney it never sat right that she and her girlfriends were kicking ass in all aspects of their careers, but were expected to resort to Jane Austen's code of etiquette when it came to approaching men. Wolfe contends that putting women in the driver's seat does not emasculate men by stripping them of their innate hunter-gatherer nature, but rather takes the pressure off males who are tired of always acting as the aggressor. Her philosophy is that this entrenched norm is not innate, but rather is borne of societal conditioning. This mentality explains Bumble's subway campaign in New York: "Life's Short, Text Him First." Because of this core philosophy, Wolfe initially wanted to call her app Leap, as according to Irish folklore February 29 is the only acceptable day for women to propose marriage. Whitney said, "I think that's the last frontier—the proposal. It doesn't seem like we're quite there yet though." The name Bumble is derived from the fact that women are in control in a bee colony, especially its queen.

Another commandment of Bumble concerns online accountability: "Thou shalt not display bad cyberspace manners." There is zero tolerance for men whose profile pic is a shirtless selfie, a shot of them in pants reminiscent of the Mae West line about whether you have a gun in your pocket, or a picture of genitals sans fig leaves. There is also a lid on nastiness. After a female user sent screenshots to Bumble of a conversation with a guy named Connor where he ranted about "gold-digging whores," the company barred him with: #LaterConnor. Another man was deleted for fat-shaming. Users regularly receive notifications to "Bee nice," along with saucy emojis.

The Bumble app claims eight hundred million matches, ten billion swipes per month, and more than five thousand engagements, giving Tinder a run for its money. And speaking of money/honey, Wolfe has appeared on Forbes' prestigious "30 Under 30" list, a nod to her personal fortune of two hundred and fifty million dollars. However, success does not mean resting on her laurels, and Whitney, who rises at 4:00 a.m., is forever abuzz with new ideas. She has added BFF, a matching service for women looking for their new bestie—something that can prove as elusive as finding a romantic partner—and Bumble Bizz, a networking app. It acquired Chappy, an app for lesbian, gay, bisexual, and transgender people looking to circumvent the landmines of many online dating agencies. The entrepreneur is also turning her hand to writing; she is working with an imprint of Penguin Press on her memoir-slash-dating guide *Make the First Move*. Bumble is also rolling out their own version of Siri called Beatrice, which calls during a date to make sure the escort is behaving in a manner befitting a gentleman.

The hub of the hive is in Austin, Texas—there are satellite offices in New York, Los Angeles, and London—all crammed full of bright yellow Bumble-branded merchandise, including T-shirts, champagne, mugs, and lip balms carrying bee logos. Jack, Whitney's giant golden Labrador, sports a Bumble neckerchief.

Ironically, the Queen Bee of online dating met her own match IRL—Internet speak for "in real life."—on Valentine's Day 2014, on a ski trip in Aspen. Not only was Michael Herd's appearance swipe-worthy, he also happens to be the heir to a multi-million-dollar oil fortune. Perhaps, "a single man in possession of a large fortune" is indeed sometimes in want of a wife. On the couple's free time, they fly to luxurious locales on his private jet. He popped the question on a sunset evening after a day of horseback riding on his Texas ranch. Ms. Wolfe accepted and is now sporting a colossal, antique pear-shaped diamond. The power couple's wedding is planned for 2017 in Positano, Italy. Whitney, by not following the rules, but by adhering to her own, is a shining example that it is still possible to love and land Mr. Darcy.

CHAPTER 36

Hats Off (2017)

An old nursery rhyme goes: "Pussy-cat, pussy-cat? Where have you been?/I've been to London to look at the Queen./Pussy-cat, pussy-cat, what did you there?/I frightened a little mouse under the chair." In the modern-day counterpart, "pussy" refers to a female body part. London is Washington, but, as with the old rhyme, she also frightened a little mouse.

Caps created for political purposes are, well, old hat. Their association with dissent goes back hundreds of years, especially during the Reign of Terror. Women known as *les tricoteuses*—immortalized by Dickens' Madame Defarge—sat by the guillotine, turning thread into red "liberty caps." These *bonnets rouges* are still a symbol associated with the figure of Marianne, the embodiment of France. Knitted hats became a tale of two cities when Washington, DC, like revolutionary Paris, mounted its rebellion.

While Trump was making a bid for the presidency, a tape surfaced, one as incriminating as Watergate's. He was caught talking to Billy Bush—cousin of George W.—wherein the Donald bragged that because of his wealth and power, he possessed sexual entitlement. "When you're a star, they let you do it. You can do anything. Grab 'em by the pussy. You can do anything." It was a remark destined never to be forgiven, never to be forgotten. Most assumed that this comment signified the death knell for his political aspirations: America would never vote for a candidate who viewed women as walking orifices. Thirty-two days later, when Trump took command of the Oval Office, the "pussies" determined to resist, a reminder to misogynists that felines also have claws.

Krista Suh, a twenty-nine-year-old Los Angeles screenwriter, like millions of others, was in mourning for Hillary Clinton's loss and decided to attend the Women's March in the nation's capital to join her sisters in a show of solidarity. Prior to the mass gathering, Krista was on a road trip with her family to celebrate her parents' anniversary. She was staring out the window, wondering what she could do at the Women's March other than merely show up. She stated how she would have been willing to become a contemporary Lady Godiva if it would have helped: "Honestly, I would have stripped naked for it if that would have been impactful." She obtained an art history degree from Barnard College and tried to think like a performance artist. How, she wondered, could she express her beliefs with a powerful punch? She toyed with the idea of a unique slogan on a handheld sign; nothing clicked. It then occurred to her as a Californian, she would be extremely cold in DC and decided to knit a hat. Her grandmother had taught her the craft, one she had honed under the tutelage of Kat Coyle, owner of the Little Knittery in Atwater Village, Los Angeles. This thought led to her *Aha!* moment; the headcovering could serve as a collective symbol of protest. She decided it would also be the antithesis of Trump's red "Make America Great Again" baseball cap. She determined that her bonnet should be pink because of the color's traditional association with females, and that she should top it off with feline ears as a gesture toward the President's sexual comment. Donald excused his words as merely being boy's banter, while many others saw them as fostering a culture of rape. Suh was fired up with enthusiasm, envisioning a sea of Barbie's signature hue, a manifestation of resistance.

Krista immediately texted Kat—a serendipitous name—excited to share her idea. She felt that Coyle, as a knitting superstar and former professional patternmaker, would turn the concept into reality.

She knew Kat would be on board, as she felt the same devastation from the election. Krista also shared her brainstorm with her close friend, thirty-nine-year-old Jayna Zweiman, a Brown graduate with a master's in architecture from Harvard. A pink protest was launched; it was time to grab back.

When Suh returned to Los Angeles, the three women were committed to the unique headgear, as distinctive as Dr. Seuss' feline. Coyle came up with the name "The Pussy Hat Project," as well as a pattern easy enough for novice knitters to follow. Within six days, the three musketeers' message had gone viral through their website, Instagram, and Facebook, requesting women around the world to participate in their visual demonstration. Knitters took up arms—in this case, knitting needles—and made them not just for themselves, but also for donation. It became standard operating procedure to tuck little notes of encouragement inside the hats before they dropped them off at designated facilities for pickup by fellow feminists.

Jayna, because of her own circumstances, reached out to those unable to travel. In 2014, she was a working wife when the walls of her life came tumbling down. On a shopping trip with her husband, she suffered a debilitating concussion when an improperly secured metal rod fell on her head. Unable to work or travel, she found solace at a makeshift Friday night Shabbat at the Little Knittery. In the Pussy Hat Project's mission statement, the founders pay homage to the traditionally female craft: "Knitting circles are sometimes scoffed at as frivolous 'gossiping circles' when really, these circles are powerful gatherings." The quiet comradery of the Little Knittery ended after the election. Unable to journey to Washington, Jayna arranged for the delivery of hats to housebound people desirous of being part of the movement.

In the 1948 Warner Brothers' animated short, Tweety Bird said, "I tawt I taw a puddy tat." Had the yellow canary been in DC for the Women's March on January 21, 2017, he would have seen thousands of them, a sea to shining sea of ears in every rosy hue: from rose to flamingo to fuchsia, some accentuated with glitter. The image resonated more than white, associated with the Suffrage Movement—or the "Nasty Woman" T-shirt, which was in homage to the woman who failed to shatter the country's highest glass ceiling. Overnight, the Pussy Hat became iconic: one image showcased Rosie the Riveter, her trademark polka dot bandana supplanted with a pink Pussy Hat. Flesh-and-blood celebrities also adopted the fashion statement: Whoopi Goldberg, Cate Blanchett, Julia Roberts, Chelsea Handler, Jessica Chastain, and the list goes on. . . . And, if there was any doubt that pink is the new black, in Italy the fashion house of Missoni had its models don the accessory for their final strut down the aisle. For Krista and Jayna, their Kelly Clarkson moment—"some people wait a lifetime for a moment like this . . ."—came when the head garment that they willed into existence graced the covers of *The New York Times Magazine*, *Time Magazine*, and *The New Yorker*.

The mad hatter duo, Krista and Jayna, are now planning further events for their creation; they have no intention of letting time put their baby in a corner. The creators of the Pussy Hat are encouraging women to keep their ears ready to "wear, share, and declare." Zweiman said, "We want to create a movement, not a moment. There's been such a strong sense of isolation throughout the election cycle. This project is about bringing people together."

Of course, as with all fashion statements, it drew its fair share of detractors. Some voiced opposition to the wearing of a headcovering christened after a vagina. They also took exception to the use of the word "pussy," a pejorative term for a woman's sexual organ as well as wimpy men. Tom Jones, in *What's New Pussycat?* had reinforced the term's patronizing connotation with the line "So go and powder your cute little pussycat nose," followed by "So go and make up your big little pussycat eyes." Petula Dvorak, columnist for *The Washington Post*, wrote against the feline display of she-power. She said that because of its cute, gimmicky nature, the Women's March of 2017, where thousands were to don the distinctive headcovering, will be remembered as "An unruly river of Pepto-Bismol roiling through the streets of the capital rather than a somber civil rights march." She likened the wearing of the pink to the 1960s Women's Movement bra-burning that has been used to dismiss the seriousness of the protest for half a century. She ended with the words that the Women's Movement should be remembered for grit, not gimmicks. After all, the March on Washington is revered for MLK's "I Have a Dream" speech, not an army of Hello Kitties.

Sue's retort for those who attack her hats is similar to that of a mother lion whose cubs have been threatened: "A feminist can wear whatever she wants. You can still be politically active while you're wearing thigh-high boots or a miniskirt or a hat with cat ears." However, thousands of women applaud the Pussy Hat Project for taking an active stand instead of indulging in a woe-is-me pity party in private.

While the wearing of the pink is a subjective matter, what is not debatable is that the fashion garment is now as famous as history's most iconic chapeaus: Napoleon's bicorne, Abraham Lincoln's stovepipe, Davy Crockett's coonskin cap, and Jackie Kennedy's pillbox hat. For that, and for showing that the power of one can lead to the empowerment of many, hats off to the founders of The Pussy Hat Project.

CHAPTER # 37

Resistance to Tyranny (2016)

Edmund Burke wrote, "The only thing necessary for the triumph of evil is for good men to do nothing." A woman in Hawaii was unwilling to be one of the proverbial monkeys—hearing, seeing, and speaking no evil was not enough. Her effort set off an earthquake that reverberated worldwide.

On the night of Donald Trump's transition from reality television star to reality president, Teresa Shook's mood turned the color of the Democratic states. She had never considered herself an activist or particularly versed in feminism. With her conviction that "Grab 'em by the pussy" was less presidential than "We have nothing to fear but fear itself," she needed a platform to vent. Her concerns mirrored those of many: the Chief Executive's vision of making America great again could entail returning to the time when women, people of color, and those with minority religions were branded second-class citizens. Teresa stated, "I was in such shock and disbelief that this type of sentiment could win. We had to let people know that is not who we are." However, Shook had few options in Maui, far from the eye of the storm.

Teresa turned to the pro-Hillary Clinton "Pantsuit Nation" Facebook page and called for women to march on the nation's capital on inauguration weekend. Historically, such venues of protest had borne substantial fruit. In 1789, the women's storming of Versailles led royal heads to feed the guillotine; in 1913, the suffragettes marched on Washington and won the vote seven years later, and in 1917, female demonstrators lined the streets of Petrograd and brought about the fall of the House of Romanov. It was time to march once more.

Teresa hoped someone else would take the lead, but when there were no takers, she asked online friends how to create a Facebook group. By the time she went to bed, there were forty RSVP's; when she awoke, there were more than ten thousand. Shook said of the event which she described as having gone ballistic, "I guess in my heart of hearts I wanted it to happen, but I didn't really think it would've ever gone viral. I didn't even know how to go viral." Responses indicated people were galvanized to action due to Trump's treatment of women—calling Miss Universe "Miss Piggy" after her weight gain, claims of sexual harassment, fear the President's appointment of Supreme Court justice could overturn *Roe v. Wade*. Shocked and awed at the promise of fantasy turning into reality, Shook was nevertheless unsure how to proceed. Organizing a massive protest was not a skill Teresa, a native of Indiana, had ever encountered in her role as attorney or as grandmother of four girls.

On the same night Shook had posted her plea five thousand miles away, Bob Bland, a fashion designer in Brooklyn, had also taken to Facebook to plan a protest. Bland had been political from the get-go, and had accrued a few thousand online followers after she had created "Nasty Woman" and "Bad Hombre" T-shirts that raised twenty thousand dollars for Planned Parenthood. Both women understood that it would take a village, yet immediately cracks appeared. Participants began to judge one another not on the content of their character but on external factors. The first fissure was the matter of race: Teresa, Bob, and all the volunteers were white. A Black activist expressed anger, "You don't just join now you're scared, too. I was born scared" and added it should be called White Women's March. Another sticking point with African Americans was they felt Shook's naming of the Million Woman March was an appropriation of the title of the 1997 gathering of thousands of Black women in Philadelphia.

Bob suggested the Million Pussy March. Polarized concerns set off a heated and divisive conversation on the Facebook page; lost in the crossfire was Lincoln's admonition, "A house divided against itself cannot stand."

Bland realized that in order to transform the march from a contentious Facebook group into a united movement, they needed help from nonwhite organizers of different demographics; they recruited African American Tamika Mallory, Hispanic Carmen Perez, and Muslim Linda Sarsour. Their challenge was to orchestrate one of the largest inauguration demonstrations in history in a two-month time frame. The first order of business was the christening, and they decided on one that invoked Martin Luther King, Jr.'s Civil Rights March of 1963—the Women's March on Washington; it received the blessing of King's youngest daughter, Bernice. She shared with them a quotation from her mother Coretta Scott King, "Women, if the soul of the nation is to be saved, I believe that you must become its soul." Despite the initial tensions, as well as Jewish women taking umbrage with Sarsour—an activist for Palestinian rights—and the animosity between pro-choice and pro-life groups, the women decided to focus on commonality: a country led by Trump could endanger universal freedoms. The organizers released their guiding vision, declaring support for Black, Native, poor, immigrant, Muslim, and LGBT women, as well as all women who "deserve to live full and healthy lives free of violence against our bodies." A sign symbolizing sisterly solidarity: "We march togetHER."

After months of agitating on social media, there was relief at getting beyond the virtual streets onto the real ones: to commiserate, to chant, to hope. On January 21, women and men congregated on all seven continents (in Antarctica, a placard proclaimed "Penguins march for peace"). More than half a million people converged on Washington for a counter-inauguration—three times as many as the turnout for the President's. The face of the opposition to the President was predominantly female. Jam-packed streets were punctuated by a preponderance of pink hats and the chant of "When they go low, we go high!" They gathered to support a liberal agenda, in sharp contrast to what Trump had laid out for his tenure. The platform focused on issues such as the rights of workers, women, and immigrants. It was a star-studded event, with celebrities such as Madonna, Scarlett Johansson, and Ashley Judd, the last of whom delivered an uninhibited speech: "They ain't for grabbing. They are for birthing new generations of filthy, vulgar, nasty, proud Christian, Muslim, Buddhist, Sikh, you name it, for new generations of nasty women." Her impassioned words continued, "I am not as nasty as a swastika on a rainbow flag, I feel Hitler in these streets. A moustache traded for a toupee." America Ferrera, whose parents hail from Honduras, stated, "It's been a heartrending time to be both a woman and an immigrant . . . but the President is not America. We are America." Feminist icon Gloria Steinem cried, "This is the upside of the downside. This is an outpouring of energy and true democracy that I have never seen in my very long life. It is wide in age and deep in diversity, and remember the Constitution does not begin with 'I the President.' It begins with 'We the People.' " The crowd showed solidarity by the waving of placards, some bearing the messages such as "Free Melania!" "Thou Shalt Not Grab," and "We Want a Leader, Not a Creepy Tweeter."

Among the marchers was Teresa, catapulted into contemporary mythology as the woman whose post ignited a movement. Strangers lavished hugs of gratitude on her. Shook wants people to know that one person can make a difference, but only if animosities are set aside. She said of the massive crowds launched by her Facebook plea, "It was an out-of-body experience, to look out and see that sea of pink bodies." Teresa said there were too many favorite moments to pick just one, but a highlight was meeting Gloria Steinem and for the feminist icon to know who she was. Bob also stepped on stage, accompanied by her infant Chloe—clad in a furry bear suit and pink hat—and her six-year-old daughter, Penny. She wanted her daughters to see that, united, women "can transform the world."

Behind the witty signs and street theater, there remained a deadly serious message: the current administration was not going to slip into the prejudice of yesteryear. There were women who rode buses for ten hours from Flint, Michigan, to remind everyone that they still do not have clean water. Some pushed wheelchairs—no small feat in the teeming wall of bodies—to express their fear of losing Obamacare. There were LGBT teens who had seen the White House lit up in rainbow colors, only to fear a future reign of homophobia. Also among the pink pussy hats were hijabs; Muslim Americans describing how they felt the welcome mat had been pulled out from under them. Mothers born in Mexico were marching to show their American-born children that America is indeed a melting pot. Fathers brought along their sons to teach a living lesson on gender equality. Like how Nero was fiddling while Rome burned, the Trump family bowled in their new Pennsylvania Avenue home.

Irony permeated the Women's March: what started as a divisive movement ended as a unified wave of sisterly solidarity. Facebook—which launched the social tsunami—had originated as Fashmash, a way to rate Harvard women based on who was hotter. But the true spirit that reigned that January morning was of the suffragettes who had paved the way. In the words of Susan B. Anthony, "Resistance to tyranny is obedience to God."

EPILOGUE

She Was Right

January derives its name from the ancient Roman God Janus; one profile looked to the left, symbolic of the past, the other to the right, symbolic of the future. The bearded deity can serve as a metaphor for the Women's Movement—to understand it, one must view it from its painful yesteryear, as well as its aspirational tomorrow.

In the 1950s, copies of *Vogue* showcased Stepford wives, flawless and impossibly-proportioned models, and manicured pointed nails painted blood-red. But there was an inconvenient truth lying behind the airbrushed images. The matrons of this milieu engaged in cleaning house, bent over stove, kissing hubby as he left to battle for home and hearth. The reigning zeitgeist was marriage as the Promised Land, and a well-prepared dinner was a litmus test of marital worth. The ladies were compliant and smiling, their only prospect a ring on finger. As Fanny Brice sang, "Sadie Sadie married lady/See what's on my hand/There's nothing quite as touching/As a simple wedding-band." *Funny Girl* indeed. Women could not take out mortgages in their names, thereby precluding them from having a room of their own. If they wanted to be fitted with a diaphragm—one of the few forms of contraception available—they had to first produce a marriage certificate. Abortion was illegal, and unmarried mothers were a disgrace; hence, many weddings were of the shotgun variety. Ironically, no such shame was attached to unmarried fathers, who were not obliged to purchase a fake gold band from Woolworths. Sex before marriage labeled the lady a slut (though a male was a stud), and pregnancy without a husband was grounds for termination in the teaching profession, one of the few acceptable jobs open to the fairer sex. Hence, a wife's identity was inextricably intertwined with that of her spouse, and she was the doctor's wife, the butcher's wife, the baker's wife, the felon's wife. . . . "The Way We Were" does not carry the whiff of nostalgia, despite Barbra Streisand's film of that name.

Since then, there have been great strides in the march toward gender equality: women have the right to bear arms in the military, wives can work without the societal pointing of a finger, and mothers can breastfeed wherever babies are hungry—at least in liberal zip codes. Law and medical schools are not estrogen-free zones, and female students who attend universities are not subjected to the smirk-laced comment that their goal is to obtain an MRS. A bride can choose to keep her own name instead of taking her husband's; Ms. can be substituted for Miss and Mrs. Language is reflective of this shift in paradigm: postman has become postal worker; fireman, firefighter; policeman, police officer. Juliet was incorrect—there is something significant in a name.

Girls do not have to wait for a Sadie Hawkins dance to make the first moves in the dating arena and can now bask in their own glory, not just a reflected one from their fathers, brothers, and sons. Hopefully, one day there will be a First Gentleman in the White House. But, in the words of Helen Reddy's song "I Am Woman," "I'm still an embryo/With a long, long way to go/Until I make my brothers understand. . . ."

201

One of the challenges in compiling the candidates to include in *Women Who Launch* is that for most of history, men have been the architects who built the world's foundations. Thus, there are no chapters on females who founded movie studios, instituted major religions, or brokered treaties that altered the geopolitical landscape. Fortunately, in the words of Bob Dylan, "the times, they are a-changin'." Yet, there are still walls that need to be scaled. This fact is exemplified by the commonality among the male tech titans who founded online empires that made them members of the billionaire Boys' Club: Google, YouTube, Facebook, Amazon, eBay, Craigslist, Oracle, Snapchat, Apple, Uber, Microsoft, LinkedIn, Etsy, Ancestry.com, Twitter, and Yelp—Yelp indeed!—and the list goes on. Similarly, car brands are often eponyms and none of the names have ever been female: Henry Ford, Walter Chrysler, Ferruccio Lamborghini, Chief Pontiac, Fernando Porsche, and the list goes on. . . .

Unenlightened as the postwar decade may have been, it was still Nirvana compared to previous eras. Therefore, the women who launched deserve all accolades considering their brainchildren grew out of unfertile soil. This paradigm is reminiscent of a quotation by Bob Thanes in his Los Angeles comic strip *Frank and Ernest*. The friends are gazing at a billboard announcing a Fred Astaire film festival with the accompanying caption, "Sure he was great, but don't forget that Ginger Rogers did everything he did . . . backwards and in high heels."

Although in the socioeconomic seesaw, girls are still in the air; gender equality is on the horizon. Susan Brownell Anthony, on her deathbed at her Rochester home, told her friend that it "seems so cruel" to die without seeing her suffrage dream come to fruition. It was her fate to be Moses, denied entry into the Promised Land. Yet her spirit remained indefatigable. At her birthday celebration in Washington, DC, a few days earlier, Anthony had spoken of those who had struggled alongside her, "With such women consecrating their lives, failure is impossible." She was right.

ACKNOWLEDGMENTS

Women Who Launch would have remained a glitter in my eye if it were not for my literary agent, Roger Williams. His words always mirror Ms. Anthony's own: "Failure is impossible." It was an honor working with him on my former book, Behind Every Great Man: The Forgotten Women Behind the World's Famous and Infamous, and I look forward to our birthing future manuscripts. Mr. Roger rocks!

A heartfelt thanks to my editor, Brenda Knight, whose emails never fail to enthuse and to encourage. No doubt her experience as an author makes her empathetic to the challenges confronting writers. Unfortunately, Roger and Brenda are not in my zip code and so I have not had the pleasure of meeting them in person. Definitely on the bucket list.

Family doubles joys and halves sorrows, and my husband, Joel Geller, and my daughter, Jordanna Geller, helped me along the smooth and rough paths that are part and parcel of publishing. They never begrudge dinners prepared compliments of Swanson; they understand that with a full-time teaching job, the hours left for writing are as scarce as the proverbial hen's teeth. I am deeply saddened that my mother, Gilda Wagman, always my greatest advocate, is not here to see my new book. Her loss is, and always will be, a never-ending sorrow.

The women profiled in these pages remain sterling examples of the power of persistence, individuals who believed that dreams do not just have to be for sleeping. Proof the latter is possible: my book in your hands. How fortunate we are to have such shoulders to stand on. Their stories share the message to keep our eyes on the prize—whatever it may be—and, despite setbacks, to persevere. They embody the truth of the quotation I chanced upon during research, "If you're not at the table, you're on the menu." It is my sincere hope that these ladies who launched have inspired readers with their intelligence and tenacity; they certainly had that effect on me.

I would love to hear from you through email: onceagaintozelda@ hotmail.com or through that great connector, Facebook (where I am Marlene Wagman), or through my website, marlenewagmangeller. com. Comments on Amazon and Goodreads would also be eagerly embraced. By the way—a woman, Elizabeth Khuri, along with her husband, Chandler, cofounded Goodreads, the world's greatest book club. It currently has fifteen million members; the Chandlers sold it to Amazon for approximately one hundred and fifty million dollars. Women who launch indeed!

—Marlene Wagman-Geller

San Diego, California (2017)

NOTES

Chapter # 1 — Julia Ward Howe

Bundy, Carol. "The woman reformer who gave us 'The Battle Hymn of the Republic'." *The Washington Post.* April 1, 2016. https://www.washingtonpost.com/opinions/the-woman-reformer-who-gave-us-the-battle-hymn-of-the-republic/2016/03/31/11307824-eaf5-11e5-a6f3-21ccdbc5f74e_story.html.

Clinton, Catherine. "Elaine Showalter on Julia Ward Howe, a poet against all the odds of her era." *Times Higher Education.* March 24, 2016. https://www.timeshighereducation.com/books/review-the-civil-wars-of-julia-ward-howe-elaine-showalter-simon-and-schuster.

Hulbert, Ann. "The Struggles of the Woman Behind 'Battle Hymn of the Republic'." *The Atlantic.* March 2016. https://www.theatlantic.com/magazine/archive/2016/03/the-civil-wars-of-julia-ward-howe/426879/

Lesser, Wendy. "The Battles Over Julia Ward Howe." *The New York Review of Books.* November 24, 2016. http://www.nybooks.com/articles/2016/11/24/the-battles-over-julia-ward-howe/.

Lepore, Jill. " 'The Civil Wars of Julia Ward Howe,' by Elaine Showalter." *The New York Times.* February 29, 2016. https://www.nytimes.com/2016/03/06/books/review/the-civil-wars-of-julia-ward-howe-by-elaine-showalter.html.

Michaud, Rosemary. "Review: 'The Civil Wars of Julia Ward Howe' reveal private battles." *The Post and Courier.* January 1, 2017 http://www.postandcourier.com/features/review-the-civil-wars-of-julia-ward-howe-reveal-private/article_dc960e50-c0b7-11e6-9692-c39a71bbefb1.html.

Ruane, Michael E. "How Julia Ward Howe wrote 'Battle Hymn of the Republic' — despite her husband." *The Washington Post*. November 18, 2011. https://www.washingtonpost.com/local/how-julia-ward-howe-wrote-battle-hymn-of-the-republic--despite-her-husband/2011/11/15/gIQAnQRaYN_story.html.

Smith, David Hugh. " 'The Civil Wars of Julia Ward Howe' tells of a woman's struggle for freedom." *The Christian Science Monitor*. March 9, 2016. https://www.csmonitor.com/Books/Book-Reviews/2016/0309/The-Civil-Wars-of-Julia-Ward-Howe-tells of-a-woman-s-struggle-for-freedom.

Soskis, Benjamin. "A Fiery Gospel." *Slate*. November 17, 2011. http://www.slate.com/articles/arts/life_and_art/2011/11/julia_ward_howe_s_battle_hymn_of_the_republic_how_it_changed_america_.html.

Steinitz, Rebecca. "The battle hymn of Julia Ward Howe." *The Boston Globe*. March 19, 2016. https://www.bostonglobe.com/arts/books/2016/03/19/the-battle-hymn-julia-ward-howe/gsBTiqY5GsdfETPwhmW1GM/story.html.

"Travails of a 19th-century feminist—Her truth marches on." *The Economist*. February 18, 2016. https://www.economist.com/news/books-and-arts/21693179-life-julia-ward-howe-who-wrote-battle-hymn-republic-her-truth-marches.

Chapter # 2 — Sarah Josepha Hale

Blakemore, Erin. "Five Fascinating Details About the Media Mogul Who May Have Written 'Mary Had a Little Lamb'." *Smithsonian Magazine*. May 24, 2016. https://www.smithsonianmag.com/smart-news/five-fascinating-details-about-media-mogul-who-might-have-written-mary-had-little-lamb-180959212/.

Collins, Gail. "How Women Won the Holidays." *The New York Times*. November 27, 2003. http://www.nytimes.com/2003/11/27/opinion/how-women-won-the-holidays.html.

Davis, Kenneth C. "How the Civil War Created Thanksgiving." *The New York Times*. November 25, 2014. https://opinionator.blogs.nytimes.com/2014/11/25/how-the-civil-war-created-thanksgiving/.

Hillinger, Charles. "U.S. Can Thank Sarah Hale for Thanksgiving." *Los Angeles Times*. November 20, 1988. http://articles.latimes.com/1988-11-20/news/vw-403_1_sarah-josepha-hale.

Kamp, Jon. " 'Thanks' to Unsung Heroine Sarah Josepha Hale." *Wall Street Journal*. November 26, 2013. https://www.wsj.com/articles/8216thanks8217-to-unsung-heroine-sarah-josepha-hale-1385511135.

Lowry, Rich. "The Mother of Thanksgiving." *National Review*. November 27, 2013. http://www.nationalreview.com/article/364996/mother-thanksgiving-rich-lowry.

Price, Rebecca. "Sarah Hale: The Woman Who Made Thanksgiving Happen." *Huffington Post*. January 22, 2012. https://www.huffingtonpost.com/rebecca-price/behind-every-american-tha_b_1108655.html.

Quigley, Paul "The Birth of Thanksgiving." *The New York Times*. November 28, 2013. https://opinionator.blogs.nytimes.com/2013/11/28/the-birth-of-thanskgiving/.

Trohan, Walter. "From the Archives: Why Lincoln set a day for Thanksgiving." *Chicago Tribune*. November 20, 2014. http://www.chicagotribune.com/lifestyles/books/ct-prj-thanksgiving-lincoln-sarah-hale-20141120-story.html.

Waxman, Olivia B. "Thanksgiving Wasn't Always a National Holiday. This Woman Made It Happen." *Time*. November 23, 2016. http://time.com/4577082/thanksgiving-holiday-history-origins/.

Chapter # 3 — Coco Channel

Dumas, Daisy. "New Coco Chanel Biography Claims To Have Proof That Fashion Icon Used Drugs, Had Lesbian Affairs And Loved A Nazi Spy." *Daily Mail*. August 2, 2011. http://www.dailymail.co.uk/femail/article-2021234/Coco-Chanel-biography-claims-used-drugs-lesbian-affairs-loved-Nazi.html.

Flanner, Janet. "31, Rue Cambon" *The New Yorker*. March 14, 1931. http://www.newyorker.com/magazine/1931/03/14/31-rue-cambon-2.

Givhan, Robin. "Book review: 'Mademoiselle,' a biography of Coco Chanel, by Rhonda K. Garelick." *The Washington Post*. December 19, 2014. https://www.washingtonpost.com/opinions/book-review-mademoiselle-a-biography-of-coco-chanel-by-rhonda-k-garelick/2014/12/19/417c539c-70ec-11e4-ad12-3734c461eab6_story.html.

Klotz, Frieda. "The Life of Coco Chanel." *Irish Independent*. January 16, 2012. http://www.independent.ie/entertainment/books/the-life-of-coco-chanel-26811856.html.

Lipton, Lauren. "The Many Faces of Coco." *The New York Times*. December 2, 2011. http://www.nytimes.com/2011/12/04/fashion/three-books-about-coco-chanel.html.

McAuley, James. "The Exchange: Coco Chanel and the Nazi Party." *The New Yorker*. August 31, 2011. http://www.newyorker.com/books/page-turner/the-exchange-coco-chanel-and-the-nazi-party.

Muhlstein, Anka. "The Cut of Coco." *The New York Review of Books.* October 9, 2014. http://www.nybooks.com/articles/2014/10/09/cut-coco-chanel/.

Picardie, Justine. "The secret life of Coco Chanel." *The Telegraph.* September 6, 2010. http://fashion.telegraph.co.uk/columns/justine-picardie/TMG7975778/The-secret-life-of-Coco-Chanel.html.

———. "The Secret Life Of Coco Chanel." *Harper's Bazaar.* July 11, 2011. http://www.harpersbazaar.com/fashion/designers/a743/coco-chanel-secret-life/.

Warner, Judith. "Was Coco Chanel a Nazi Agent?" *The New York Times.* September 2, 2011. http://www.nytimes.com/2011/09/04/books/review/sleeping-with-the-enemy-coco-chanels-secret-war-by-hal-vaughan-book-review.html.

Chapter # 4 — Emma Lazarus

Benfey, Christopher. "The Convert." *The New York Review of Books.* February 15, 2007. http://www.nybooks.com/articles/2007/02/15/the-convert/.

Crain, Caleb. "Mother of Exiles." *The New York Times.* December 31, 2006. http://www.nytimes.com/2006/12/31/books/review/mother-of-exiles.html.

Mettler, Katie. " 'Give me your tired, your poor': The story of poet and refugee advocate Emma Lazarus." *The Washington Post.* February 1, 2017.

Reilly, Katie. " 'Give Me Your Tired, Your Poor': The Story Behind the Statue of Liberty's Famous Immigration Poem." *Time*. January 28, 2017. http://time.com/4652666/statue-of-liberty-give-me-your-tired-poor/.

Scharper, Diane. "Lazarus Rising." *The Weekly Standard*. July 21, 2014. http://www.weeklystandard.com/lazarus-rising/article/796384.

Chapter # 5 — Helena Rubenstein

Berman, Eliza. "How One Woman Built an Empire on Lipstick and Lotion." *Time*. March 4, 2015. http://time.com/3723935/helena-rubinstein/.

Gladwell, Malcolm. "The Color of Money." *The New Yorker*. March 28, 2011. http://www.newyorker.com/magazine/2011/03/28/the-color-of-money.

Haslam, Nicky. " 'Helena Rubinstein: The Woman Who Invented Beauty', by Michèle Fitoussi – review." *The Spectator*. April 13, 2013. https://www.spectator.co.uk/2013/04/park-avenue-princess/.

Stonehouse, Cheryl. "Helena Rubinstein, the penniless refugee who built a cosmetics empire." *Express*. March 16, 2013. http://www.express.co.uk/life-style/style/384696/Helena-Rubinstein-the-penniless-refugee-who-built-a-cosmetics-empire.

Chapter # 6 — Elizabeth Magie

Gayle, Damien. "The real story behind Monopoly: How a secretary designed the board game more than 100 years ago in protest against property moguls of the day." *Daily Mail*. February 17, 2015. http://www.dailymail.co.uk/news/article-2957197/The-real-story-Monopoly-secretary-designed-board-game-100-years-ago-protest-against-property-moguls-day.html.

Pilon, Mary. "Monopoly's Inventor: The Progressive Who Didn't Pass 'Go' " *The New York Times*. February, 13, 2015. https://www.nytimes.com/2015/02/15/business/behind-monopoly-an-inventor-who-didnt-pass-go.html.

Pilon, Mary. "The secret history of Monopoly: the capitalist board game's leftwing origins." *The Guardian*. April 11, 2015. https://www.theguardian.com/lifeandstyle/2015/apr/11/secret-history-monopoly-capitalist-game-leftwing-origins.

Wise, Sarah. "The Monopolists by Mary Pilon: review." *Telegraph*. April 7, 2015. http://www.telegraph.co.uk/culture/books/bookreviews/11514047/The-Monopolists-by-Mary-Pilon-review.html.

Chapter # 7 — Juliette Gordon Law

Associated Press. "Girl Scouts mark 100 years of closing gender gaps." *Daily Herald*. March 4, 2012. http://www.dailyherald.com/article/20120303/news/703039971/.

Finnerty, Amy. "Saluting a Centennial." *The Wall Street Journal*. February 11, 2012. https://www.wsj.com/articles/SB10001424052970203711104577200831260449326.

Gambino, Megan. "The Very First Troop Leader." *Smithsonian.com*. March 7, 2012. https://www.smithsonianmag.com/history/the-very-first-troop-leader-116645976/.

"Great Lives Series: Juliette Gordon Low." *Washington Independent Review of Books*. March 15, 2012. http://www.washingtonindependentreviewofbooks.com/features/great-live-series-juliette-gordon-low.

Kehe, Marjorie. "That 'Crazy Daisy' who started the Girl Scouts." *The Christian Science Monitor*. March 12, 2012. https://www.csmonitor.com/Books/chapter-and-verse/2012/0312/That-Crazy-Daisy-who-started-the-Girl-Scouts.

Kleiber, Shannon Henry. "Juliette Gordon Low, who had no children of her own, started Girl Scouts in 1912." *The Washington Post*. March 9, 2012. https://www.washingtonpost.com/lifestyle/kidpost/juliette-gordon-low-who-had-no-children-of-her-own-started-girl-scouts-in-1912/2012/02/28/gIQA5CBO1R_story.html.

Marcotte, Amanda. "The Girl Scouts Have Always Been Ahead of Their Time." *Slate.com*. March 11, 2012. http://www.slate.com/blogs/xx_factor/2012/03/09/girl_scouts_100th_anniversary_juliette_gordon_low_s_group_has_always_been_ahead_of_its_time_.html.

Roberts, Cokie. " 'Juliette Gordon Low: The Remarkable Founder of the Girl Scouts' by Stacy A. Cordery and 'On My Honor: Real Life Lessons from America's First Girl Scout' by Shannon Henry Kleiber." *The Washington Post*. April 7, 2012. https://www.washingtonpost.com/entertainment/books/juliette-gordon-low-the-remarkable-founder-of-the-girl-scouts-by-stacy-a-cordery-and-on-my-honor-real-life-lessons-from-americas-first-girl-scoutby-shannon-henry-kleiber/2012/04/07/gIQAR1G61S_story.html.

Sayeau, Ashley. " 'Juliette Gordon Low,' by Stacy A. Cordery." *SFGate*. March 18, 2012. http://www.sfgate.com/books/article/Juliette-Gordon-Low-by-Stacy-A-Cordery-3413807.php.

Tuttle, Kate. "Boy Scouts Are From Mars, Girl Scouts Are From Venus." *The Atlantic*. March 5, 2012. https://www.theatlantic.com/national/archive/2012/03/boy-scouts-are-from-mars-girl-scouts-are-from-venus/253957/.

Wilson, Craig. "One smart cookie founded the Girl Scouts 100 years ago." *USA Today*. March 12, 2012. www.usatoday.com/life/books/news/story/2012-03-07/juliette-gordon-low-girl-scouts-anniversary/53406500/1.

Williams, Jasmin K. "Juliette Gordon Low." *New York Post*. March 13, 2008. http://nypost.com/2008/03/13/juliette-gordon-low/.

Wong, Brittany. "Girl Scouts' 100th Anniversary: Founder Juliette Gordon Low's Surprising Divorce History." *Huffington Post*. March 12, 2012. http://www.huffingtonpost.com/2012/03/12/girl-scouts-100th-anniver_n_1340050.html.

Chapter # 8 — Anne Jarvis

MacLean, Maggie. "Anna Jarvis." *Civil War Women*. February 9, 2007. https://www.civilwarwomenblog.com/anna-jarvis/.

Mapes, Josh. "Anna Jarvis: Mother of Modern Mother's Day." *Biography*. May 12, 2012. https://www.biography.com/news/anna-jarvis-mother-of-modern-mothers-day-20826125.

Mulinix, Jonathan. "The Founder of Mother's Day Later Fought to Have It Abolished." *Mental Floss*. May 4, 2017. http://mentalfloss.com/article/30659/founder-mothers-day-later-fought-have-it-abolished.

Oliphint, Joel. "The Founder of Mother's Day Was Sorry She Ever Invented the Holiday." *BuzzFeed.* May 8, 2015. https://www.buzzfeed.com/joeloliphint/anna-jarvis-was-sorry-she-ever-invented-mothers-day.

Rouvalis, Cristina. "For the mother of Mother's Day, it's just never been right." *Pittsburgh Post-Gazette.* May 11, 2008. http://www.post-gazette.com/frontpage/2008/05/11/For-the-mother-of-Mother-s-Day-it-s-just-never-been-right/stories/200805110164.

Strauss, Valerie. "Why Mother's Day founder came to hate her creation (and more on moms, gifts, baby names etc.)." *The Washington Post.* May 13, 2012. https://www.washingtonpost.com/blogs/answer-sheet/post/why-mothers-day-founder-came-to-hate-her-creation-and-more-on-moms-gifts-baby-names-etc/2012/05/13/gIQAyOH8LU_blog.html.

Varma, Arjun. "Mother's Day history and origin: How and when the special sentimental day came into existence." *International Business Times.* May 8, 2016. http://www.ibtimes.co.in/mothers-day-history-origin-how-when-special-sentimental-day-came-into-existence-677672.

Wilson, Jacqueline. "Shocking History of Mother's Day." *Huffington Post.* May 8, 2017. https://www.huffingtonpost.com/jacqueline-wilson/shocking-history-of-mothers-day_b_7242766.html.

Chapter # 9 — Caresse Crosby

Lyle, Peter. "The Crosbys: literature's most scandalous couple." *The Telegraph.* June 19, 2009. http://www.telegraph.co.uk/culture/5549090/The-Crosbys-literatures-most-scandalous-couple.html.

Ruane, Michael E. *The Washington Post*. November 11, 2014. "Caresse Crosby, who claimed the invention of the bra, was better known for her wild life." https://www.washingtonpost.com/local/caresse-crosby-who-claimed-the-invention-of-the-bra-was-better-known-for-her-wild-life/2014/11/09/99c55f7e-3f39-11e4-b03f-de718edeb92f_story.html.

Stampler, Laura. "The 100-Year History of the Modern Bra Is Also the History of Taking Off Bras." *Time*. November 3, 2014. http://time.com/3553997/modern-bra-history-1914/.

Chapter # 10 — Margaret Sanger

Cooke, Rachel. "Woman Rebel: The Margaret Sanger Story by Peter Bagge – review." *The Guardian*. January 6, 2014. https://www.theguardian.com/books/2014/jan/06/woman-rebel-margaret-sanger-review.

Hagelin, Rebecca. "Planned Parenthood founded on racism, belief in protecting society against 'the unfit'." *The Washington Times*. April 23, 2017. http://www.washingtontimes.com/news/2017/apr/23/margaret-sanger-founded-planned-parenthood-on-raci/.

Latson, Jennifer. "What Margaret Sanger Really Said About Eugenics and Race." *Time*. October 14, 2016. http://time.com/4081760/margaret-sanger-history-eugenics/.

"Margaret Sanger Is Dead at 82; Led Campaign for Birth Control." *The New York Times*. September 7, 1966. http://www.nytimes.com/learning/general/onthisday/bday/0914.html.

Wagman-Geller, Marlene. *Eureka!: The Surprising Stories Behind the Ideas That Shaped the World*. TarcherPerigee, 2010.

Chapter # 11 — Rosie Monroe

Bruk, Diana. "Meet The 95-Year-Old Real-Life Rosie The Riveter." *Harper's Bazaar*. September 7, 2016 http://www.harpersbazaar.com/culture/features/news/a17573/real-life-rosie-the-riveter/.

Counter, Rosemary. "Why You Keep Reading Obituaries for Rosie the Riveter." *Vanity Fair*. May 7, 2015. https://www.vanityfair.com/culture/2015/05/why-you-keep-reading-obituaries-rosie-riveter.

Daily Mail Reporter. "Model who inspired the Rosie the Riveter 'We Can Do It!' WWII poster campaign dies at 86." *Daily Mail*. December 31, 2010. http://www.dailymail.co.uk/news/article-1342877/Geraldine-Hoff-Doyle-model-inspired-We-Can-Do-It-WWII-poster-campaign-dies-86.html.

Dunlap, Tiare. "See Rosie the Riveter at 95: Woman Who Inspired WWII Poster Was Lost to History for 7 Decades.". *People*. October 5, 2016. http://people.com/celebrity/rosie-the-riveter-meet-the-woman-who-inspired-the-iconic-poster/.

Marcano, Tony. "Famed Riveter In War Effort, Rose Monroe Dies at 77." *The New York Times*. June 2, 1997. http://www.nytimes.com/1997/06/02/us/famed-riveter-in-war-effort-rose-monroe-dies-at-77.html.

Chapter # 12 — Estée Lauder

Bender, Marylin. "Youth Dew Did It." *The New York Times*. November 17, 1985. http://www.nytimes.com/1985/11/17/books/youth-dew-did-it.html.

Boyer, G. Bruce. "Estée Lauder and the Business of Beauty." *The Washington Post*. November 24, 1985. https://www.washingtonpost. com/archive/entertainment/books/1985/11/24/estee-lauder-and-the-business-of-beauty/e0659750-60c4-4717-9940-b2f2f8edae2a.

"Estée Lauder." *The Telegraph*. April 27, 2004. http://www.telegraph. co.uk/news/obituaries/1460329/Estee-Lauder.html.

"Estée Lauder: From rags to riches." *Daily Mail*. April 26, 2004. http://www.dailymail.co.uk/news/article-259381/Estee-Lauder-From-rags-riches.html.

Mirabella, Grace. "Beauty Queen: Estée Lauder." *Time*. December 17, 1998. http://content.time.com/time/subscriber/article/0,33009,989786,00. html.

Severo, Richard. "Estée Lauder, Pursuer of Beauty And Cosmetics Titan, Dies at 97." *The New York Times*. April 26, 2004. http://www. nytimes.com/2004/04/26/nyregion/estee-lauder-pursuer-of-beauty-and-cosmetics-titan-dies-at-97.html.

Chapter # 13 — Lillian Vernon

Arnold, Laurence. "Lillian Vernon, who created mail-order catalog business, dies at 88." *The Washington Post*. December 14, 2015. https://www.washingtonpost.com/business/lillian-vernon-who-created-catalog-business-dies-at-88/2015/12/14/f4cffec8-a2bc-11e5-b53d-972e2751f433_story.html.

————. "Lillian Vernon, queen of mail-order catalogs, dies at 88." *Chicago Tribune*. December 15, 2016. http://www.chicagotribune. com/business/ct-lillian-vernon-dies-20151215-story.html.

————. "Lillian Vernon: Businesswoman whose idea of selling monogrammed bags and belts became a brand loved in the US." *The Independent*. January 12, 2016. http://www.independent.co.uk/news/obituaries/lillian-vernon-businesswoman-whose-idea-of-selling-monogrammed-bags-and-belts-became-a-brand-loved-a6808251.html.

Hochberg, Fred. "On the Passing of My Mother, Lillian Vernon." *Huffington Post*. December 22, 2016. http://www.huffingtonpost.com/fred-hochberg/on-the-passing-of-my-moth_b_8864026.html.

Povich, Lynn. "Lillian Vernon, Creator of a Bustling Catalog Business, Dies at 88." *The New York Times*. December 14, 2015. https://www.nytimes.com/2015/12/15/business/lillian-vernon-creator-of-a-bustling-catalog-business-dies-at-88.html.

Chapter # 14 — Abigail Van Buren and Anne Landers

Anderson, Jon. "Advice columnist Ann Landers dead at 83."*Chicago Tribune*. June 22, 2002. http://www.chicagotribune.com/news/chi-020622landers-story.html.

Coburn, Marcia Froelke. " 'Dear' Sisters- An Inside Peek At Rival Twins Abby And Ann." *Chicago Tribune*. November 8, 1987. http://articles.chicagotribune.com/1987-11-08/entertainment/8703240171_1_eppie-lederer-dear-ann-landers-dear-abby.

Felsenthal, Carol. "Dear Ann." *Chicago Magazine*. February 1, 2003. http://www.chicagomag.com/Chicago-Magazine/February-2003/Dear-Ann/.

Noveck, Jocelyn. "Pauline Phillips a.k.a. 'Dear Abby' leaves legacy of wit and warm advice." *The Christian Science Monitor.* January 17, 2013. https://www.csmonitor.com/The-Culture/Latest-News-Wires/2013/0117/Pauline-Phillips-a.k.a.-Dear-Abby-leaves-legacy-of-wit-and-warm-advice.

Shapiro, Samantha M. "Abigail Van Buren." *The New York Times.* December 21, 2013. https://www.nytimes.com/news/the-lives-they-lived/2013/12/21/abigail-van-buren/.

Strochlic, Nina. "Words of Wisdom: The Best of 'Dear Abby'." *The Daily Beast.* January 17, 2013. http://www.thedailybeast.com/words-of-wisdom-the-best-of-dear-abby.

Witt, Linda. "The Friedman Twins Find You Can Go Home Again, Especially If You're Ann Landers and Dear Abby." *People.* July 12, 1976. http://people.com/archive/the-friedman-twins-find-you-can-go-home-again-especially-if-youre-ann-landers-and-dear-abby-vol-6-no-2/.

Chapter # 15 — Ruth Handler

Horwell, Veronica. "Ruth Handler." *The Guardian.* May 1, 2002. https://www.theguardian.com/news/2002/may/02/guardianobituaries.veronicahorwell.

Kershaw, Sarah. "Ruth Handler, Whose Barbie Gave Dolls Curves, Dies at 85." *The New York Times.* April 29, 2002. http://www.nytimes.com/2002/04/29/arts/ruth-handler-whose-barbie-gave-dolls-curves-dies-at-85.html.

Latson, Jennifer. "The Barbie Doll's Not-for-Kids Origins." *Time.* March 9, 2015. http://time.com/3731483/barbie-history/.

Leith, Sam and Catherine Elsworth. "Barbie creator dies, survived by 1bn dolls." *The Telegraph.* April 29, 2002.

http://www.telegraph.co.uk/news/worldnews/northamerica/usa/1392569/Barbie-creator-dies-survived-by-1bn-dolls.html.

"Ruth Handler." *The Economist.* May 2, 2002. http://www.economist.com/node/1109674.

"Ruth Handler." *The Telegraph.* May 3, 2002. http://www.telegraph.co.uk/news/obituaries/1392978/Ruth-Handler.html.

Wagman-Geller, Marlene. *Eureka!: The Surprising Stories Behind the Ideas That Shaped the World.* TarcherPerigee, 2010.

Wansell, Geoffrey. "The curse of Barbie: How the world's most famous toy destroyed the sordid lives of her two creators." *Daily Mail.* March 10, 2009. http://www.dailymail.co.uk/femail/article-1160823/The-curse-Barbie-How-worlds-famous-toy-destroyed-sordid-lives-creators.html.

Woo, Elaine. "Barbie Doll Creator Ruth Handler Dies." *The Washington Post.* April 29, 2002. https://www.washingtonpost.com/archive/local/2002/04/29/barbie-doll-creator-ruth-handler-dies/76bfe4ad-d4aa-431f-9c45-16b9b33046fd/.

Chapter # 16 — Rachel Carson

Cataneo, Emily. "On Farther Shore." *The Christian Science Monitor.* September 11, 2012. https://www.csmonitor.com/Books/Book-Reviews/2012/0911/On-a-Farther-Shore.

Flannery, Tim. "A Heroine in Defense of Nature." *The New York Review of Books.* November 22, 2012. http://www.nybooks.com/articles/2012/11/22/heroine-defense-nature/.

Hickman, Leo. "What is the legacy of Rachel Carson's Silent Spring?" *The Guardian.* September 27, 2012. https://www.theguardian.com/global/blog/2012/sep/27/rachel-carson-silent-spring-legacy.

Lear, Linda. *Rachel Carson: Witness for Nature.* H. Holt, 1997. Reprint, Mariner Books, 2009. Also available, in part, online, http://www.washingtonpost.com/wp-srv/style/longterm/books/chap1/rachelcarson.htm.

Milne, Lorus and Margery. "There's Poison All Around Us Now." *New York Times Books.* September 23, 1962.

http://www.nytimes.com/books/97/10/05/reviews/carson-spring.html.

"Rachel Carson Dies of Cancer; 'Silent Spring' Author Was 56." *The New York Times.* Accessed April 14, 2017. http://www.nytimes.com/learning/general/onthisday/bday/0527.html.

Radford, Tim. "Silent Spring by Rachel Carson – review." *The Guardian.* September 30, 2011. https://www.theguardian.com/science/2011/sep/30/silent-spring-rachel-carson-review.

Royte, Elizabeth. "The Poisoned Earth- 'On a Farther Shore,' by William Souder." *The New York Times.* September 14, 2012. http://www.nytimes.com/2012/09/16/books/review/on-a-farther-shore-by-william-souder.html.

Stewart, Amy. "Book review: William Souder's 'On a Farther Shore: The Life and Legacy of Rachel Carson'." *The Washington Post.* September 28, 2012. https://www.washingtonpost.com/opinions/book-review-william-souders-on-a-farther-shore-the-life-and-legacy-of-rachel-carson/2012/09/28/0d7313ae-f616-11e1-8b93-c4f4ab1c8d13_story.html.

Chapter # 17 — Mahalia Jackson

Bucktin, Christopher. "Martin Luther King: The story behind the famous 'I have a dream' speech that changed course of America." *The Mirror.* September 10, 2013. http://www.mirror.co.uk/news/world-news/martin-luther-king-story-behind-2178797.

Hansen, Drew. "Mahalia Jackson, and King's Improvisation." *The New York Times.* August 27, 2013. http://www.nytimes.com/2013/08/28/opinion/mahalia-jackson-and-kings-rhetorical-improvisation.html.

"Jackson, Mahalia 1911–1972." Contemporary Black Biography. *Encyclopedia.com.* October 23, 2017. http://www.encyclopedia.com/education/news-wires-white-papers-and-books/jackson-mahalia-1911-1972.

Kot, Greg. "How Mahalia Jackson defined the 'I Have a Dream' Speech." *BBC Culture.* October 21, 2014. http://www.bbc.com/culture/story/20130827-a-song-that-made-america-believe.

Reuters Reporter and James Nye. "Key aide reveals Martin Luther King almost never said 'I have a dream' during speech which changed America." *Daily Mail.* August 27, 2013. http://www.dailymail.co.uk/news/article-2402161/Aide-reveals-Martin-Luther-King-said-I-dream.html.

Wikipedia contributors. "Mahalia Jackson." *Wikipedia, The Free Encyclopedia.* Accessed January 15, 2017. https://en.wikipedia.org/w/index.php?title=Mahalia_Jackson&oldid=798870064.

Whitman, Alden. "Mahalia Jackson, Gospel Singer, And a Civil Rights Symbol, Dies." The Learning Network, *The New York Times.* January 28, 1972. http://www.nytimes.com/learning/general/onthisday/bday/1026.html.

Younge, Gary. "Martin Luther King: the story behind his 'I have a dream' speech." *The Guardian*. August 9, 2013. https://www.theguardian.com/world/2013/aug/09/martin-luther-king-dream-speech-history.

Chapter # 18 — Eunice Kennedy

Baranauckas, Carla. "Eunice Kennedy Shriver, Influential Founder of Special Olympics, Dies at 88." *The New York Times*. August 11, 2009. http://www.nytimes.com/2009/08/12/us/12shriver.html.

Dailey, Kate. "Eunice Kennedy Shriver, The Special Olympics, And The Power Of Sports." *Newsweek*. August 11, 2009. http://www.newsweek.com/eunice-kennedy-shriver-special-olympics-and-power-sports-222176.

McCrum, Robert. "Eunice Kennedy and the death of the great American dream."

The Guardian. August 15, 2009. https://www.theguardian.com/world/2009/aug/16/eunice-kennedy-family-us-politics.

Mcmurran, Kristin. "To Eunice Shriver, the Most Compassionate and Competitive Kennedy, Life Is a Special Olympics." *People*. August 27, 1979. http://people.com/archive/to-eunice-shriver-the-most-compassionate-and-competitive-kennedy-life-is-a-special-olympics-vol-12-no-9/.

Orth, Maureen. "Remembering Eunice Kennedy Shriver, A Woman Who Got Her Way." *Vanity Fair*. August 2009. https://www.vanityfair.com/news/2009/08/remembering-the-indomitable-eunice-kennedy-shriver.

Shriver, Eunice Kennedy. "My sister Rosemary." *Saturday Evening Post.* September 22, 1962. Reprinted in *The Guardian.* August 12, 2009. https://www.theguardian.com/world/2009/aug/13/rosemary-kennedy-eunice-kennedy-shriver.

Wagman-Geller, Marlene. *Eureka!: The Surprising Stories Behind the Ideas That Shaped the World.* TarcherPerigee, 2010.

Chapter # 19 — Norma McCorvey

Carlson, Michael. "Norman McCorvey. Obituary." *The Guardian.* February 19, 2017. https://www.theguardian.com/us-news/2017/feb/19/norma-mccorvey-obituary.

Carpenter, Julia. "The fascinating life of Norma McCorvey, the 'Jane Roe' in Roe v. Wade." *The Washington Post.* January 22, 2016. https://www.washingtonpost.com/news/soloish/wp/2016/01/22/the-fascinating-life-of-norma-mccorvey-the-jane-roe-in-roe-v-wade/.

Fagan, Kevin. "PAGE ONE -- 'Roe's' Conversion Doesn't Surprise Partner, Friends." *SFGate.* August 12, 1995. http://www.sfgate.com/news/article/PAGE-ONE-Roe-s-Conversion-Doesn-t-Surprise-3027430.php.

Green, Michelle and Lois Armstrong. "The Woman Behind Roe v. Wade." *People.* May 22, 1989. http://people.com/archive/the-woman-behind-roe-v-wade-vol-31-no-20/.

" 'Jane Roe' Joins Anti-Abortion Group." *The New York Times.* August 11, 1995. http://www.nytimes.com/1995/08/11/us/jane-roe-joins-anti-abortion-group.html.

Mcfadden, Robert D. "Norma McCorvey, 'Roe' in Roe v. Wade, Is Dead at 69." *The New York Times*. February 18, 2017. https://www.nytimes.com/2017/02/18/obituaries/norma-mccorvey-dead-roe-v-wade.html.

Prager, Joshua. "The Accidental Activist." *Vanity Fair*. February 2013. https://www.vanityfair.com/news/politics/2013/02/norma-mccorvey-roe-v-wade-abortion.

Verhovek, Sam Howe. "New Twist for a Landmark Case: Roe v. Wade Becomes Roe v. Roe." *The New York Times*. August 12, 1995. http://www.nytimes.com/1995/08/12/us/new-twist-for-a-landmark-case-roe-v-wade-becomes-roe-v-roe.html.

Wikipedia contributors. "Norma McCorvey." *Wikipedia, The Free Encyclopedia*. Accessed October 31, 2017. https://en.wikipedia.org/w/index.php?title=Norma_McCorvey&oldid=805737189.

Chapter # 20 — Anita Roddick

"Anita Roddick, capitalist with a conscience, dies at 64." *The Independent*. September 10, 2007. http://www.independent.co.uk/news/uk/this-britain/anita-roddick-capitalist-with-a-conscience-dies-at-64-402014.html.

Farouky, Jumana. "Anita Roddick, the Queen of Green." *Time*. September 11, 2007. http://content.time.com/time/business/article/0,8599,1660911,00.html.

"Green made good." *The Economist*. September 13, 2007. http://www.economist.com/node/9803795.

Horwell, Veronica. "Dame Anita Roddick." *The Guardian*. September 12, 2007. https://www.theguardian.com/news/2007/sep/12/guardianobituaries.business.

Lyall, Sarah. "Anita Roddick, Body Shop Founder, Dies at 64." *The New York Times*. September 12, 2007. http://www.nytimes.com/2007/09/12/world/europe/12roddick.html.

Press Association. "Anita Roddick dies aged 64." *The Guardian*. September 27, 2007. https://www.theguardian.com/business/2007/sep/10/ethicalliving.lifeandhealth.

Sullivan, Patricia. "Anita Roddick, 64; Founder Of Activist Cosmetics Firm." *The Washington Post*. September 11, 2007. http://www.washingtonpost.com/wp-dyn/content/article/2007/09/10/AR2007091002360.html.

Chapter # 21 — Ingrid Newkirk

Bowen, Alison. "Why PETA president posed nude, hanging from hook on Chicago billboard." November 7, 2017. http://www.chicagotribune.com/lifestyles/ct-peta-billboard-bacon-fest-lifestyles-0419-20170419-story.html.

Cadwallader, Carole. "Peta's Ingrid Newkirk: making the fury fly." *The Guardian*. March 30, 2013 https://www.theguardian.com/world/2013/mar/31/peta-ingrid-newkirk-making-fur-fly.

Mejia, Paula. "Peta Founder Newkirk Explains Her 'Unique' Will: Barbecue Me And Send My Eyeballs To The Epa." *Newsweek*. October 24, 2014. http://www.newsweek.com/peta-founder-ingrid-newkirk-explains-her-unique-will-barbecue-me-and-send-my-279794.

"Put Your Ethics Where Your Mouth Is." *The New York Times*. April 20, 2012. http://www.nytimes.com/interactive/2012/04/20/magazine/ethics-eating-meat.html.

Reed, Susan. "Activist Ingrid Newkirk Fights Passionately for the Rights of Animals; Some Critics Say Humans May Suffer." *People*. October 22, 1990. http://people.com/archive/activist-ingrid-newkirk-fights-passionately-for-the-rights-of-animals-some-critics-say-humans-may-suffer-vol-34-no-16/.

Specter, Michael. "The Extremist." *The New Yorker*. April 14, 2003. http://www.newyorker.com/magazine/2003/04/14/the-extremist.

Usborne, Simon. "Ingrid Newkirk: 'It's bizarre to kill animals for a sandwich'." *The Independent*. November 17, 2013. http://www.independent.co.uk/news/people/profiles/ingrid-newkirk-its-bizarre-to-kill-animals-for-a-sandwich-8944582.html.

Wagman-Geller, Marlene. *Eureka!: The Surprising Stories Behind the Ideas That Shaped the World*. TarcherPerigee, 2010.

Chapter # 22 — Jenny Craig

Craig, Jenny. *The Jenny Craig Story: How One Woman Changes Millions of Lives*. Wiley, 2004.

Dennis Hevesi. "Sidney Craig, 76, a Founder of Jenny Craig, Dies." *The New York Times*. July 24, 2008. http://www.nytimes.com/2008/07/24/business/24craig.html.

Rizzo, Monica. "Painful Silence." *People*. May 3, 1999. http://people.com/archive/painful-silence-vol-51-no-16/.

Wagman-Geller, Marlene. *Eureka!: The Surprising Stories Behind the Ideas That Shaped the World*. TarcherPerigee, 2010.

Chapter # 23 — The Guerilla Girls

Brockes, Emma. "The Guerrilla Girls: 30 years of punking art world sexism." *The Guardian*. April 29, 2015. https://www.theguardian.com/artanddesign/2015/apr/29/the-guerrilla-girls-interview-art-world-sexism.

Goldstein, Jessica. "Guerrilla Girls: 'Feminist masked avengers' win acceptance in art world they target." *The Washington Post*. July 1, 2011. https://www.washingtonpost.com/lifestyle/style/guerrilla-girls-feminist-masked-avengers-win-acceptance-in-art-world-they-target/2011/06/27/AGufp8tH_story.html.

Ryzik, Melena. "The Guerrilla Girls, After 3 Decades, Still Rattling Art World Cages." *The New York Times*. August 5, 2015. https://www.nytimes.com/2015/08/09/arts/design/the-guerrilla-girls-after-3-decades-still-rattling-art-world-cages.html.

Toobin, Jeffrey. "Girls Behaving Badly." *The New Yorker*. May 5, 2005. http://www.newyorker.com/magazine/2005/05/30/girls-behaving-badly.

Williams, Zoe. "Going Ape." *The Guardian*. June 29, 2006. https://www.theguardian.com/artanddesign/2006/jun/29/art.gender.

Chapter # 24 — Evelyn Lauder

Associated Press. " 'She was our pillar of strength': Family's heartfelt tributes as Evelyn Lauder - the founder of the breast cancer pink ribbon campaign - dies aged 75." *Daily Mail.* November 14, 2011. http:// www.dailymail.co.uk/femail/article-2060960/Evelyn-Lauder-dies-75-Breast-cancer-pink-ribbon-campaign-founder-died.html.

Associate Press in New York. "Evelyn Lauder, founder of pink ribbon breast cancer campaign, dies aged 75." *The Guardian.* November 13, 2011. https://www.theguardian.com/world/2011/nov/13/evelyn-lauder-pink-ribbon-breast-cancer.

"Evelyn Lauder." *The Telegraph.* December 25, 2011. http://www.telegraph.co.uk/news/obituaries/medicine-obituaries/8977365/Evelyn-Lauder.html.

Hammel, Sara. "Evelyn Lauder Dies at 75." *People.* November 13, 2011. http://people.com/celebrity/evelyn-lauder-dead-remembered-for-championing-breast-cancer-research/.

Horwell, Veronica. "Evelyn Lauder obituary." *The Guardian.* November 30, 2011. https://www.theguardian.com/fashion/2011/nov/30/evelyn-lauder-obituary.

Horyn, Cathy. "Evelyn H. Lauder, Champion of Breast Cancer Research, Dies at 75." *The New York Times.* November 12, 2011. http://www.nytimes.com/2011/11/13/nyregion/evelyn-h-lauder-champion-of-breast-cancer-research-dies-at-75.html.

Maume, Chris. "Evelyn Lauder: Founder of the pink ribbon campaign for breast cancer awareness." *The Independent.* November 15, 2011. http://www.independent.co.uk/news/obituaries/evelyn-lauder-founder-of-the-pink-ribbon-campaign-for-breast-cancer-awareness-6262269.html.

"Obituary: Evelyn Lauder, Daughter-in-law of Estée and founder of the breast cancer pink ri." *Express*. November 19, 2011. http://www.express.co.uk/expressyourself/284698/Obituary-Evelyn-Lauder-Daughter-in-law-of-Est-e-and-founder-of-the-breast-cancer-pink-ri.

Chapter # 25 — Ellen Fein

Bittman, Kate. "Take Cover: A New Set of Rules Is Coming." *The New Yorker*. June 24, 2011. http://www.newyorker.com/books/page-turner/take-cover-a-new-set-of-rules-is-coming.

Brady, Lois Smith. "Ellen Fein and Lance Houpt." *The New York Times*. August 9, 2008. http://www.nytimes.com/2008/08/10/fashion/weddings/10VOWS.html.

Broughton, Philip Delves. "Woman who wrote 'The Rules' for a happy marriage files for divorce

in New York." *The Telegraph*. March 26, 2001. http://www.telegraph.co.uk/news/worldnews/1328071/Woman-who-wrote-The-Rules-for-a-happy-marriage-files-for-divorce.html.

Frey, Jennifer. "The Exception That Proves 'The Rules'?" *The Washington Post*. May 10, 2001. https://www.washingtonpost.com/archive/lifestyle/2001/05/10/the-exception-that-proves-the-rules/adeb04bf-ca58-40da-b46e-f535174dd9e7/.

Gleick, Elizabeth. "Playing Hard To Get." *Time*. June 24, 2001. http://content.time.com/time/magazine/article/0,9171,136591,00.html.

Guinness, Molly. "Women, beware these women." *The Spectator*. January 13, 2013. https://www.spectator.co.uk/2013/01/women-beware-these-women/.

"Playing by the rules." *Irish Examiner*. April 27, 2011. http://www.
irishexaminer.com/viewpoints/analysis/playing-by-the-rules-152834.html.

Roiphe, Katie. "Why we all want a happy ending." *The Guardian*.
March 27, 2001. https://www.theguardian.com/world/2001/mar/27/
gender.uk.

Tresniowski, Alex. "There Goes the Bride." *People*. April 16, 2001.
http://people.com/archive/there-goes-the-bride-vol-55-no-15/.

Chapter # 26 — Sue Ellen Cooper

"Five go mad in a tea shop." *The Guardian*. April 24, 2005. https://
www.theguardian.com/world/2005/apr/25/gender.uk1.

"Red Hat ladies frivolous at fifty." *The Telegraph*. February 19,
2005. http://www.telegraph.co.uk/news/worldnews/northamerica/
usa/1483905/Red-Hat-ladies-frivolous-at-fifty.html.

Walker, Rob. "Middle Age? Bring It On." *The New York Times*.
January 30, 2005. http://www.nytimes.com/2005/01/30/magazine/
middle-age-bring-it-on.html.

Chapter # 27 — Sara Blakely

Bankoff, Caroline. "How Selling Fax Machines Helped Make Spanx
Inventor Sara Blakely a Billionaire." The Vindicated, *NYMag*. October
31, 2016. http://nymag.com/vindicated/2016/10/how-selling-fax-
machines-helped-sara-blakely-invent-spanx.html.

Couric, Katie. "Sara Blakely Entrepreneur." *Time*. April 18,
2012. http://content.time.com/time/specials/packages/
article/0,28804,2111975_2111976_2112100,00.html.

Cronin, Emily. "Thanks, Mrs Spanx! Meet billionaire underwear guru Sara Blakely." *The Telegraph*. July 24, 2016." http://www.telegraph.co.uk/fashion/people/thanks-mrs-spanx-meet-billionaire-underwear-guru-sara-blakely/amp/.

Hesse, Monica. "Essay: at Spanx, the battle of the bulges is on." *Chicago Tribune*. December 27, 2012. http://www.chicagotribune.com/lifestyles/sns-wp-washpost-bc-spanx-essay26-20121226-story.html.

Jacobs, Alexandra. "Smooth Moves." *The New Yorker*. March 28, 2011. https://www.newyorker.com/magazine/2011/03/28/smooth-moves.

Walker, Harriet. "Sara Blakely: Spanx a billion." *The Independent*. March 10, 2012. http://www.independent.co.uk/news/people/profiles/sara-blakely-spanx-a-billion-7547334.html.

Wood, Zoe. "Sara Blakely: a woman with a great grasp of figures." *The Guardian*. March 10, 2012. https://www.theguardian.com/theobserver/2012/mar/11/observer-profile-sara-blakely-spanx.

Chapter # 28 — Arianna Huffington

Andrews, Suzanna. "Arianna Calling!" *Vanity Fair*. December 2005. https://www.vanityfair.com/news/2005/12/huffington200512.

Collins, Lauren. "The Oracle- The many lives of Arianna Huffington." *The New Yorker*. October 13, 2008. http://www.newyorker.com/magazine/2008/10/13/the-oracle-lauren-collins.

Gabbatt, Adam. "Arianna Huffington: profile of the multimillion-dollar blogger." *The Guardian*. February 7, 2011. https://www.theguardian.com/media/2011/feb/07/arianna-huffinton-profile.

Skidelsky, William. "Arianna Huffington: 'Going to bed with Bernard Levin was a liberal education'." *The Guardian.* July 14, 2012. https://www.theguardian.com/theobserver/2012/jul/15/arianna-huffington-post-journalism-interview.

Chapter # 29 — Tarana Burke

Garcia, Sandra E. "The Woman Who Created #MeToo Long Before Hashtags." *The New York Times.* October 20, 2017. https://www.nytimes.com/2017/10/20/us/me-too-movement-tarana-burke.html.

Michallon, Clemence. " 'It wasn't built to be a viral campaign!' Meet the women's rights activist who came up with the #MeToo movement 10 YEARS ago to help women of color who had been abused." *Daily Mail.* October 18, 2017. http://www.dailymail.co.uk/femail/article-4994392/Tarana-Burke-started-MeToo-movement-Alyssa-Milano.html.

Ohlheiser, Abby. "The woman behind 'Me Too' knew the power of the phrase when she created it — 10 years ago." *The Washington Post.* October 19, 2017. https://www.washingtonpost.com/news/the-intersect/wp/2017/10/19/the-woman-behind-me-too-knew-the-power-of-the-phrase-when-she-created-it-10-years-ago/.

Wellington, Elizabeth. "Me Too movement can't end with a hashtag, its founder says." *The Inquirer.* October 23, 2017. http://www.philly.com/philly/columnists/elizabeth_wellington/philly-me-too-movement-founder-tarana-burke-20171023.html.

Chapter # 30 — Sophie Amoruso

Baitz, Alison. "The 'Nasty Gal' Invasion: Sophia Amoruso Wants to Create an Army of #GIRLBOSSes." *The Daily Beast*. August 5, 2014. https://www.thedailybeast.com/the-nasty-gal-invasion-sophia-amoruso-wants-to-create-an-army-of-girlbosses.

Gittleson, Kim. "Nasty Gal's Sophia Amoruso: 'Shoplifting saved my life'." *BBC News*. May 19, 2014. http://www.bbc.com/news/business-27414760.

Hess, Amanda. "Netflix Embraces a Nasty Gal, Based on the Real Deal." *The New York Times*. April 19, 2017. https://www.nytimes.com/2017/04/19/arts/television/netflix-girlboss-nasty-gal-sophia-amoruso.html.

Luckhurst, Phoebe. " 'I'm not good at doing what I'm told': meet real-life Girlboss Sophia Amoruso." *The Guardian*. May 11, 2017. https://www.theguardian.com/lifeandstyle/2017/may/11/girlboss-feminism-sophia-amoruso-nasty-gal-netflix-cinderella-tech-tv-series.

Merian, Anna. " 'Everything Really Hit Rock Bottom': How Nasty Gal's Culture Went Nasty." *Jezebel*. June 17, 2015. https://jezebel.com/everything-really-hit-rock-bottom-how-nasty-gals-cultu-1711454805.

Morning Joe Staff. "Sophia Amoruso is taking your questions." *MSNBC*. May 28, 2014. http://www.msnbc.com/morning-joe/excerpt-sophia-amorusos-girlboss.

Perlroth, Nicole. "Naughty in Name Only." *The New York Times*. March 24, 2013. http://www.nytimes.com/2013/03/25/technology/nasty-gal-an-online-start-up-is-a-fast-growing-retailer.html.

Schaefer, Kaylene. "What Comes After Scandal and Scathing Reviews? Sophia Amoruso Is Finding Out." *Vanity Fair*. April 26, 2017. https://www.vanityfair.com/style/2017/04/sophia-amoruso-girlboss-netflix-nasty-gal.

Shuster, Yelena. "NastyGal Founder Sophia Amoruso on How to Become a #GirlBoss." *Elle*. May 5, 2014. http://www.elle.com/culture/career-politics/a12716/nastygal-sophia-amorusa-girl-boss/.

White, Adam. "The real Girlboss: the rise and fall of Nasty Gal founder Sophia Amoruso." *The Telegraph*. April 28, 2017. http://www.telegraph.co.uk/tv/0/real-girlboss-rise-fall-nasty-gal-founder-sophia-amoruso/.

Wright, Jennifer. " 'Girlboss' is a feminist fraud." *New York Post*. April 22, 2017. http://nypost.com/2017/04/22/girlboss-is-a-feminist-fraud/.

Chapter # 31 — Cindy Gallop

Blair, Olivia. "Make Love Not Porn founder Cindy Gallop: Emma Watson was wrong to call for feminist alternatives to porn." *The Independent*. July 30, 2016. http://www.independent.co.uk/news/people/cindy-gallop-make-love-not-porn-founder-on-de-stigmatising-sex-and-why-emma-watson-was-wrong-to-call-a7163901.html.

Buckley, Cara. "Spreading the Word (and Pictures) on 'Real' Sex." *The New York Times*. September 9, 2012. http://query.nytimes.com/gst/fullpage.html?res=9906EFDE113FF93AA3575AC0A9649D8B63

Lovatt, Phoebe. "Sex tech pioneer Cindy Gallop: 'a man is not a financial strategy'." *The Guardian*. February 27, 2017. https://www.theguardian.com/careers/2017/feb/27/sex-tech-pioneer-cindy-gallop-a-man-is-not-a-financial-strategy.

Saner, Emine. "Cindy Gallop: 'Advertising is dominated by white guys talking to white guys'." *The Guardian*. June 26, 2016. https://www.theguardian.com/media/2016/jun/26/cindy-gallup-advertising-white-men-sex-tapes.

Chapter # 32 — Alicia Garza

Chokshi, Niraj. "How #BlackLivesMatter Came to Define a Movement." *The New York Times*. August 22, 2016. https://www.nytimes.com/2016/08/23/us/how-blacklivesmatter-came-to-define-a-movement.html.

Day, Elizabeth. "#BlackLivesMatter: the birth of a new civil rights movement." *The Guardian*. July 19, 2015. https://www.theguardian.com/world/2015/jul/19/blacklivesmatter-birth-civil-rights-movement.

Eligon, John. "One Slogan, Many Methods: Black Lives Matter Enters Politics." *The New York Times*. November 18, 2015. https://www.nytimes.com/2015/11/19/us/one-slogan-many-methods-black-lives-matter-enters-politics.html.

Hunt, Elle. "Alicia Garza on the beauty and the burden of Black Lives Matter." *The Guardian*. September 2, 2016. https://www.theguardian.com/us-news/2016/sep/02/alicia-garza-on-the-beauty-and-the-burden-of-black-lives-matter.

King, Jamilah. "#blacklivesmatter- How three friends turned a spontaneous Facebook post into a global phenomenon." *The California Sunday Magazine*. March 1, 2015. https://stories.californiasunday.com/2015-03-01/black-lives-matter/.

Meyerson, Collier. "The Founders of Black Lives Matter: 'We Gave Tongue To Something That We All Knew Was Happening.' " *Glamour*. November 1, 2016. https://www.glamour.com/story/women-of-the-year-black-lives-matter-founders.

Chapter # 33 — Sheryl Sandberg

Alter, Charlotte. "Sheryl Sandberg Explains Why Young Women Should Mentor Each Other." *Time*. June 23, 2016. http://time.com/4379072/sheryl-sandberg-young-women-mentorship-interview/.

Applebaum, Anne. "How to Succeed in Business." *The New York Review of Books*. June 6, 2013. http://www.nybooks.com/articles/2013/06/06/sheryl-sandberg-how-succeed-business/.

Associated Press. The new book club? Women desperate to kickstart their careers are forming 'Lean In' circles inspired by Facebook's Sheryl Sandberg." *Daily Mail*. April 26, 2016. http://www.dailymail.co.uk/femail/article-2315376/Facebooks-Sheryl-Sandberg-inspires-Lean-In-circles-women-desperate-kickstart-careers.html.

Bonos, Lisa. "A year after 'Lean In,'" these are Sheryl Sandberg's truest believers." *The Washington Post*. March 7, 2014. https://www.washingtonpost.com/opinions/a-year-after-lean-in-these-are-sheryl-sandbergs-truest-believers/2014/03/07/407b0e8e-9dac-11e3-a050-dc3322a94fa7_story.html.

Holmes, Anna. "Maybe You Should Read the Book: The Sheryl Sandberg Backlash." *The New Yorker*. March 4, 2013. https://www.newyorker.com/books/page-turner/maybe-you-should-read-the-book-the-sheryl-sandberg-backlash.

Nathan, Sara. "PICTURE EXCLUSIVE: From teenage aerobics instructor to Facebook's billion-dollar woman and is the next stop the White House? The astonishing rise and rise of Sheryl Sandberg." *Daily Mail.* March 1, 2013. http://www.dailymail.co.uk/news/article-2286584/ Facebooks-Sheryl-Sandberg-teen-aerobics-instructor-COO--stop-White-House.html.

Slaughter, Anne-Marie. "Yes, You Can. Sheryl Sandberg's 'Lean In'." *The New York Times.* March 7, 2013. http://www.nytimes.com/2013/03/10/ books/review/sheryl-sandbergs-lean-in.html.

Chapter # 34 — Jennifer Kempton

Batha, Emma. "Former sex slave helps women reclaim their branded bodies with new tattoos." *Reuters.* November 27, 2016. https://www. yahoo.com/news/former-sex-slave-helps-women-reclaim-branded-bodies-001558006.html.

Goldsmith, Belinda. "Sex and labor trafficking survivors call for funding and jobs, not pity." *Reuters.* April 25, 2017. http://www.dailymail. co.uk/wires/reuters/article-4445404/Sex-labor-trafficking-survivors-call-funding-jobs-not-pity.html.

Hodal, Kate. "Jennifer Kempton death: 'A strong, brilliant woman who loved all the way'." *The Guardian.* May 19, 2017. https://www. theguardian.com/global-development/2017/may/19/jennifer-kempton-death-strong-brilliant-woman-who-loved-all-the-way.

Kelly, Annie. " 'I carried his name on my body for nine years': the tattooed trafficking survivors reclaiming their past." *The Guardian.* November 15, 2014. https://www.theguardian.com/ global-development/2014/nov/16/sp-the-tattooed-trafficking-survivors-reclaiming-their-past.

Trott, Florence. "Our sex traffickers branded us, but they won't own us forever." *Cosmopolitan*. November 28, 2014. http://www. cosmopolitan.com/uk/reports/a31517/survivors-ink-jennifer-kempton/.

Chapter # 35 — Whitney Wolfe

Alter, Charlotte. "Whitney Wolfe Wants to Beat Tinder at Its Own Game." *Time*. May 15, 2015. http://time.com/3851583/bumble-whitney-wolfe/.

Bennett, Jessica. "With Her Dating App, Women Are in Control." *The New York Times*. March 18, 2017. https://www.nytimes.com/2017/03/18/fashion/bumble-feminist-dating-app-whitney-wolfe.html.

Black, Julia. "Tinder Co-founder Whitney Wolfe on Why Bumble Is Different." *Elle*. March 26, 2015. http://www.elle.com/culture/tech/a27505/the-new-dating-appwhich-nudges-women-to-make-the-first-movemay-be-just-the-social-crutch-we-needed/.

Ellis-Petersen, Hannah. "WLTM Bumble – A dating app where women call the shots." *The Guardian*. April 12, 2015. https://www.theguardian.com/technology/2015/apr/12/bumble-dating-app-women-call-shots-whitney-wolfe.

Ensor, Josie. "Tinder co-founder Whitney Wolfe: 'The word 'feminist' seemed to put guys off, but now I realise, who cares?'." *The Telegraph*. May 23, 2015. http://www.telegraph.co.uk/women/womens-business/11616130/Tinder-co-founder-Whitney-Wolfe-The-word-feminist-seemed-to-put-guys-off-but-now-I-realise-who-cares.html.

Frankel, Todd C. "Whitney Wolfe, founder of dating app Bumble, has had quite the year. She just can't discuss parts of it." *The Washington Post*. December 2, 2015 https://www.washingtonpost.com/news/the-switch/wp/2015/12/02/whitney-wolfe-founder-of-dating-app-bumble-has-had-qu.

Lepore, Meredith. "Bumble Is Becoming a Platform for Non-Creepy Networking." *Observer*. October 27, 2016. http://observer.com/2016/10/bumble-is-becoming-a-platform-for-non-creepy-networking/.

Milligan, Lauren. "What's the Buzz About Bumble?" *Vogue*. March 7, 2016. http://www.vogue.co.uk/article/bumble-dating-app-founder-whitney-wolfe-interview.

Mulkerrins, Jane. "Meet Whitney Wolfe, the queen bee of digital dating." *Daily Mail*. March 4, 2017. http://www.dailymail.co.uk/home/you/article-4271840/Meet-Whitney-Wolfe-queen-bee-digital-dating.html.

Rao, Priya. "The Dating Game." *Harper's Bazaar*. March 18, 2015. http://www.harpersbazaar.com/culture/features/a10312/bumble-dating-app-0415/.

Chapter # 36 — Krista Suh

Bravo, Tony. "Pussyhats and the power of pink." *San Francisco Chronicle*. January 27, 2017. http://www.sfchronicle.com/style/article/Pussyhats-and-the-power-of-pink-10884232.php.

Kahn, Mattie. "The Pussyhat Is an Imperfect, Powerful Feminist Symbol That Thousands Will Be Wearing This Weekend in DC." *Elle*. January 15, 2017. http://www.elle.com/culture/career-politics/news/a42152/pussyhat-project-knit-protest/.

Pearl, Diana. " 'Pussyhats' Galore: Inside the Pink Toppers Thousands Will Wear to the Women's March on Washington." *People.* January 21, 2017. http://people.com/politics/pussyhats-galore-inside-the-pink-toppers-thousands-will-wear-to-the-womens-march-on-washington/.

Pearson, Catherine. "Thousands Are Knitting 'Pussy Hats' For The Women's March On Washington." *Huffington Post.* January 3, 2017. http://www.huffingtonpost.com/entry/thousands-are-knitting-pussy-hats-for-the-womens-march-on-washington_us_586bb22ee4b0d9a5945c636a.

"Pussyhats. How one woman created the unofficial uniform for the Women's March." Women in the World, *The New York Times.* January 25, 2017. http://nytlive.nytimes.com/womenintheworld/2017/01/25/how-one-woman-created-the-unofficial-uniform-for-the-womens-march/.

Raymer, Miles. "Those Pink Women's March Hats Are Part of a Grand Tradition of Protest Fashion." *Esquire.* January 23, 2017. http://www.esquire.com/style/mens-accessories/news/a52493/pussyhat-womens-march-protest-fashion/.

Reimel, Erin and Krystin Arneson. *Glamour.* January 22, 2017. https://www.glamour.com/story/the-story-behind-the-pussyhats-at-the-womens-march.

Reuters in Los Angeles. "Casting off Trump: the women who can't stop knitting 'pussy hats'." *The Guardian.* January 15, 2017. https://www.theguardian.com/world/2017/jan/15/casting-off-trump-the-women-who-cant-stop-knitting-pussy-hats.

Tribune News Service. "How these LA-born pink hats became worldwide symbol of anti-Trump women's march." *San Francisco Examiner.* January 16, 2017. http://www.sfexaminer.com/la-born-pink-hats-became-worldwide-symbol-anti-trump-womens-march/.

Walker, Rob. "The D.I.Y. Revolutionaries of the Pussyhat Project." *The New Yorker*. January 25, 2017. http://www.newyorker.com/culture/culture-desk/the-d-i-y-revolutionaries-of-the-pussyhat-project.

Chapter # 37 — Teresa Shook

Alter, Charlotte. "How the Women's March Has United Progressives of All Stripes." *Time*. January 20, 2017. http://time.com/4641575/womens-march-washington-coalition/.

Blair, Tim. "All Shook Up." *The Daily Telegraph*. January 5, 2017. http://www.dailytelegraph.com.au/blogs/tim-blair/all-shook-up/news-story/664fe81ea1a13df7abed925cdf3e62f9.

Felsenthal, Julia. "These Are the Women Organizing the Women's March on Washington." *Vogue*. January 10, 2017. http://www.vogue.com/article/meet-the-women-of-the-womens-march-on-washington.

Kahn, Mattie. "The Women's March on Washington: How It Came to Be and What You Need to Know." *Elle*. January 12, 2017. http://www.elle.com/culture/news/a42067/womens-march-on-washington-timeline-logistics/.

Stein, Perry. "The woman who started the Women's March with a Facebook post reflects: 'It was mind-boggling'." *The Washington Post*. January 31, 2017. https://www.washingtonpost.com/news/local/wp/2017/01/31/the-woman-who-started-the-womens-march-with-a-facebook-post-reflects-it-was-mind-boggling/.

Stein, Perry and Sandhya Somashekhar. "It started with a retiree. Now the Women's March could be the biggest inauguration demonstration." *The Washington Post.* January 3, 2017. https://www.washingtonpost.com/national/it-started-with-a-grandmother-in-hawaii-now-the-womens-march-on-washington-is-poised-to-be-the-biggest-inauguration-demonstration/2017/01/03/8af61686-c6e2-11e6-bf4b-2c064d32a4bf_story.html.

St. Martin, Victoria. "Hawaii retiree who came up with march idea is 'blown away'." *The Washington Post.* January 21, 2017. https://www.washingtonpost.com/local/2017/live-updates/politics/womens-march-on-washington/hawaii-woman-who-came-up-with-march-idea-blown-away/.

Tolentino, Jia. "The Somehow Controversial Women's March on Washington." *The New Yorker.* January 18, 2017. http://www.newyorker.com/culture/jia-tolentino/the-somehow-controversial-womens-march-on-washington.

Woerner, Meredith. "Who started the march? One woman." *Los Angeles Times.* January 21, 2017. http://www.latimes.com/nation/la-na-pol-womens-march-live-who-started-the-march-one-1485033621-htmlstory.html.

ABOUT THE AUTHOR

Marlene Wagman-Geller received her BA from York University and her teaching credentials from the University of Toronto and San Diego State University. Currently she teaches high school English in National City, California. Reviews from her first three books (Penguin/Perigree) have appeared in *The New York Times* and the Associated Press article was picked up in dozens of newspapers such as *The Denver Post, The Huffington Post,* and *The San Diego Union-Tribune.*